SEABLINDNESS

SEABLINDNESS

*How Political Neglect
Is Choking American Seapower
and What to Do About It*

SETH CROPSEY

Encounter Books
New York • London

First American edition published in 2017 by Encounter Books, an activity of Encounter for Culture and Education, Inc., a nonprofit, tax-exempt corporation. Encounter Books website address: www.encounterbooks.com

Manufactured in the United States and printed on acid-free paper. The paper used in this publication meets the minimum requirements of ANSI/NISO Z39.48–1992 (R 1997) (*Permanence of Paper*).

FIRST AMERICAN EDITION

LIBRARY OF CONGRESS CATALOGING-IN-PUBLICATION DATA
Names: Cropsey, Seth, author.
Title: Seablindness : how political neglect is choking American seapower and what to do about it / by Seth Cropsey.
Other titles: How political neglect is choking American seapower and what to do about it
Description: New York : Encounter Books, [2017] | Includes bibliographical references and index. |
Identifiers: LCCN 2017006242 (print) | LCCN 2017024026 (ebook) | ISBN 9781594039164 (Ebook) | ISBN 9781594039157 (hardcover : alk. paper)
Subjects: LCSH: Sea-power–United States. | United States–Military policy. | United States–Strategic aspects. | Security, International. | Naval strategy.
Classification: LCC VA58.4 (ebook) | LCC VA58.4 .C76 2017 (print) | DDC 359/.030973–dc23
LC record available at https://lccn.loc.gov/2017006242

PRODUCED BY WILSTED & TAYLOR PUBLISHING SERVICES
Copy editor Nancy Evans   *Proofreader* Melody Lacina
Designer Nancy Koerner   *Indexer* Robert Swanson

For Mihaela and Gabriel Ethan Cropsey,
whose loving support made this book possible.

CONTENTS

PREFACE

The United States, bounded on three of its five sides by the seas, is a maritime state. We depend on safe transit over the Earth's watery surface for a large portion of our commerce. We depend on the same freedom of maneuver upon the seas for our ability to communicate with allies, to project power as we did at Normandy in 1944, to prevent crises from reaching our shores, and to block enemies from using the oceans to their advantage. I hope that the observations in this discussion about the importance of seapower to a maritime state will endure.

What I hope will not endure is the dangerous condition of depleted seapower that existed as an administration elected in 2008 transferred power to the one that Americans chose in 2016. This account is in large measure a picture of where American seapower stood as one administration ended and another took power. It is a description of the challenge that faces the recently elected president.

Measured in size, the U.S. combatant fleet today stands

at 276 ships, the smallest since before World War I. Propelled by the prospect of aging ships—built during the Reagan buildup and which must be withdrawn from service—world events, and the rise of would-be competitors, the U.S. Navy plans for a larger fleet—over the next thirty years.

When complete, the fleet that the George W. Bush administration planned for construction over this three-decade period would have numbered 375 vessels. The fleet size that the Obama administration planned to reach at the end of thirty years shrank to 306 vessels, a reduction of nearly one-fifth. Both the Congressional Research Service (CRS) and the Congressional Budget Office (CBO) agree that achieving even the reduced fleet size requires significantly more money than the average amount that the Navy has received for shipbuilding over recent decades. At the same time, the actual fleet size fell by 3 percent during the Obama administration. These numbers say nothing about the problematic combat readiness of U.S. seapower, logistic support, and the infrastructure needed to support a fleet. Years of diminished funding have resulted in a hollow Navy as well as a similar hollowing out of the other armed services of the United States.

This book is not a political document. Responsibility for the state of American seapower in 2017 rests not with a single administration nor with a single Congress. Rather, it is the sum of decisions made by policy makers of both major parties and in both the executive and legislative branches of government as Cold War tensions lifted and as elected and appointed officials turned their gaze from great power issues to terrorism and wars in the Middle

East, all the while assuming that the transoceanic dominance of the United States was a given.

Like sheep that have gone astray, we forgot that competition among the great powers may recede or abate, but only temporarily. Great power competition to establish the terms of international order is one of history's defining characteristics. Throughout history, great maritime powers that forgot, neglected, or were otherwise distracted from the oceanic anchor of their commerce and security fell from their high positions. Such amnesia or strategic befuddlement is called *seablindness*.

The assumption of American dominance at sea is as unwarranted as the supposition that the history of great power competition has come to an end. What follows is a portrait of the actual and possible consequences of the political decision to permit American seapower to fade. It is in large measure an illustration of how U.S. seapower fared at what may turn out to be the pivotal moment when the electorate gave its mandate to a candidate who promised to rebuild America's defenses. It is neither my intent nor is it within the scope of this book to answer the difficult question of how the restoration of America's armed forces can be financed—which remains a vexing obstacle to restoring the armed forces of the United States. But history provides clear answers about the dire consequences for a great maritime state if it neglects its seapower. The risk that the United States will follow Britain, Spain, Holland, and ancient Athens into a naval decline that preceded and in large measure caused their descent from great power status is real. Descriptions of the current woes of American seapower appear in this book's chapters. The Trump administration's proposed 10 percent increase in defense spending will likely go to restocking depleted weapons inventories, purchasing spare parts, repairing equipment that has been overused, and other important accounts that have been drawn down so that the United States could maintain its global presence. The administration's proposed 10 percent increase in defense spending will not begin to address the large capital costs of rebuilding or modernizing an aging fleet, much less reconfiguring it to meet the growing threat that China and Russia pose.

Large existing debt and the prospect of servicing an even larger debt obligation make the choice that the United States faces unusually serious. Simultaneous with the American electorate's apparent call for a reinvigoration of its military, events unfolded that American policy makers twenty-five years ago agreed must never recur. This was the rise of another great power to challenge the United States and the world order that American policy sought to shape throughout the twentieth century. What follows is a snapshot of how American seapower—the most effective strategic guarantor for keeping threats at a distance and preserving the liberal international order—stands on the cusp.

I am grateful to the Smith Richardson Foundation for their generous support in the research and writing of *Seablindness*. Very few other such organizations continue to demonstrate Smith Richardson's breadth of strategic vision. I am grateful as well to my literary agent, Don Fehr, for his belief in the importance of this subject and his efforts on the book's behalf. I am indebted to a host of able, highly motivated, and dedicated researchers and interns whose work I depended on as this book took shape. In particular, I would like to thank Kevin Truitte, Harry Halem, Chris Zeller, Elias Riskin, Justus Vorwerk, Kevin Philpott, Iris Hsu, Liam Cardon, Titus Techera, Matt Whiting, and Craig Hooper.

Finally, I am deeply grateful to Roger Kimball at Encounter Books for his confidence in this project, and for the support of Katherine Wong and Wilsted and Taylor's Christine Taylor and Nancy Evans, whose editorial judgment turned a manuscript into a book.

SEABLINDNESS

CHAPTER I

WHAT IS A HOLLOW MILITARY?

Mao Zedong dismissed the United States as *zhilaohu*, a paper tiger. All imperialist states, he said, were weak because of their appetite to enlarge. Their militaries looked strong, he admitted, but overextension had gutted them. Mao's description missed the mark. Overextension did not tax the United States or its allies. America's economic and military strength allowed its resolute policy to win the Cold War. The system of purges that strove for ideological purity and of an absolute embrace of a centrally controlled economy died with Mao. It was replaced by one that, while still authoritarian, repressive, and ruled by a single party, encouraged the Chinese people's enterprising character.

A couple of decades after Mao's "paper tiger" expression became common usage, Army Chief of Staff General Edward "Shy" Meyer coined another phrase along parallel lines, "hollow army." A troubled economy helped created the vacant space at the core of U.S. forces. After President Nixon ordered and then gradually lifted wage and price controls in the early 1970s, and following the Federal Reserve's historically low interest rates, companies sought to make up for lost earnings. Inflation began to rise.

At this point, the administration replaced conscription with the all-volunteer force (AVF). Military salaries couldn't keep pace with inflation rates, which ballooned from nearly 9 percent in 1973, the year that the AVF began, to 14 percent in 1980, the year that President Carter lost his campaign for reelection. Sailors who helped launch and recover planes aboard aircraft carriers earned less than hamburger flippers at McDonald's. Among some of the youngest enlisted personnel, salaries fell below the federal government's poverty level,[1] which made the military less attractive to new recruits and more likely to lose qualified people, along with their experience and skills.

In 1979, the Navy reported that it had 20,000 fewer petty officers than it needed.[2] The Army missed its recruitment goal by 15,000 soldiers.[3] In that year, six out of the ten Army divisions on U.S. soil were deemed "not combat ready." This was troubling because the burden of stopping and reversing a possible Soviet invasion of Western Europe rested on the ability of U.S. forces to return to the continent and fight. If the U.S. Army's predicament at home wasn't sufficiently alarming, in Europe itself, one out of four U.S. combat divisions were rated as "not combat ready."

The military responded by filling the ranks with large numbers of the unqualified. As the 1970s drew to a close, fresh recruits caused enough disciplinary problems or proved so unqualified that 40 percent of them had to be fired. Combat unreadiness was central to the military's hollowness. General Frederick Kroesen, who had commanded U.S. troops in World War II and risen to become commander of the U.S. Army in Europe, described the U.S. Army in Europe as "obsolescent."[4]

What the military calls "modernization," the replacement of old equipment with new and more technologically advanced hardware, added to the hollowing effect of the 1970s. A chart of money spent on procurement since 1948 looks like jagged wide-angle pictures of Wyoming's Grand Teton Mountains: sharp peaks divided by deep precipices. The summits occur during the Korean conflict, the Vietnam War, the Reagan buildup, and the Iraq and Afghanistan wars. As the defense budget started to climb out of the trough that followed the end of the Vietnam War, Defense Department leaders wanted to replace antiquated weapons with new technologically superior ones.

The bottom of the post-Vietnam War dip in weapons procurement occurred in 1977 and 1978. New systems such as the Navy's Aegis radar—which integrates a ship's tracking and fire control systems—had been developed to replace twenty-five-year-old technology. The Defense Department started purchasing these and other systems, such as the Air Force's F-15 fighter and the Army's Apache attack helicopters, to modernize the entire military.

But there was a cost. Defense budgets couldn't pay for both modernization and readiness. Fuel, flight hours, spare parts—all part of the large amount of logistics needed for training—are some examples of what's required to keep a military force ready to fight.

The same logic applies in other competitive human activities. If an aspiring Olympic downhill skier can't find financial support for training, lodging, food, and transportation—in addition to equipment—the athlete will lack the necessaries to hone his competitive skill.

Insufficient resources for readiness compounded the problem of attracting the high-quality personnel who are needed to operate more technologically advanced equipment and magnified the weakness that Army Chief of Staff General Meyer described as a hollow military.

Fundamental differences between the Navy's idea of its role in protecting the nation and basic security assumptions of the Nixon and Carter administrations cannot be separated from the especially acute readiness problems that U.S. seapower faced. The Navy saw its mission as responding to crises around the world, while the White House, throughout the 1970s, concentrated on shoring up the central front in Europe against the Soviet-led Warsaw Pact. Naval leadership would align its strategy later, but at the time the Navy had yet to articulate a strategic idea that fit administration policy.[5] An official from the Carter administration's Office of Management and Budget told the Navy "to get its act together."

Then events intervened. The Soviet invasion of Afghanistan, the failure of the Carter administration's attempt to rescue American hostages held in Tehran, the hollow force's emergence as an issue in the 1980 presidential campaign, and Republican president nominee Ronald Reagan's arguments that peace depended on strength occurred in less than a year. These events prepared a solid base for popular support of large increases in defense spending. The defense budget measured 5.5 percent of gross domestic product (GDP) in 1979. Seven years later it had climbed by over a fifth to 6.8 percent of GDP.[6] In constant (2015) dollars, defense spending during the same period rose from slightly over $400 billion to slightly over $600 billion annually.[7] The hollow force disappeared.

But not before the new administration learned the scope of naval unpreparedness. When John Lehman became secretary of the Navy at the beginning of the first Reagan term, he found that the Navy had "less than a week's supply of most major defensive missiles and torpedoes."[8] The magazines of the fleet's 479 ships were incomplete, and the shelves of logistics dumps were not full enough to replenish them. The media reported that $9 billion was needed to buy enough ammunition to reach authorized levels.[9]

Spare parts for ships and aircraft were one-third of the amount required. Such critical aircraft as the anti-submarine carrier-based S-3 Viking were so poorly supplied with spare parts that only three out of ten were capable of performing their missions.[10] The Navy was so short on reserve aircraft that if they were used to fill gaps in the service's twelve existing air wings—one wing per carrier—there were enough planes for only nine carriers.[11] Insufficient funding was responsible for a backlog of twenty-six ships awaiting overhaul. The new Navy secretary reported that maintenance had been put off at the Great Lakes Naval Training Center's gym for so long that the building "collapsed flat on the ground in 1981."[12]

A similar hollowing affected the Navy's fleet size. Measured in displacement, the U.S. Navy possessed more tonnage—3.5 times as much—in every category of combatant than the Soviets in the mid-1960s. Then, the U.S. Navy decommissioned aging World War II ships, and the So-

viet fleet increased modestly. By the mid-1970s, absent resources to preserve the U.S. lead, the Soviets had caught
up sufficiently so that its surface and submarine fleets,
excluding the immense U.S. lead in aircraft carriers, out-
displaced that of the United States.[13]

Displacement comparisons don't tell the whole story.
At the height of the hollow force of the 1970s, about 1978,
the Soviet fleet consisted of 446 surface combatants to
the United States's 217. The advantage that the United
States enjoyed in aircraft carriers, twenty-one to three,
could never compensate for a numerically superior surface
fleet's ability to cover key global choke points, maintain
presence, conduct convoy operations, deny access, or challenge denied access.

Other comparisons give a better picture. Ship-days
measure the amount of time a single naval ship spends
on patrol out of its home waters. Fewer ships mean fewer
possible ship-days. In 1965, Soviet ship-days in the Caribbean and Mediterranean Seas as well as in the Atlantic,
Indian, and Pacific Oceans numbered 7,500. For the same
places and in the same year, the United States recorded
almost 110,000 ship-days. Nine years later, U.S. ship-days
had dropped to 61,300. Soviet ship-days had increased to
53,100.[14]

In other words, just as the Navy needed to modernize
a fleet that was being decimated because of age, the Johnson administration was shifting defense budgets away
from military hardware needed in the future and spending
money on current operations in Vietnam. Its pre–Vietnam
War level of shipbuilding funds was halved throughout
the war.

6

The prospect of a hollow military has returned. Beginning with Leon Panetta, President Obama's first secretary of Defense, all three secretaries of Defense of the Obama administration pointed out this possibility. A few months after taking office, Panetta, responding to the administration's plan to decrease defense spending by $350 billion over ten years, said that additional cuts "would have devastating effects" on the Defense and State departments. As the Obama administration ended, those cuts totaled at least three times as much. Panetta added that going beyond the proposed $350 billion reduction would "result in hollowing out the force," and "weaken our ability to respond to the threats in the world."[15]

Robert Gates followed Leon Panetta as secretary of Defense. As he was preparing to leave office, Gates told the graduating class at Notre Dame in May 2011 that an adequately funded U.S. military "cannot be taken for granted." Specifically, he said, "our military credibility, commitment and presence are required to sustain alliances, to protect trade routes and energy supplies, and to deter would-be adversaries." Gates warned that across-the-board spending cuts—like sequestration—such as those that followed the Vietnam War and the Cold War, would hollow out the military.[16]

After Gates left office, he spoke more candidly. About sequestration, he told CBS that "there may be a stupider way to do things, but I can't figure out what it is. . . . The result is a hollow military and we will pay for it in the same way we paid for it every time we have done this in the past. And that is, in the next conflict, and there will be a next conflict, with the blood of our soldiers."[17]

Until now, the current form of U.S. military hollowness has been a matter of will rather than of financial embarrassment. The U.S. military as a whole replicates the deficiencies of American seapower that were sketched earlier. Hobbled by budget-induced problems of readiness, maintenance, operational capacity, and an inability to modernize, the military is hard-pressed to carry out the national military strategy of the Joint Chiefs of Staff.

Where two Army corps were once stationed in Europe, the United States today maintains two permanent brigades, with a rotating armored brigade to be added in 2017.[18] One corps is made of two divisions and includes between 40,000 and 100,000 troops. One brigade is made up of between 3,000 and 5,000 troops. The Army reports that only twenty of its sixty brigades—with members from active duty, reserves, and the National Guard—are combat ready, eleven of which are committed to ongoing missions.[19] Russian forces in the regions that abut Eastern Europe are at least twenty times the size of U.S. ground forces. They are equipped with modern and effective weapons, both offensive and defensive.

The Air Force chief of staff, General David L. Goldfein, told Congress in 2016 that, contrary to the nation's military strategy, the U.S. Air Force (USAF) is not fully prepared to handle more than one of the required two major regional contingencies.[20] The United States has been shrinking the size and, by failing sufficiently to modernize, the capability of its entire armed forces as our potential adversaries grow in numbers and combat ability.

These facts inclined the Obama administration's third secretary of Defense, former Nebraska Senator Chuck

Hagel, to share his immediate predecessors' views. His experience in the Vietnam War as an Army infantry soldier also contributed to his understanding. He spoke to the Veterans of Foreign Wars in July 2013 on the sixtieth anniversary of the armistice that ended the hostilities of the Korean War: "Many of you—especially those veterans of the Korean War—have seen the costs, measured in precious American lives, that come with sending a hollow force into battle. We cannot repeat the mistakes of the past."[21]

Hagel meant that we should not repeat the mistakes of the past. We did.

IT'S AN OLD STORY

History warns of the consequences. The falls of the Dutch and English from their positions as great seapowers and great powers are commonly cited. The eclipse of Spanish naval power was more dramatic. It shows how seapower is linked to superpower status and how quickly—and simultaneously—both can unravel.

The Spanish Empire of the sixteenth century was so extensive that a priest, Fray Francisco de Ugalde, earned a small place in history when he told his sovereign, Charles I, that Spain had become *"el imperio en el que nunca se pone el sol,"* the empire on which the sun never sets. The Spanish Empire extended from its northern and southern European possessions, including the Kingdom of Naples, to the Atlantic islands, widely separated African outposts, and millions of square miles in the Americas. Charles's son, Philip II, solidified and expanded Spain's imperial holdings in the islands named for him, the Philippines.

But reach exceeded grasp. Empires must be held together, and only ships could link such large and glittering
imperial jewels with the crown in Madrid. Alfred Thayer
Mahan writes in *The Influence of Sea Power upon History*, "Spain
. . . afforded an impressive lesson of the weakness caused
by . . . separation when the parts are not knit together by
a strong sea power."[22]

Key to the collapse of Spain's maritime dominance was
the disastrous Spanish Armada of 1588. The "Invincible"
Armada was ill-prepared and poorly equipped. Built amid
consistent royal bankruptcies and a treasury stretched thin
by Spanish struggles in the Netherlands, the Armada that
sailed for England was short on leadership, training, and
tactics. Notwithstanding advances in naval weaponry that
improved the range and accuracy of its guns, the Spanish
navy's doctrine required Spanish ships to travel in tight
formation.

The Armada, weighed down by its lumbering troop
transports, proceeded very slowly and was at a serious disadvantage to England's swifter and more maneuverable
warships.[23] In the event, this mattered little. Only six Spanish ships of the 129-vessel invasion force were destroyed as
a direct result of naval combat. Dirty weather favored the
English. So did the fighting spirit of England's indomi-
table queen. Elizabeth I told her forces, assembled at Til-
bury to quash a possible Spanish march up the Thames,
that "I know I have the body but of a weak and feeble
woman; but I have the heart and stomach of a king—and
of a king of England too."

At least fifty ships were lost during the North Atlantic
storms that decimated the fleet as it attempted to return

to Spain past Ireland's west coast. More than 13,500 sailors and soldiers died, not from English cannon fire, but as the result of insufficient supplies, disease, and deficient leadership—a hollow military if ever there were one. Had Spain's 27,000-strong invasion force reached England, the survival of Elizabeth's Protestant realm would have been at serious risk.[24]

While the riches of the Western Hemisphere still flowed across the Atlantic, the Spanish treasury was pushed time and again to its breaking point. The debt of the Spanish Empire had become crippling. The royal bankruptcies of 1596, 1607, 1627, and 1645 weighed heavily on a nation engaged in land campaigns against England, France, and various opponents in the melee of the Thirty Years' War.[25] Spain's attachment to the Mediterranean tactics of boarding enemy galleys blinkered its high command to the lessons of firepower and maneuverability. The English understood these tactics and applied them on the high seas. The distraction of continental warfare left Madrid seablind.

The Council of Finance's reluctant and consistently slow financial support to the *Junta de Armadas*, a royal advisory group with directive powers over the navy, resulted in a naval force that experienced sharp rises and declines in size and capability. As do his successors the world over, Martin de Aróztegui, the secretary of the Spanish navy, argued that the *consistent* provision of money was the "principal foundation" of naval preparations, and without proper funding nothing could be accomplished.[26] David Goodman writes in his analysis of the decline of Spanish naval power that every aspect of Spain's naval planning and preparation was subject to delay and collapse owing to insufficient funding. It is rare to encounter documents, he writes, that are free from warnings of serious consequences if funds were not forthcoming.[27]

By 1663, the Spanish treasury had become so strained that the president of finance, Juan de Góngora, announced that he had not one *real* to give to the fleet.[28] The *Junta de Armadas* warned that the fleet was being left with "only the bones and scraps" and, shortly after Philip IV's death, announced it had no funds, only debts.[29] The term "hollow force" did not exist at the time, but Spain's was a hollow force caused by the twin enemies of a robust one: strategic distraction in the form of land wars and accompanying impoverishment.

The Council of War and the *Junta de Armadas* had failed to establish a fleet that could answer imperial commitments, a goal they struggled to achieve for almost half a century. Spain never recovered from the rout of its great Armada. While there were limited successes in the early seventeenth century, Spain's navy had begun a decline from which neither it nor the state recovered. In less than a century, Spanish seapower descended from the top drawer to a third-rate force. So low had Spanish naval power fallen that, by the late seventeenth century, the Spanish coast was navigated by a few Dutch ships and seamen hired by the Spanish. Shipping from the Indies to Spain could be conducted easily by Dutch shipping in peacetime but was easily interrupted in time of war.[30] Spain maintained skeletal parts of its former global power, holding lands and influence in the Americas until the early nineteenth century. But seapower hollowed by penuriousness withered the muscle and rotted the empire's connective tissue.

FROM GALLEONS TO GUIDED MISSILE CRUISERS

The initial signs of a hollow U.S. naval force existed long before sequestration. The wars in Iraq and Afghanistan redirected U.S. military spending priorities throughout the 2000s, just as the Vietnam War had affected subsequent military budgets and resulted in a hollow force. The United States's post–Cold War military drawdown shrank the Navy from its 594-ship high to 316 ships by September 2001.[31] Combat operations from then on shifted funding away from the Navy and Marine Corps. U.S. ship numbers steadily declined during the Iraq War as the Navy pared its surface warship fleet down from 127 to 118, cut its submarine fleet by four boats, and trimmed its amphibious fleet from 41 to 33 ships.[32] Force cuts alone might not create a hollow navy, but, combined with the concept of "transformation" and the financial squeezes of the Iraq and Afghan wars, these force cuts indicate that this is exactly what happened.

Secretary of Defense Donald Rumsfeld and much of the U.S. national security establishment championed the idea of force transformation.[33] This harkened back to the "military revolution" of the early modern period, when the combination of gunpowder technology, massed infantry tactics, and improved logistics transformed how wars were fought. The 2001 Quadrennial Defense Review defined transformation as the result of "the exploitation of new approaches to operational concepts and capabilities, the use of old and new technologies, and new forms of organization that more effectively anticipate new or still emerging strategic and operational challenges and opportunities and that render previous methods of conducting war obsolete."[34] President Bush expanded on this concept, stating that the force should be "defined less by size and more by mobility and swiftness, one that is easier to deploy and sustain, one that relies more heavily on stealth, precision weaponry, and information technologies."[35] This force would "redefine war on our terms."[36]

Proponents of transformation argued that the overwhelming victory of the United States in the First Gulf War was due to the nation's major technological edge over its adversary. Precision-guided missiles and bombs, along with stealth aircraft and immediate air supremacy, ensured America's victory over Saddam Hussein's million-man army. By combining these advanced technologies with the power of computer networks, U.S. force planners hoped to create a better-informed, more advanced military that could apply precise force at any location on the planet. Maintaining this technological advantage was therefore the key to preserving American military dominance and deterring future threats to U.S. power. By revolutionizing warfare, the United States could ensure its dominance for decades to come.

Asymmetric conflicts in Iraq and Afghanistan only encouraged these ideas. In urban operating spaces crowded with noncombatants, minimizing collateral damage was, and remains, a crucial U.S. military objective. "Smart weapons" were meant to achieve this objective.

Transformation affected every service. While the F-22 and F-35 tactical aircraft are the most public demonstrations of the approach, the strategy had the greatest impact on the Navy, since fleet construction takes place over decades, not months or years. Transformation called for placing experimental technologies on platforms under construction in order to get ahead of America's adversaries, much as the innovative Royal Navy Admiral Jacky Fisher did when constructing the HMS *Dreadnought*.

Two important examples are the *Gerald R. Ford*–class supercarrier and the *Zumwalt*-class destroyer. The *Ford*-class substitutes a highly efficient electromagnetic catapult for the old steam-powered ones. The new ship's reactors generate over three times more power than its *Nimitz*-class predecessors, allowing it to use directed energy weapons.[37] The *Zumwalt*-class was designed as the nation's first stealth fighting ship and can fire a guided land-attack 5-inch shell.[38]

None of this was cheap. Both projects have seen major cost overruns: the *Ford*-class is $2.3 billion over its projected cost,[39] while the three ships of the *Zumwalt*-class are expected to cost nearly $12.8 billion, a result partly caused by greatly reducing the number of ships purchased.[40] Such overruns also delayed the delivery date of the new ships.

President Bush's defense budgets accelerated the hollowing out of American seapower. The Bush administration's critics still fault the former president for his high defense expenditures, arguing that the economic costs of the wars in Iraq and Afghanistan outweigh strategic benefits. Bush's supposedly bloated defense budgets, his critics argue, undermined American prosperity and stability while giving the military too much power in setting foreign policy.

This view of Bush-era defense spending misses the most important issue. President Bush came into office promising a $1.35 trillion tax cut. A modest defense budget would be only part of a broader policy to shrink the U.S. government and keep debt under control. Bush inherited the advantage of the Clinton-Gingrich revenue surplus from 1997 to 2001.[41] Executing the president's transformation vision would require subordinating operational and manpower budgets to high-tech advances in network warfare. The military services as a whole resisted such efforts, emphasizing already low operational budgets.[42]

The September 11th attacks forced the new administration to act quickly and decisively. The military was shifted to a war footing as the administration poured funds into operational budgets, particularly for the Army and Air Force. The Navy proved its worth as a rapid reaction force: carrier-based aircraft flew three-quarters of the strike missions in the opening phases of the Afghan War.[43] However, the service was encouraged to act as a support element for ground troops rather than as a global force with an international role and strategy. Chief of Naval Operations Admiral Vern Clark's Fleet Response Plan reconfigured the Navy for this role. The service was now redesigned to "surge" when needed, leaving unnecessary ships in port to decrease operational costs.[44]

The Navy was caught in a bind. Expensive transformation projects continued, but the service was required to maintain a high operational tempo to support engaged ground forces. An evaluation of the Bush administration's defense budgets purely by the numbers thus yields a skewed picture. Despite high defense budgets, the Navy was hollowed out during the first decade of the twenty-first century.

President Obama's cuts simply continued to squeeze

the Navy. Sequestration—explained in full in chapter 8—extended the hollowing process by further reducing funding. Since the Navy's global missions have remained static, the sea service has been forced to choose between funding current operations and long-term procurement. As a result, operational efficacy, future development, and personnel funding have suffered.

Force hollowness has had a material effect on the Navy. The major projects of the past decade—the *Zumwalt*-class destroyer and *Ford*-class carrier—are good demonstrations. Initial plans for construction of thirty-two *Zumwalt*-class destroyers were slashed to three.[45] This has had a major impact on available weapons systems. Weapons like the Navy's guided land-attack 5-inch shell—a rocket-assisted round with a range of 100 miles, fired by a standard 5-inch naval gun—are no longer viable because of the project's high cost compared to its volume of output.[46]

The *Ford*-class has been plagued by delays to its new technological systems. To keep the Navy at the congressionally mandated eleven-carrier minimum, the service commissioned the *Gerald R. Ford* while retiring the *Enterprise*, even though the *Ford* is not combat ready.

The littoral combat ship (LCS) project has also experienced major cuts. A December 2015 memo from the secretary of Defense ordered the Navy to cut its LCS procurement from fifty-two to forty ships. This reduction is significant: after much wrangling over its initial design, which was deemed insufficiently defensible, the LCS's firepower was increased with the expectation that it would become the Navy's future frigate.[47] Questions about the LCS's lethality in combat remain. However, there is no doubt that frigates are indispensable to commanding the sea in such strategic places as the South China Sea.

Force hollowness is also evident in the Navy's tactical fighter fleet. The F-35 project is unhappily famous for its cost overruns and major delays. Slated for initial operational capability in 2006, the F-35 was not fielded until 2016, and even then in limited numbers. The project is over $160 billion above its initial budget projections.[48] Concurrently, the Navy's fighter fleet of F/A-18 Hornets, Super Hornets, and Growlers is degrading over time: the service must rely on airframes from the Cold War.

When discussing the Navy's difficulties during the post–Vietnam War drawdown, Admiral Thomas Hayward, the twenty-first chief of naval operations, said:

> The Admirals back in Washington had so many pressures on them, so many diversions, they forgot their primary job is to make sure that the fleet is ready to go with highly trained and motivated sailors. The problem particularly manifests itself when the budget is way down.[49]

Just as after the Vietnam War, morale and motivation in today's fleet has significantly declined. A combination of high operational tempo and poor funding has created force hollowness among personnel, a phenomenon even more dangerous than material hollowness.

Officer retention rates are telling. The junior officer corps combines technical knowledge with command authority, overseeing specialized warrant and petty officers in their various subspecialties. Not only is the junior officer corps the future of the service but its morale and quality are also an immediate concern for the Navy's combat efficacy. The Navy commissioned a study in 2013 that discovered startlingly low retention rates for its junior officer corps throughout the service. Naval aviation had a retention rate of 36 percent, far below the 45 percent minimum acceptable threshold. Electronic warfare officers and strike fighter pilots were the hardest hit by the shortfall.[50]

The surface warfare community had an even lower retention rate of 35 percent.[51] Junior surface warfare officers have begun leaving the service after their first shore tour. Junior officers who leave the service are meaningful indicators of force hollowness and morale issues. Unlike senior officers, who have spent two decades or more in uniform and have earned retirement options, junior officers choose to exit the Navy after nearly a decade, but with no retirement benefits. They see better opportunities outside of the military, despite the lack of financial compensation on retirement. Post-command retention has also declined. From 2010 to 2012, the number of naval aviators who retired after their first command assignment jumped from seven to twenty.[52] A study of twenty-five executive officer prospects revealed that 70 percent were preparing to transition out of the military.

Just as hard ship numbers can mask material force hollowness, so retention numbers can mask human force hollowness. Despite the issues noted above, the Navy has been able to fill all its billets in each of its subspecialties. However, as officers with extensive operational experience in Iraq and Afghanistan retire, the Navy will begin to lose its most experienced leaders. This is likely to produce a negative effect on the junior officer corps, which is likely to influence the enlisted ranks.

A combination of low funding, long deployments, decreasing commitment to overseas conflicts, and increasingly competitive pay as the private sector returns to life are leaching top talent away from the Navy. When this talent drain is associated with an aging fleet and a Navy that lacks the funding to operate enough modern combatants, the signs of force hollowness are evident.

Pundits and politicians frequently remind Americans that the United States has the largest and best military the world has ever seen. No other nation fields eleven nuclear-powered aircraft carriers, can deploy a division anywhere in the world in a matter of days, and can maintain a constant strategic deterrence.

However, America's multiplying adversaries can see the signs of force hollowness. Just as Spain, Holland, and England did, America will face increasing challenges to its maritime power. A hollow military increases the risk of folding under this pressure, catching fire like a paper tiger at the light of a match.

CHAPTER II

WHY SEAPOWER?

For a maritime state, which the United States—bounded by water on three sides—assuredly is, an overseas bulwark of vigorously supported allies helps contain dangerous enemies, limits their ability to use the oceans as an invasion route, and allows the United States to apply power around the globe. A healthy network of politically like-minded allies also discourages the rise of hegemonies and the spread of their often inimical ideologies that would have unfavorable economic, security, and political consequences for America. A wisely fashioned alliance structure helps a global maritime power secure key choke points in the world's oceanic trade routes, on whose safety the United States depends for the health of its foreign trade.

Alliances are expensive to maintain, frustrating to preserve, and risky when promises to defend them must be honored. Alliances are also very useful, especially in persuading a hostile state not to test them. America's allies are a retaining wall that lies flush against potential adversaries on the Eurasian continent, from Russia to Iran to China and North Korea. U.S. alliances fortify the broad geographic girdle composed of states that border both the world's great oceans and the heartland of the Eurasian continent, from which the most serious current and likely future external threats to American security come.

"The British army should be a projectile to be fired by the British Navy."[1] Were the United States required to take the offensive at some future point, this observation by Lord Edward Grey, a British foreign secretary in the early twentieth century, would have strategic meaning. Its network of global alliances provides the United States with the space to insert U.S. ground troops onto the Eurasian land mass. Where allies are found wanting, for reasons of either geography or politics, the U.S. Marine Corps, an integral portion of American seapower, would be a "projectile," insofar as Lord Grey's remark applies to us.

The presence of American seapower sustains and inspirits our allies, all of whom are weaker than we are. Seapower protects the ever-increasing volume of global trade and, in an extremity, the transportation of military supplies. It deters conflict and succors the international order on which increasing prosperity rests. Strategically located allies—as all of ours are—offer logistic support for U.S. military power in the troubled neighborhoods where it matters. Allies create a defensive barrier that adds diplomatic, economic, and military power to the geographic advantage the United States enjoys from the oceans that separate us from Eurasia. For a maritime nation, the symbiotic relationship of seapower and alliances safeguards the nation's strategic depth—the broad sweep of its encircling seas—as it ensures that challenges to its security remain at a distance.

The idea of alliances is going through a rocky patch in the United States today. As a presidential candidate, Donald Trump spoke of "putting America first," an expression of views held by many who are dubious about the length and extent of American engagement beyond its borders since the attacks of 2001. Along the same line were questions about our allies in the North Atlantic Treaty Organization (NATO) who have failed to meet the defense spending obligations that the alliance requires. NATO members have been shirking their responsibility to spend 2 percent of their GDP on their own defense for decades. This is not a new story.

Only five NATO members—the United States, Greece, Poland, the United Kingdom, and Estonia—met the Atlantic Alliance's 2 percent of GDP requirement. Trump's suggestion would affect the other Baltic States, Germany, and the rest of the 82 percent of alliance members who failed to meet their NATO defense obligations. It might encourage them to take their commitments more seriously. Some already are. Romania, Lithuania, and Latvia will meet the 2 percent target before the end of 2018. Nevertheless, the choice of the electorate in the 2016 campaign implies a diminution of Western security and is a fair representation of the doubts with which Americans today regard an outward-looking foreign policy.

Some of the national media took note of candidate

Trump's comment. However, the U.S. electorate's general shrug at the threat to hold fellow alliance members responsible for their obligations indicates that the idea of a U.S.-led international order based on allies and supported by naval presence, deterrence, and, if necessary, seaborne expeditionary warfare no longer possesses the acceptance it had enjoyed since the end of World War II.

Skepticism about alliances is not limited to one party. President Obama began his administration by returning a bust of Winston Churchill to the British embassy. He said that then–Prime Minister David Cameron bore responsibility for the violence that followed Muammar Qaddafi's death when "he [the prime minister] became distracted by other things."[2] When Islamist terrorists attacked the *Charlie Hebdo* magazine in Paris in 2015, killing eleven staff members, heads of state from Europe to the Middle East marched through the French capital's streets in solidarity. The White House sent no one.

Relations between the United States and Israel declined precipitously in the Obama administration. The media blamed this on frosty personal relations between Prime Minister Benjamin Netanyahu and President Obama. More likely, the latter believed that West Bank settlements are the cause of friction between Israel and the Palestinian Authority and that this tension is key to resolving the Middle East's problems.

Additional examples of the Obama administration's cool relations with allies point in the same direction, showing a profound doubt about the wisdom of the U.S. military's intercession as a keystone of alliance relations, a certainty that U.S. engagement is more provocative than stabilizing, and an abiding faith that important strategic regions of the world can best achieve equilibrium if left to their own devices. The Obama administration's deep hope of concluding large strategic agreements with states—Iran, for example—that regard the United States with enmity is the obverse face of its ambivalent view of allies. The ambivalence did not begin with President Obama.

The attempt to patch things up with powers that regard the United States as hostile started well before he took office. A senior foreign policy official of George W. Bush's administration asked a highly respected elder academic, one of America's leading experts on Turkey and the Middle East, about the advisability of building bridges to Iran's radical clerics. The professor answered that the effort would "earn nothing except the enmity of the Iranian people and the contempt of their rulers."[3]

President Obama also tried his hand at grand bargains. He sought to "reset" relations with Russia, notwithstanding Vladimir Putin's 2008 invasion of Georgia. The remaking of U.S. foreign policy did not end with Russia's rejection of Obama's overtures. Echoing Obama's 2013 televised wishes to Iran, Secretary of State John Kerry wrote the same year of his commitment "to resolving the differences between Iran and the United States, and continuing to work toward a new day in our relationship."[4]

Iran's leadership was unfazed. In early May 2016, the deputy commander of Iran's Islamic Revolutionary Guard Corps, General Hossein Salami, threatened to close the Strait of Hormuz to the United States and its allies. He added that "Americans cannot make safe any part of the world."[5] The Iranian general's overstated claims aside, he has a point.

Most of America's allies are medium-sized states located where geography and the nation's broad political interest in containing potential adversaries combine. Asked to define Central Europe, a senior Polish statesman once sought refuge in geography, calling it "the area between the Baltic and the Black Seas."[6] This description includes, among others, the Baltic States and the Visegrad Group of the Czech Republic, Hungary, Poland, and Slovakia, as well as states that abut the Balkan Peninsula, Romania and Bulgaria. These mostly democratic states sit on or near Russia's western border, so that the center of the entire area brackets Russia while its littoral extremities touch the seas through which Russian ships must pass to reach the Atlantic or the Mediterranean. Geography, containment, and politics combine in favor of the United States. Wise policy will exploit these strengths by supporting the Atlantic Alliance.

The post–Cold War commitment of the United States to the independence and security of Central and Eastern European states has added to Western Europe's strategic depth as it nourished democratic stability in the cradle of the wars that convulsed Europe beginning more than a century ago. The same American commitment has countered Moscow's effort to control utterly the flow of energy westward and corrode NATO, an alliance whose ability to preserve freedom on the western end of the Eurasian continent remains vital if there is to be such a thing as "the West."

The Middle East is significantly different from Europe and Asia because America's most important ally, Israel, is a regional power that has successfully withstood neighboring enemies' attacks since reassuming its position as a Jewish state nearly seventy years ago. Otherwise, America's generally weak allies are mostly grouped together along the Persian Gulf, where their self-interest in resisting Iran and maintaining peaceful seas over which their oil can be transported has aligned with America's large interest in an unmolested supply of Middle Eastern oil and—now—growing interest in containing Iran.

Finally, there is China, where American allies, friends, and partners bracket the East Asian mainland from Japan to South Korea to Taiwan, the Philippines, the Australian continent, Singapore, Vietnam, Thailand, and the subcontinent, India. The U.S.-led network of bilateral alliances has supported the progress of democracy, large strides in regional prosperity, and increased markets for U.S. goods and services. As with the European peninsula's oceanic borders, the dependable presence and deterrent ability of American seapower has been pivotal in supplying the hard power to ensure the safety of free sea-lanes, defend allies and friends, and convince a growing potential adversary that nothing is to be gained from war with the United States.

While a peaceable U.S. presence has remained a constant in the region since the end of World War II, its effects have changed. Where U.S. interest once offered stability in which East Asian states prospered, today the bilateral relationships that exist between these states and the United

States are a land moat against Chinese regional hegemony as well as a breakwater against China's ambitions in the island chain that lies further east in the Pacific. Because half the world's population lives in Asia, regional hegemony there has a meaning unlike anywhere else.

The allies, partners, and friends that successive U.S. administrations have constructed into a global system since World War II share several important characteristics. They are all at great distances from the United States but quite close to potential adversaries. They ring the Eurasian continent. Besides the Arab states and Vietnam, they are democracies. With very few exceptions, they sit astride vital sea lines of communication or choke points through which a large fraction of international shipping passes. From their shores, seapower can be exercised, whether it is to guarantee the safety of the world's navigational routes, command the proximate seas, project force ashore, encourage allies by a U.S. naval presence, or supply the bases that support America's entire network of global alliances.

If budget cuts, loss of interest, disengagement, or other obstacles decimate American power, the nation will lose its ability to make safe the parts of the world in which it has a strategic interest. This will result in historically unprecedented international chaos, from the South and East China Seas to the Persian Gulf to the Mediterranean and, most immediately, to Russia.

The seagoing inklings of this chaos are in full sight as the United States concentrates on combating terror at the expense of reinvigorating its ability to defeat such potential adversaries as Russia and China. The steel sinews of

American seapower not only have guarded our ability to ship goods abroad and communicate with allies but also, since the end of World War II, have provided an unequaled ability to respond to crises, remain present in troubled regions, provide disaster relief and humanitarian assistance, and apply force from sea to land. Our seapower has served as the single strongest guarantor of such order as exists in the world today.

No one alive today knows a world in which general principles of order do not exist. Although practiced imperfectly and selectively, most states acknowledge them as the standard of international behavior. Respect for national sovereignty, government by consent of the governed, freedom of navigation on the high seas, and economic systems based on capitalism are some of the better-known elements of the order. All have been objectives of American foreign and security policy since the nation's founding.

Today's order has its intellectual roots in the transition from ancient to modern political theory that took place as human nature's concern with life in society replaced virtue as the aim of politics. For practical purposes, the international system we know began with the Treaties of Westphalia, which were signed in 1648 and which ended the Thirty Years' War. The war had been an exceptionally barbaric European free-for-all over religion. At its end, the duke of the religiously divided northern European duchy of Pomerania described the long conflict as having "driven [the poor] to such unnatural and inhuman food as buds of trees and grass, and even to the flesh of their own children and of dead bodies."[7]

In the event, a balance of state powers and practicality lighted Europe's path away from repeated violent explosions of religious dissension fueled by the collision of imperial ambition, aspiring states, and lesser principalities. As with the Magna Carta, in which the nobility's specific complaints against King John led to a broader acceptance of individual rights, the Westphalian agreements set in motion today's international order.

Since World War II, America's allies, its military, and its diplomacy have been the most important guarantor of the international system. When fascists in Europe and Asia sought its destruction, the United States together with its allies defeated them. Faced with a challenge from the Soviet Union, the United States and its allies contained it.

In all cases, the ability of the United States to communicate with allies and demonstrate solidarity with them reinforced our partners' determination and fighting spirit. From Normandy to Inchon to Danang to Baghdad, the United States did more than encourage and reinforce. It fought. These engagements were not altruistic. Such actions as deposing a Panamanian dictator, heading off a military coup against an elected Philippine leader, or preventing additional genocide in the Balkans were aimed at local and regionalized threats. But the large contests, undertaken against large threats, had the collateral effect of preserving the international system.

Both diplomacy and force supported the international system. The single most important military enabler has been seapower. The United States used it to sustain England in the fight against Hitler, to transport men and matériel across the Atlantic, and to return to the European continent by force. The island-hopping approach to Japan during World War II would have been impossible without naval and amphibious forces.

Had the Warsaw Pact invaded Western Europe, U.S. seapower would have been indispensable to NATO's defense or to succor a second invasion had one been needed to free the continent. The ballistic missiles carried aboard U.S. submarines guaranteed the means of retaliation if the United States were struck first. The Cold War could not have ended well if U.S. seapower had consisted of either a regional or a coastal navy.

Threats to the international system did not stop with the Cold War. They went into a remission, which has ended. Today, China and Russia, respectively, threaten international order by seeking to incorporate the South and East China Seas' international waters as sovereign ones; and by violating the sovereign territory of Ukraine, by projecting power from Crimea throughout the Black Sea, by challenging the security of the Baltic States, and by assisting Syria's criminal ruler in preserving his grip in the Middle East, including on the Mediterranean's eastern shore. North Korea is an international miscreant armed with nuclear weapons and missiles of increasing range. As with other surprising achievements of this impoverished and despotic state, it is a question of time until North Korea miniaturizes nuclear devices sufficiently to mount them on missiles of increasing range. Iran's support for terror and such Sunni terror organizations as Hamas aim at the heart of democratic governance. The order that any of these states or non-state actors represent would change a tolerably messy world into a brutal one.

Global reach is essential to preventing such a transformation. The U.S. Navy is this nation's chief instrument of global reach. To name a few examples of its influence, American warships make regular port visits around the world, conduct exercises with friends and allies, engage in humanitarian missions, lead anti-piracy patrols in the Gulf of Aden, and maintain freedom of navigation. It provides the sinews on which the international system's preservation rests. Allies were critical when America fought for independence. They have been essential in the major and lesser conflicts and confrontations of the past century. As great power competition once again characterizes international relations, America's allies are indispensable to our security.

CHAPTER III

SINEWS CHALLENGED: RUSSIA

Challenges to the international order are synonymous with today's threats to the United States, whose position as the world's dominant maritime power is at risk because of increasing threats and decreasing political will to pay for a military to deter them. An understanding of the development of the naval forces of our potential adversaries is essential to grasp the challenge that U.S. seapower faces today.

RUSSIA

A sense of loss or humiliation felt by an entire people is powerful. Germany's response to its loss of World War I and the terms that the victorious allies imposed were an important part of Hitler's rise. China's anger at Europe's nineteenth-century colonization remains an animating force throughout the Middle Kingdom. Russians may be pleased that the tyranny to which they are subject is no longer exercised by communists. But they are not pleased at Russia's descent from its status as one of the world's two superpowers. Understanding what Russia was is essential to understanding what Russia seeks once again to be. In no category of national power is this more important than in the strategic influence that a strong navy gave the Soviet Union.

The professional career of Commander-in-Chief of the Soviet Navy Admiral Sergei Gorshkov poses a problem for Leo Tolstoy's idea that history is shaped more by the actions of multitudes rather than by great men. Gorshkov single-handedly transformed the Russian navy from a marginally effective coastal force into a genuine threat to American and Western naval superiority. Much like Imperial Germany's *Großadmiral* Alfred von Tirpitz, Gorshkov combined an advanced understanding of politics with a keen mind for naval strategy. He managed to remain in command of the Soviet navy under five general secretaries, a feat that no other individual of similar standing accomplished in the Union of Soviet Socialist Republics (USSR). While the U.S. Navy had eight chiefs of naval operations during the same time, Gorshkov's unified vision directed the growth of the Soviet navy for more than a quarter century.[1]

During the 1930s, multiple purges cut Soviet naval ambitions short. World War II did not help. The USSR's greatest adversary, Nazi Germany, abandoned its ambition of a powerful surface fleet after Karl Doenitz replaced Erich Raeder as chief of the *Kriegsmarine*. Thus, the Soviets had little reason to create naval forces beyond those needed to protect allied convoys that carried war matériel to the northern port of Archangel. The "Red Navy" received only 6.6 percent of the military budget in 1944, and more than 400,000 Soviet sailors were sent into battle on the Eastern Front as infantrymen.[2]

Immediately after the war ended, the USSR captured a number of German U-boat engineers, who helped chart a course toward a major increase in the quality of Soviet submarines. Nevertheless, the renamed Soviet navy was placed behind the army, strategic missile forces, air force, and air defense forces in service seniority rankings. Gorshkov began a decades-long campaign to convince the Politburo that naval forces were necessary for the country's future. Drawing upon the successes of the Russian navy in the early 1700s, he argued that the new Soviet fleet would be used predominantly to support the Red Army.

The United States's 1962 naval quarantine during the Cuban Missile Crisis helped convince Soviet leaders of the need for a stronger navy. The Soviet Union had little flexibility in responding to the U.S. blockade, a fact that narrowed its options during the crisis and forced Nikita Khrushchev into a high-risk game of nuclear brinksmanship with President Kennedy. Gorshkov used the groundwork he had laid over the previous six years as admiral of the fleet to secure greater funding for the Soviet navy. He began to create a major blue-water force.

Gorshkov addressed the difficulties of cold northern environments by developing the world's largest and most advanced icebreaker fleet to facilitate year-round operations. The Soviet navy was also faced with multiple choke points, such as the Greenland–Iceland–United Kingdom (GIUK) gap and the Dardanelles, which the Western powers routinely patrolled. Geography constrained the movement of ships into the open ocean. Resupplying these ships on ma-jor patrols was no less a challenge. Unlike the U.S. Navy, the Soviet Union did not have an extensive network of bases abroad. Diplomacy, threats, luck, and an increasing presence prevailed. By the mid-1970s, the Soviet navy rou-tinely deployed to Cuba, Africa, and the Indian Ocean.

Soviet naval strategy centered on area denial. Gorshkov wanted to prevent the United States and its allies from moving large numbers of troops and supplies to Europe to support a prolonged ground campaign. To accomplish this, Gorshkov built a fleet centered on submarines, which were supplemented with various surface combatants that carried anti-air and anti-ship missiles.[3]

Kynda- and *Kresta*-class guided-missile cruisers, launched in the mid-1960s, were both comparable to American air-defense cruisers at the time and carried a wide variety of anti-air, anti-surface, and anti-submarine warfare combat systems. Nimble Soviet destroyers and frigates such as the *Kashin-* and *Krivak*-class surface combatants bristled with long-range anti-ship missiles and anti-submarine mines and torpedoes. By the late 1970s, the Soviets had begun work on a very short takeoff and landing aircraft car-rier, similar to the United Kingdom's *Invincible*-class anti-submarine warfare carriers, but with a heavier surface-to-surface armament.[4]

Still, Gorshkov's pride was his submarines. According to Soviet naval doctrine, surface ships would engage air threats while undersea forces would shoulder the bulk of offensive action. By the late 1970s, the Soviet navy operated close to two hundred attack submarines, the majority of which were diesel electric.[5] The Alfa-class—NATO's designation—nuclear-powered submarine was the fastest in the world at the time of its construction in 1977. The Soviets also developed more than a dozen Charlie-class nuclear-powered submarines that carry cruise missiles, designed to stay at sea on extended patrols and attack NATO ships with their long-range missiles. The Soviet Oscar-class submarines, under construction at the end of the 1970s, were long-range, high-endurance guided-missile boats comparable to America's.

By the early 1980s, the Soviet navy operated around 260 attack, cruiser, and guided-missile submarines, a fleet larger than the American submarine force at that time.[6] Gorshkov's navy supplemented its surface and subsurface fleet with substantial land-based naval aviation. A modified version of the Tu-95 Bear bomber was used for long-range reconnaissance. Strike aircraft included the Tu-22M Backfire bomber and Il-38 May anti-submarine warfare aircraft.[7]

In addition, Soviet strategic naval forces at that time included seventy ballistic-missile nuclear submarines (SSBNs) of varying types, the most advanced of which could slip undetected through the narrow passage between the Kola Peninsula and the main Russian land mass. The Yankee- and Delta-class SSBNs formed the backbone of the USSR's sea-based deterrent force. Gorshkov assigned these boats to targets in North America, reserving European targets for the less-advanced Hotel- and Golf-class submarines.[8] This choice eliminated the need for older, louder boats to transit the GIUK gap and increased the Soviet nuclear arsenal's efficiency. The Soviet construction program of ten submarines per year between 1968 and 1977 facilitated this rapid increase in subsurface forces.

Amphibious capabilities were the one area that the Soviet navy neglected during the 1970s. Power projection was
never the goal of Soviet sea control strategy; creating an
extensive amphibious fleet would have been counterpro-
ductive. Nevertheless, Gorshkov initiated some modernization of amphibious capabilities, constructing three *Ivan
Rogov*–class amphibious ships.[9] These vessels could operate offshore, dispatching assault troops from a well deck,
or discharge tanks and armored personnel carriers directly
onto a beach in an opposed landing. Each ship could carry
520 marines and twenty-five tanks, or a maximum of fifty-
three tanks and eighty armored personnel carriers. Even in
amphibious capabilities, the Soviets were slowly catching
up to the United States.

Gorshkov's Soviet navy could not execute the same
range of missions that Admiral Elmo Zumwalt's U.S. Navy
could during the 1970s, even before the Reagan buildup.
However, the Soviet navy was more than capable of challenging the free use of critical sea-lanes by U.S. forces for
transport and combat. At the same time, the U.S. Navy was
shrinking as World War II ships were decommissioned,
with the expectation that the administration and Congress
would support replacing them with modern combatants.

1972–1980—THE USSR IN AFRICA AND LATIN AMERICA

As U.S. military power declined during the 1970s, America's rivals became bolder, taking advantage of increasing volatility in the Middle East, Africa, and, later, Latin
America. America's withdrawal from Vietnam and its ensu-
ing global reset had not decreased the range of its commit-

ments, but it had emboldened its adversaries. A resurgent Soviet navy with a true global reach allowed the USSR to exert its influence on several continents. It helped shape Soviet foreign policy throughout the last two decades of the USSR's existence, reinforcing Moscow's stock in the Third World and its position as a global power.

Nixon's presidency initiated the period of rapprochement with the USSR known as détente. This policy represented a shift toward a traditional balance-of-power diplomacy, with the goal of creating a tense but stable international environment. American military power would prevent the Soviet Union from expanding its dominance into Western Europe. But the Soviets would refrain from undue provocations globally in return for a relaxation of the West's economic barrier against the Eastern Bloc. Simultaneously, Nixon and his successors pursued a strategic reset with China intended to safeguard American interests in the Pacific, while whipsawing the Soviets and raising questions about China's reliability as a fraternal socialist partner.

For the first half of the decade, this policy was largely successful. Zumwalt's slowly modernizing U.S. Navy remained dominant over its Soviet adversary, and American conventional and strategic forces in Europe deterred Soviet aggression. The State Department undertook arms control initiatives that produced arguable results.

Still, a host of factors undermined détente after 1975, resulting in increasing challenges to American power. The post–Vietnam War decline in American military power and the United States's refocus toward Europe's central front allowed adversaries to exploit openings in Africa and Latin America. Moreover, the relative economic strength of the United States compared to its allies, particularly Japan, had declined. The period of unquestioned American economic dominance ended simultaneously with America's military drawdown after the Vietnam War.

Political and strategic reasons dictated the USSR's decision to increase its influence in Latin America and Africa. Both continents were fertile grounds for postcolonial Marxist and nationalist movements, offering Soviet emissaries ideological access to various governments and rebel groups. Strategically, Soviet military planners recognized that the South Atlantic could influence NATO's main line of communications. NATO might bottle up Russian submarines and surface combatants in such choke points as the GIUK gap, but Soviet naval forces deployed in Africa and Latin America would, at a minimum, tie down significant American assets in the South Atlantic and hold out the hope of distracting the United States from supplying its fellow NATO members during a central European conflict.

The Soviet Union began by targeting Latin America. Latin American stability has been a major U.S. interest since the 1820s. Putting pressure on the United States in this theater made obvious sense to Soviet strategic planners. Cuba became the linchpin of Soviet activities in Latin America. Cuba's extensive revolutionary activities throughout the region gave the Soviet Union easy access to multiple guerrilla groups throughout Latin and South America. In return, the Soviet Union funneled huge quantities of arms to Castro's regime, with arms shipments in 1981 reaching 63,000 tons.[10] By 1980, Soviet military aid to Cuba alone was ten times the United States's military assistance to the entirety of South and Central America.[11]

Nicaragua served as the other pillar of Soviet regional policy. Throughout the 1970s, the Soviet Union progressively increased its support for the Sandinista National Liberation Front (*Frente Sandinista de Liberación Nacional*, or FSLN), a Marxist revolutionary group that sought to topple Nicaragua's dictator Anastasio Somoza. Beginning in 1978, the Soviet-equipped and -trained FSLN escalated their attacks on government forces, leading to a full-scale civil war between the Somoza regime and the Sandinistas.[12] Significant Soviet support allowed the Sandinistas to overthrow the regime and establish control of Nicaragua in July 1979. Not since 1959 had a country in the Western Hemisphere fallen to communist rule. The Soviet Union bankrolled the new Nicaraguan military, enabling it to grow to 45,000 men by the mid-1980s.[13] Throughout Latin America, left-wing rebel groups and insurgencies increased their activities, typically with external Soviet backing. By 1980, the USSR supported two major communist regimes, a third friendly regime in Peru, and two insurgent groups in El Salvador and Costa Rica.[14]

In response to growing Soviet power, President Carter reactivated Operation Condor, the Department of State–Department of Defense–CIA program initiated by President Nixon and Secretary of State Henry Kissinger to train, equip, and finance anti-communist rebels and governments throughout the continent. Nevertheless, instability persisted and grew in Latin America. The Soviets were enjoying a measure of success made possible by Admiral Gorshkov's increasingly capable navy.

Russian ships operated out of Cuban ports from 1957 onward, and the Kremlin frequently requested that nations

—including Peru, Ecuador, and Chile—provide the Soviet navy with basing facilities.[15] Soviet ships routinely escorted arms shipments from Russia in and out of Latin American ports. The presence of Soviet naval vessels increased the risk of conflict at sea to prevent arms shipments. Any confrontation between Soviet and American ships had the potential to escalate. Even without direct Soviet combat support, the expanding militaries of Nicaragua and Cuba threatened the heavily used sea lines of communication in the Gulf of Mexico. This factor would significantly complicate crisis planning in the event of hostilities. In Latin America, the Soviet navy clearly influenced and facilitated Soviet foreign policy throughout the 1970s and into the 1980s.

Africa was also identified as a target of opportunity. Postcolonial Africa had become hospitable for revolutionary Marxism, which combined with tribal loyalties and various Pan-African ideologies to encourage political instability. The pervasiveness of left-wing ideology gave the Soviet Union and its Cuban ally an inroad into the continent. In Angola, the Soviet Union and Cuba supported the People's Movement for the Liberation of Angola (MPLA), another revolutionary leftist organization with the goal of overthrowing the Angolan government and establishing a revolutionary Marxist regime.[16]

Wary of being drawn into a multi-factional conflict, especially after seeing the experience of the United States in Vietnam, the USSR restricted itself to financial and technical support of the rebels.[17] Throughout the decade, the Soviets attempted to convince the MPLA to allow them to construct a naval base on Angola's coast. Although this never came to be, during 1978 and 1979 it seemed entirely possible that the USSR could obtain its first international naval base in a strategically critical location. Submarines and surface combatants based in Angola would have directly threatened American shipping and communication in any major conflict. The USSR also supported Ethiopia in its war against Somalia in 1978, to assert its influence in the Horn of Africa.

The Soviet navy played a role in Africa similar to that in Latin America. Russian vessels carried vital supplies to the various Kremlin-backed rebel groups in Angola and operated out of multiple foreign ports. However, the Soviet navy's actions in Africa were much more aggressive than in Latin America. Soviet ships provided gunfire support to the MPLA in 1976 and attacked Ethiopian rebels in 1978.[18] The USSR deployed its modern, long-range cruise missiles to ships operating off the West African coast, increasing the efficacy of Soviet naval fire support. In 1980, the USSR deployed a helicopter carrier and supporting squadron to Mozambique.[19] Soviet naval presence was both visible and consequential throughout Africa during the 1970s and later in the 1980s.

Admiral Gorshkov transformed what Soviet rulers initially regarded as an appendage into an effective instrument of national power that generated positive strategic value for the Soviet regime. However, the fleet sailed into shoal waters and went aground as the Soviet Union's economy collapsed in the late 1980s. The communist regime temporized at first and later began a descent from which it would not recover.

The Soviet hammer-and-sickle flag was lowered over

the Kremlin for the last time on Christmas Day, 1991. Russian military spending went into free fall. Fighters and bombers, whose design necessitated far more attention than Western military aircraft, sat on aprons for lack of maintenance and spare parts. Insufficient fuel immobilized tanks, while naval vessels rusted at their moorings. As one consequence, Chechen rebels turned back a large Russian assault in the 1996 battle for Grozny, the capital city of Chechnya.

During the mid-1990s, the Russian military budget dwindled to a trickle. Penury forced operating military units to forage to pay for ammunition and fuel.[20] In August 2000 the Russian navy conducted its first major fleet exercise in a decade, in the Barents Sea. An Oscar-class nuclear-powered submarine, the *Kursk*, which carried anti-ship cruise missiles and torpedoes, experienced a series of explosions and fires that sank the boat, killing all 118 sailors aboard.

But a crippled military was not part of Vladimir Putin's design for Russia's return as a major power. Moscow reversed its military spending decline in 1999, when funding for its armed forces reached a nadir of a little more $20 billion.[21] Spending climbed to more than $90 billion annually in 2012, a 27 percent increase over its level just after the Cold War ended. Not only the rise in oil revenues but also Vladimir Putin's will account for the quadrupling of the military budget in thirteen years. Falling energy prices have battered Russia's rearmament, but Moscow's rulers have persisted in their effort to modernize the nation's military forces, despite economic setbacks.

RUSSIAN NAVAL MODERNIZATION

In the United States, we take for granted the necessity of openness to ideas from afar, technological innovation, and a vigorous economy able to supply revenue for national defense. This combination is one of our virtues. Not all countries share it. Peter the Great's construction of a Russian navy required an efficient taxation system where none existed as well as a defense industry that met or exceeded the standard of the times. During Peter's reign as czar—from 1682 to 1721—some ships were built with green wood and fastened together with wooden pegs. They would sink in the absence of any external force.[22]

One hundred seventy-seven years after Peter died, Leo Tolstoy published an essay titled "Famine or Not Famine" in the *Russian Gazette*. Tolstoy was responding to a private letter he had received from a Mrs. Sokolóv, who described the impoverishment and hunger of peasants in the Vorónezh district, the northern border of which is 200 miles south of Moscow. Vorónezh is known for the richness of its black soil and its exceptional ability to produce sugar beets, grain, potatoes, sunflowers, and livestock. Tolstoy listed several causes for the region's hunger: indifference to spiritual matters, dejection of spirit, contempt for agricultural labor, and inertia. In particular, he wrote about the peasants'

> unwillingness to change their habits and their condition. During all these years, when in the other governments [i.e., districts] of Russia, European plows, iron harrows,

new methods of sowing seeds, improved horticulture, and even mineral manures were coming into use, in the center, everything remained the same—the wooden sokha [a primitive plow that cuts the earth but does not turn it over], and all the habits and customs of Rurik's time [the ninth century].[23]

In many respects Russia remains a technologically backward state. Even today, the technology for extracting hydrocarbons from Russian oil fields comes from the West. Modernization, where it exists in Russia, demands firm resolve, uninterrupted purposefulness, and iron commitment. Notwithstanding the general population's backwardness, the Soviets demonstrated that these qualities could be mustered.

A revival of this applied determination is under way again. Russia's navy has now awakened from the state-imposed hibernation of the years that immediately followed the end of the Cold War. Russian nuclear-powered submarines were deployed for 1,500 days in 2015, a 50 percent increase over the preceding year, according to a Russian navy spokesman.[24] One of the several classes of nuclear-powered subs that saw more deployments was the Oscar-class guided-missile submarine *Smolensk*.[25] With twenty-four anti-ship cruise missiles each, the eight Oscar-class boats are particularly well-suited to attack U.S. aircraft carriers and their accompanying surface escorts.

Russian naval planning calls for these boats to be modernized with updated sonar, electronic intercept capabilities, and fire control. Without modifying the hull, the modernized boat will triple its missile-carrying ability. The changes substantially augment Russia's ability to threaten the access of American surface ships to such places as the Baltic and Mediterranean Seas and the approaches from the Atlantic to the North Sea between Greenland and Iceland and northern Great Britain.

In May 2016, the Russian navy launched the sixth and final modernized Kilo-class submarine. *Kolpino*, named for a municipality of St. Petersburg, was built for service in the Black Sea. This inland sea is the center of festering conflicts and tensions from Turkey to Transnistria to the Donbass region of eastern Ukraine to Abkhazia, South Ossetia, and large swaths of Georgia that have been the source of tension and bloodshed between Georgia and Russia. Naval control of the Black Sea advances Russia's interest in reasserting control over the region. *Kolpino* and the modernized members of its class are longer than the Kilo boats after which they were modeled. They can launch torpedoes as well as cruise missiles aimed at land and sea targets. One boat of the class, *Rostov-na-Donu*, named for the city of Rostov-on-Don near the Sea of Azov in south Russia, fired cruise missiles at Syrian targets from the Mediterranean in December 2015.

The improvements have allowed Russian submarine operations in the Atlantic to return to Cold War levels. The Russian navy's submarine activity is matched by its advanced technology. Royal Navy Vice Admiral Clive Johnstone, commander of NATO's Maritime Command, says that "through an extraordinary investment path not mirrored by the West," Russia has made "technology leaps that are remarkable." He adds that Russian submarines possess "longer ranges, they have better systems, [and] they're freer to operate," and notes "a rise in professionalism and ability to operate their boats that we haven't seen before."[26]

The Royal Navy's views are shared on this side of the Atlantic. Rear Admiral David Johnson, former director of the Navy's submarine design programs, told a Naval Submarine League symposium in 2014 that "We'll be facing tough potential opponents. One has only to look at the *Severodvinsk* [a nuclear-powered attack submarine that entered service in 2014]. I am so impressed with this ship," said Admiral Johnson, "that I had . . . a model [built] from unclassified data."[27] The boat's submerged displacement is greater than that of the *Virginia*-class U.S. attack submarine; it has been tested with the Kalibr land-attack supersonic-capable cruise missile as well as the same missile system's anti-ship and anti-submarine missiles. The Kalibr is the missile that Russia says its submarines in the Eastern Mediterranean and Caspian Sea launched respectively in 2015 and 2016 at Syrian targets.

The commander of the U.S. 6th Fleet, Vice Admiral James Foggo III, wrote in June 2016 that, "Combined with extensive and frequent submarine patrols throughout the North Atlantic and Norwegian Sea, and forward-deployed forces in Syria, Russia has the capability to hold nearly all NATO maritime forces at risk. No longer is the maritime space uncontested. For the first time in almost 30 years, Russia is a significant and aggressive maritime power. . . . The clear advantage that we enjoyed in anti-submarine warfare during the Cold War is waning."[28] Just as in both World Wars, the cat-and-mouse maneuvers of the Cold War's great maritime confrontation contested the control of the sea lines of communication between democracies on both shores of the Atlantic. Although there is no doubt that the United States controls the Atlantic's vast expanses today, Russia's reemergence as a naval power raises troubling and important questions about the future.

WHAT IS PUTIN UP TO?

When the Soviet Union ceased to exist in December 1991, the so-called republics that girdled Russia to its south and west had already declared independence and become sovereign nations. These states had not been republics; they were run by communist parties controlled from Moscow. The dissolution of the empire ended in the creation of fifteen states that reached from the Baltic Sea, southeast to include Ukraine, and continuing along the Black Sea's eastern coast to the Caspian and beyond, deep into the eastern frontier of Kazakhstan, which touches Mongolia.

The results of the breach were large. Before December 1991, the USSR's population stood at about 290 million. Moscow controlled more than 22 million square kilometers, approximately one-sixth of the earth's land surface. Dissolution cost the Soviet Union 139 million citizens. Russia was left with a total population of 151 million. Its land area had been reduced by nearly one-fourth.

In his 2005 state of the nation address to Russia's parliament, Vladimir Putin called the collapse of the Soviet Union and the attendant diminution of Russia "the greatest geopolitical catastrophe of the [twentieth] century."[29] If Russia's shrunken borders lead toward a more stable region, Putin is wrong. So far, however, his efforts suggest that the catastrophe lies not in the Soviets' loss but rather in their successors' attempt to reconstruct the shattered pedestal from which the USSR fell. If Russian policy triumphs, animated by the same kind of resentment at having lost an empire that consumed Germany after losing World War I, history may judge Putin's remark as an understatement.

Russia's subjugation of Georgia in 2008, along with Moscow's recognition of two breakaway Georgian regions as sovereign states (one of which—Abkhazia—possesses more than 100 miles of coastline on the Black Sea), was a lackluster military operation. But it sent a clear message that Russia's economic, demographic, and political misfortunes would not prevent her rulers from rekindling the fear of domination that has been a fact of life in the region since before the Russian Revolution.

Vladimir Putin's invasion of Crimea in 2014, along with his military support for the ethnic Russians in eastern Ukraine who needed no prodding to take up arms against their own government, emphasized Moscow's ambition to reassert regional hegemony. The armed conflict between Ukraine's democratically elected government and Russian-backed separatists in eastern Ukraine continues today.

Putin's ambitions do not end in Ukraine. Extending their reach beyond border states, Russian military forces intervened on behalf of Syrian dictator Bashar al-Assad in 2015, four years after the Syrian civil war began. The intervention improved Moscow's access to a Syrian port, Latakia, on the Mediterranean and a nearby airfield that is used to conduct missions in support of Assad. It also enabled Iran to plant a violent foot in Syria in the form of an expanding network of Shiite terror groups.

The late-2016 fall of Aleppo, the center of Syrian resistance to Assad, was a major success for Putin. Where U.S. policy makers saw only failed outcomes, Putin gambled that Russia would not become enmeshed in a prolonged civil conflict. He won. The victory established Russia as the major external power in the Levant, consolidated his position of strength in the Black Sea and Eastern Mediterranean, and underlined the retreat of the United States from its previous influence in the region.

Russia's access to the world's great seas and oceans offers at once opportunities to complicate the effectiveness of the United States and its allies operating in the same bodies of water, to disrupt communications between the United States and its allies, and to project global force. A revanchist power couldn't ask for much more. Russia has largely succeeded in monopolizing the energy output of its former possessions in Central Asia. Neutering NATO, replacing the United States as the major external power in the Middle East, and reestablishing control over the Baltic States as well as Ukraine would help right the wrongs that Vladimir Putin believes were perpetrated when the Russian Federation replaced the Soviet Union.

Putin is acting as purposefully at sea as he has on land. Usually the two are linked. With its seizure of the Crimea, Russia regains the access to the Black Sea that the USSR exploited to keep its littoral client states in line and to make Turkey nervous. Today, as before, the Black Sea provides a gateway to the Bosphorus and the Mediterranean.

Moreover, Russia understands the same lesson that China, Iran, North Korea, and every other potential adversary learned from Desert Storm: defeating the United States at sea today is much harder than denying it the access needed to apply American land and seapower. Russian possession of the Crimea allows its modern effective anti-surface and surface-to-air missiles to challenge access to the region by NATO vessels, including those of the United States, which conduct presence and deterrence missions in the Black Sea. Moscow's maritime and continental efforts to restore its position in the Black Sea region are particularly effective as Western national security policy makers concentrate their attention on Russia's increasing threat to the Baltic States.

Examples of Russian military preparation in the Baltics include increased long-range anti-ship missiles and beefed-up air-defense systems in the Kaliningrad military district. In April 2016, Russian tactical jets flew several high-speed passes dangerously close to the destroyer USS *Donald Cook* in the Baltic Sea.[30] The Russian defense ministry is also tightening its belt; its month-long investigation into its Baltic Sea fleet command led to the firing of fifty senior naval officers for leadership and operational misjudgment in early July 2016.[31]

But in the revised Russian Marine Doctrine that was published in July 2015, Putin's naval focus is the Atlantic Ocean and the Arctic. "We emphasize the Atlantic," states the document, "because NATO has been developing actively of late and coming closer to our borders, and Russia is . . . responding to these developments."[32] This is meant for a domestic audience that is receptive to Putin's claim that he protects them from Western states bristling with weaponry and bent on subduing Russia. It's nonsense. Eighty-five percent of NATO's member states currently fail to meet the alliance's goal of spending 2 percent of GDP on defense. NATO's largest single military power, the United States, is experiencing sufficient difficulty in keeping a single aircraft carrier deployed in the Western Pacific and the Persian Gulf so that intervals have been introduced into the carriers' operational schedules, during which no carrier is on station.

Closer to the truth is the Russian document's seeming non sequitur that follows its point about the Atlantic's importance: "The second reason [for emphasizing the Atlantic] is that Crimea and Sevastopol have been reunited with Russia and we need to take measures for their rapid integration into the national economy. Of course, we are also restoring Russia's naval presence in the Mediterranean."[33]

The Atlantic is important to Russia's revanchist goals because an Atlantic presence challenges America's ability to sustain NATO if there is a war on the European continent. Russia has two routes to the Atlantic: through the Baltic Sea and through the Black Sea and the Mediterranean. Moscow's ability to command these long passages, or, at a minimum, to deny NATO and U.S. seapower the ability to operate in them, opens the Atlantic to the kind of warfare that the Nazis conducted in World War II, during which more than 72,000 allied sailors and merchant seamen lost their lives and 3,500 ships were sunk, with a loss of 14.5 million gross tons.

The other focus of Russia's stated maritime doctrine is the Arctic Sea. The overwhelming preponderance of

Russia's nearly 24,000-mile coast lies between Severod-vinsk on the White Sea bay of the Arctic and the Bering Sea, where the Arctic Sea empties into the North Pacific. The Arctic today is open to Russian shipping for a couple of months a year, if that, but ships there still require assistance from the world's only nuclear-powered icebreaker fleet—Russia's.

The U.S. Geological Survey estimates that the Arctic contains 1.6 trillion cubic feet of natural gas and 44 billion barrels of natural gas liquids, of which 84 percent lies offshore.[34] Plentiful mineral resources, such as bauxite, copper, iron ore, and nickel, also lie beneath the seabed. Russia manufactures little. Its economy depends largely on using Western technology to exploit its abundant natural resources. The contest for these resources and control of the seas above them is a certain point of future international friction.

Russian maritime doctrine supports Putin's goal of re-establishing Russia as a great power by using its navy to challenge the United States's ability to communicate with its European allies, fill the power vacuum left in the Mediterranean by the United States, and threaten NATO on its northern and southern flanks. Expanding its fleet of nuclear-powered icebreakers and assigning more naval combatants to Arctic duty advances Russia's goals as it seeks to establish Moscow as the preeminent Arctic power.

Vladimir Putin is building a modern and technologically sophisticated fleet. Russia's combatants and its ground and air forces are competitive in air defenses, unconventional warfare, electronic warfare, and naval gunfire. Moscow's cyber abilities have proved sufficiently advanced to influence American and other democratic states' politics. The program is guided by a strategic vision of advancing Russia's economic interest in further cornering the world's energy market while reestablishing a dominant Russian naval presence in the seas that flank the European peninsula. Simultaneously, Putin seeks to offset the ability of U.S. seapower to counter these threats and to shake NATO by interrupting the sea lines of communication that link the United States to its European allies. Along with China's sale of its capable modern weaponry to such states as Iraq and North Korea, Russia adds to the threat of denying U.S. forces the access they require to succor allies and apply effective force globally.

Changes in the threats that face the United States must have consequences. There is no point in any state's armament other than to advance its interests in a material way. Many saw Nazi Germany and Japan's preparations for war in the 1930s, but Western governments' record of publicizing these was spotty. Harder still was imagining how the preparations could result in disaster. A description of a military's condition and those that might oppose it is incomplete if it does not attempt to imagine the effects of changes in the balance of power.

CHAPTER IV

FAILURE OF IMAGINATION

Scenarios are the military's time-tested instrument for juxtaposing current or anticipated forces alongside possible crises. Called "war games," "command post," or "table-top" exercises, they enlist the participation of senior civilian and military officials or defense experts to understand how they react to events that could happen. If such exercises are sufficiently difficult and innovative, they can yield valuable clues about strategy, tactics, escalation, logistics, and a host of other variables that challenge commanders in peace, in the dim light between peace and war, and in war itself. The U.S. Naval War College has long specialized in war games. Fleet Admiral Chester Nimitz wrote of his experience there in the early 1920s that "the enemy of our games was always—Japan," adding that, because of his preparation, "nothing that happened in the Pacific was strange or unexpected."[1]

By 1939, American cryptanalysts could read Japan's highest level of diplomatic code, which they code-named

Purple. The yield from this rich vein was referred to as "Magic." In late September 1941, U.S. codebreakers intercepted a message from Tokyo to an agent in Hawaii.[2] Two weeks later, the message was decoded and passed along to Army, Navy, and State Department recipients. In the message, Japan's Hawaiian agent was asked to divide the relatively small (ca. 5 square miles) naval area of the harbor into five zones. He was further instructed to report on the location and type of ships in each zone.

Chief of Naval Operations Admiral Harold R. Stark read the report. He admired Japan's efficient intelligence services and their attention to detail. Opinion remains divided today about Admiral Stark's failure to send this intelligence to Admiral Husband E. Kimmel, commander of the U.S. Pacific Fleet. On December 3, the U.S. high command was also aware that the Japanese had destroyed their codes and encryption devices in Asian consulates as well as in London and Washington. In congressional investigations that followed the end of World War II, Admiral Kimmel stated correctly that not all Japanese codes were being destroyed and that "Such reports had been made to me three or four times in the course of the year."[3]

Less senior officers peered into the approaching whirlwind's opacity with similar results. Because of a November 28 war-warning message from Washington, Lieutenant General Walter Short, who was responsible for Hawaii's defense, changed the Aircraft Warning Service's (AWS) watch, which had lasted from 0600 to 1130. Thus, radar screens would now be manned from 0400 to 0700, the general's estimate of the most likely time for an attack.

However, the watch standers and their immediate superiors were not told the reason for the added hours. Fewer than ten minutes after sunrise—at 0703—on December 7, the watch stander at the Opana radar station, just south of Kawela Bay at the northern tip of Oahu, saw planes approaching the islands 137 miles to the north and reported it to an Army lieutenant at the AWS center. The lieutenant, who was wholly inexperienced, judged that the unidentified aircraft were a flight of B-17s that was due to arrive from the mainland in the morning.

As with most mishaps, hindsight uncovered a host of other miscalculations, errors, and faulty interpretations. But the nub of the attack's success was the failure of imagination among American political leadership and the high command. The idea that Japan could dispatch six aircraft carriers across the Northern Pacific undetected to strike Hawaii did not fit with what civilian and military policy makers believed was possible. As Roberta Wohlstetter observes:

> For every signal that came into the information net in 1941 there were usually several plausible alternative explanations, and it is not surprising that our observers and analysts were inclined to select the explanations that fitted the popular hypotheses. They sometimes set down new contradictory evidence side by side with existing hypotheses, and they also sometimes held two contradictory beliefs at the same time. . . . Apparently human beings have a stubborn attachment to old beliefs and an equally stubborn resistance to new material that will upset them.[4]

The 9/11 Commission reached similar conclusions. Established by Congress and the president, the bipartisan commission found that the attacks of September 11, 2001, revealed failures in imagination, policy, capabilities, and management. The commission report listed "imagination" first.

The 9/11 Commission report noted that, following the crash of TWA flight 800 in 1996, which the FBI concluded was not the result of a crime, President Bill Clinton had established a commission headed by Vice President Al Gore. The Gore Commission was scrupulously exhaustive in its concentration on the dangers of bringing explosives aboard civilian aircraft, as had been planned—but foiled—in the so-called Manila plot of 1995, in which Islamists planned to place bombs aboard eleven passenger aircraft and destroy them as they flew from Asia to the United States. The Gore Commission identified a lack of rigor in searching passengers before they boarded. It did not mention the possibility of using aircraft themselves as weapons.

Other oversights complement that of the Gore Commission. In August 1999, the Federal Aviation Administration's Civil Aviation Security intelligence office worried that al-Qaeda might try to hijack a plane. One of its scenarios was a suicide hijacking operation. The scenario was dismissed within the FAA because, as the 9/11 Commission recorded, "it does not offer an opportunity for dialogue to achieve the key goal of obtaining [i.e., releasing Omar Abdel-] Rahman and other key captive extremists."[5] "A suicide hijacking," said FAA analysts, "is assessed to be an option of last resort."[6]

In short, scholarly and official inquiries into the two largest and most lethal attacks against the U.S. military and the American homeland in the past three-quarters of a century identify a failure of imagination as critical in the unpreparedness that preceded disaster. Imagination is as essential in thinking about the consequences of sharply reduced or strategically distracted seapower as it is in considering future threats.

STRATEGIC CHANGE

The threats the United States faces have changed radically in a little over one generation. In 1991 Mikhail Gorbachev resigned his position as president of the Soviet Union. He was succeeded by Boris Yeltsin, president of the newly formed independent state of Russia. U.S. policy makers bent their efforts to ensure that the United States would never again face a peer competitor that could cripple the nation in minutes and destroy it within hours.

Embers of the Soviet Union ignited in the Balkans, and Russia faced a constitutional crisis that was resolved by force. Terrorism grew. A short war was fought at the northern end of the Persian Gulf. China started its rise and began to invest heavily in arms. But great power competition seemed to have ended as the Soviet Union was replaced by a weak state, whose natural resources were more valuable than the finished products manufactured from them.

A single generation later, all has changed. The United States today faces a heretofore unfamiliar strategic challenge: the possibility of three linked hegemonies that span the Eurasian land mass. Russia is on the ramparts in Ukraine, Georgia, and the Middle East. Its Baltic State ambitions are no secret. NATO's failure to respond in a real crisis means the end of the alliance and a maturing Russian hegemony that stretches from Central Asia to the Atlantic. China actively seeks to become Asia's hegemon, while its unruly satellite North Korea has become a nuclear power. Iran's rulers, armed with missiles of increasing range, added financial resources, and the likelihood of nuclear weapons, have their eye on dominating the strategic space between Moscow's influence and Beijing's.

A single hegemony on the Eurasian land mass threatens U.S. markets, our ability to keep conflict at a distance, regional stability, and democracy. At a minimum, the three hegemonies would overturn the current liberal international order. If the United States does not take effective action to prevent this, its run as a preeminent global power will end. Proximity to the oceans and seas offers the United States the opportunity to leverage its still-dominant seapower as the key to countering or, if necessary, opposing the three would-be hegemons.

Since Woodrow Wilson, the goal of American foreign policy has been to prevent regional hegemony. Two decades after Wilson, President Franklin D. Roosevelt led the United States in another global conflict, against Nazi Germany and the Empire of Japan. Both Europe and Asia were—and remain—critical to our hopes for greater prosperity, security, and an increasingly democratic world. The United States and its allies destroyed both totalitarian hegemons. Finally, the United States contained the Soviet Union for almost half a century, blunting its threat to Europe, and confronting its expanding influence in Asia, Africa, the Middle East, and Latin America.

Emerging from this century of nearly continuous global conflict, the United States was the unquestioned global power. No state could challenge it economically, politically, or militarily. The United States destroyed the Iraqi military twice in slightly over a decade, and put a stop to ethnic cleansing in the Balkans.

New threats have ended this brief period of America's benevolent international leadership. Three competitors are at odds with the American-led international system. The sum of their ambitions is to undermine U.S. global power.

A resurgent Russia aims to reclaim its previous glory and capitalize on the current U.S. administration's idea that America can make itself great again with a minimum of cooperation from others.

The European refugee crisis and potential destabilization in the European Union challenge the American alliance system in Europe—the cornerstone of American security policy since the end of World War II. America's remaining allies show little resolve. Meager European defense budgets make matters worse. They offer ammunition to demagogic politicians who seek to exploit the undercurrent of American isolationism.

In Asia, a rising China focuses on cultivating and marshaling its economic resources to develop its military power. China's island-building campaign aims to extend its territorial claims into international waters and directly confronts the international order. As Admiral Harry Harris, commander of U.S. forces in the Pacific, told Congress in early 2017, "China has fundamentally altered the physical and political landscape in the South China Sea."[7] Beijing combines its land reclamation campaign with high-tempo presence operations conducted by the People's Liberation Army Navy (PLAN) and coast guard in contested areas of the South and East China Seas. The Chinese are also accelerating their ability to project naval power and control the seas by constructing troop transports, large surface combatants, and a second aircraft carrier.

This situation bears a resemblance to the world America faced before World War II, when Nazi Germany and Imperial Japan initially overwhelmed the European powers that had refused to rearm following World War I.

But the semblance is passing. America faces not two aspiring hegemons, but three. The Middle East is the critical link between Europe and Asia. Its oil-rich states supply a large amount of the world's energy resources and facilitate exchange between the two hemispheres. With the Red Sea, Persian Gulf, and Arabian Sea in the south, the Mediterranean to the west, and the Caspian and Black Seas to the north, the Middle East is more like an island than a contiguous land mass.

On this island, Iran attempts to assert its dominance. Russia aids Iran with weapons transfers and its support of Iranian proxy Bashar al-Assad in Syria. Relieved of sanctions, the Islamic Republic has begun to receive massive financial inflows and has actively directed some of its profits toward obtaining dual-use military technology such as jet engines. Iranian Special Forces, known as the Quds Force, conduct paramilitary operations in Iraq and Syria, expanding Tehran's influence over its neighbors.

Although America's adversaries have worked with one another in the past, the current degree of cooperation between China, Russia, and Iran is a strategic terra incognita. Iranian oil shipped into Chinese ports generates financial resources that the Islamic Republic uses to purchase advanced weapons from Russia. Russia helps Iran fight its proxy wars, while Iran supports growing Russian influence in the Eastern Mediterranean.

America's three strategic competitors oppose the United States in similar ways. China, Russia, and Iran understand the lessons of the First Gulf War. Since the Cold War's end, America's style of warfare has been to build coalitions, amass men and resources in neighboring countries, and launch combined arms assaults that overwhelm the enemy technologically and operationally. In the First Gulf War, the American-led coalition of nearly 1 million soldiers eviscerated an entrenched Iraqi army of more than 1.5 million. However, without neighboring Saudi Arabia's willingness, the United States would have been unable to conduct the operation. A naval assault would have been smaller, and Kuwait's crowded coastline could have meant high casualties.

The First Gulf War suggested a clear strategy to counter the United States. Deny American forces access to a region, and the United States loses power. Chinese, Russian, and Iranian efforts have all focused on denying America access to their respective regions. As it turns up the heat on the Baltic States, Russia is proscribing options for a rapid buildup by deploying long-range air-defense and strike missiles at NATO's borders.

This is consistent with U.S. European Command commander General Philip Breedlove's February 2016 statement to Congress that "President Putin has sought to undermine the rules-based system of European security and attempted to maximize his power on the world stage."[8] China's land reclamation campaign, increasing naval power, and anti-ship missiles aim to keep American forces at a distance from which effective combat power cannot readily be applied. Iran's low-cost missile boats, midget subs, large numbers of ballistic and cruise missiles, as well as mines, and its influence at the Strait of Hormuz seek to offset American escalation. Instability in Iraq and America's shaky relations with Pakistan further restrict staging points for an American attack.

Declining U.S. military budgets and a shrinking force combined with poor treatment of critical allies have made things worse, calling into question the ability of the United States to honor its commitments. The Obama administration's 2009 abrogation of ballistic-missile defense agreements with Poland and the Czech Republic; its prolonged interruption of defensive arms sales to Taiwan; and its failure to keep the Saudis informed about its 2015 deal with Iran (the Joint Comprehensive Plan of Action) are examples of treating allies shabbily. Thus, the United States is less able to rely on adequate basing rights where they are needed both to deter and, if necessary, to fight.

President Trump faces a new challenge to U.S. national security that calls for changes to American strategy. The access that once allowed us to deter the Soviets has been eroded. Its resurrection in today's Europe is unlikely. Such access is largely nonexistent in the Middle East and is tenuous in East Asia.

Coalitions of allied and partner nations remain extremely important—as they have since the United States became a major power. U.S. ground forces will not go it alone. They rarely have. Even the 1994 operation to remove Haiti's military junta engaged coalition partners: Poland and Argentina. A combat operation, had one been necessary, would have been staged out of the mainland United States, Puerto Rico, and Guantanamo.

Equally reliable options are limited in Eurasia. While alliances and partnerships—for example, of Sunni states opposed to ISIS—are vital, they may not always be available or dependable. If North Korea were to invade the South, there is no guarantee that Japan would allow its bases to be used for repelling the invaders or for striking deep into North Korea.

Seapower possesses the advantages of geography, mobility, and—with sufficient investment—numbers and growing technological edge. It will be essential in future conflicts because it allows us to depend less on nearby bases. Logistics ships in sufficient number can keep battle groups, including amphibious forces, on station, present, and combat ready largely independent of basing agreements. Maritime coalitions will likely offer more security in the future. But there is no alternative to dominant U.S. seapower today. Allies like Japan lack the industrial capacity to make up the deficit between the U.S. Navy and the expanding Chinese PLAN. Newer partners like Vietnam cannot hope to hold out against a Chinese onslaught without American support. Taiwan can defend against a PRC assault, but not indefinitely. Seapower is the surest means to ensure constant access to effective combat capability in the Western Pacific.

The same shift in thinking applies to the greater Middle East. Its gulfs and seas allow access that is largely independent of diplomatic agreements. Robust seapower may not be sufficient to cover our security interests in the Middle East, but its usefulness increases proportionately to the territorial holdings on which ISIS has staked its claim as a caliphate. The Persian Gulf and Gulf of Oman are Iran's southwest and southern borders. It's a long haul from there or from the Eastern Mediterranean to Tehran, but a doable one with refueling tankers based in Gulf States or, in the foreseeable future, carrier-launched drones that can refuel a ship's strike aircraft.

The Cold War plan to mass land forces in defense of Europe has been voided by continental hopes that perpetual peace has arrived. Even the most stalwart American partners, such as the United Kingdom, have cut military capacity and capability. But Europe is a peninsula. It is surrounded by accessible waters from St. Petersburg to the Crimea. Seapower cannot stop a Russian ground invasion of the Baltics, but it can snap the supply lines of an attack and give such ground forces as NATO can muster a chance to prevail. The ability of naval vessels to control the Baltic Sea and project power inland can also deter Russia from launching an attack.

The United States has emerged into a new world. To the potential for nuclear warfare with China—a would-be peer competitor—that American statesmen most wished to avoid after the Cold War have been added threats from a nuclear-armed Russia, North Korea, and, sooner or later, Iran. The more immediate prospect of a triple hegemony may not be an existential threat, but its outcome would unravel such order as exists in the world, cripple our markets, shatter our alliances, and imperil us at home. All this can be avoided by a grand strategy that continues to hold threats at a distance as it relies on the independence, accessibility, and technological superiority of seapower.

What will the consequences be if U.S. strategy proves as insufficient as the nation's ability to execute it, owing to a lack of seapower?

CHAPTER V

THE INVASION OF ESTONIA

The object of this and subsequent scenarios is to illustrate the challenges that American seapower faces
today and will face in the future: a diminishing fleet; unresolved strategic decisions; and miscalculations in fleet design (which can be the result of insufficient funding, slow
adaptation to large geopolitical shifts, or the swift pace of
technological change, to name a few). One important element of creating useful war games, scenarios, or plans is
imagination. War and architecture on a grand scale, for
example, are two complex human activities that require
forethought, organization, and decisive leadership. But a
civil engineer does not have to worry that a river will alter
its course to avoid a planned bridge. Intelligent military
officers know that this is exactly what the enemy will do:
change his plan to achieve his goal. This fact puts a pre-
mium on imagination and thus exacts a very high price for
failures of imagination.

During the Cold War's final years, U.S. maritime strategy came to regard the land mass from the Soviet Union's western border to the Atlantic as a peninsula surrounded on the north by the Baltic and North Seas and on the south by the Mediterranean. Both NATO and the Warsaw Pact's high commands believed that a conventional war would most likely spark where the two sides' forces abutted one another: in the center of Germany. American naval strategists operated two aircraft carrier battle groups in the Mediterranean, whose 140 tactical aircraft could attack targets in the USSR proper and help cut off Moscow's supply lines that would sustain an armed thrust into Western Europe.

To the north, U.S. aircraft carriers accompanied by attack submarines were added to the mix. Together with its Mediterranean fleet, the United States had effectively encircled the European peninsula—just as the Royal Navy had done during the Napoleonic Wars. If, as the expression of the time had it, "the balloon went up," U.S. naval forces would hunt for and destroy Soviet ballistic-missile submarines that hid in the northern seas waiting for the order to launch their weapons against North American targets. According to the then-current theory, the submerged Soviet arsenal guaranteed that whatever might happen to the rest of Moscow's nuclear forces, one part would remain intact and lethal.

The ability to roll back and eventually destroy this so-called second-strike nuclear capability would—American strategists thought—help deter Moscow from launching a first strike. At the same time, U.S. aircraft carrier attacks against Soviet naval bases and infrastructure in the vicinity of Murmansk were planned to distract attention from the central front—just as aircraft carriers were expected to attack key southern targets from the Mediterranean.

No one ever learned whether this scheme would have worked. However, the presence of powerful U.S. naval forces on the Soviets' northern flank helped divert the Warsaw Pact leader's intelligence, logistic, air, and naval defenses from the center. Washington saw this as a good thing.

A Scenario In 2025, thirty-four years after the fall of the Soviet Union, the U.S. naval fleet was less than one-third the size of its Cold War predecessor. An extraordinarily wealthy autocrat at the top of a small pyramid of oligarchs ruled Russia, much as the czar did before the Bolsheviks seized power. Vladimir Putin had announced in 2013 his plan to spend 4 trillion rubles, or $132 billion, to expand Russia's combat fleet over the next seven years. As those seven fat years ended, Putin promised to spend an additional $150 billion on naval modernization by 2027. Several U.S. analysts had noted that the delivered—and promised—largesse was close to 30 percent more than the United States planned to spend on shipbuilding during the same period. No one paid them any attention—except in Moscow and Beijing.

Between Putin's announcement and 2025, eighteen new frigates had joined the Russian Federation combat fleet, along with twenty-four missile-carrying corvettes and a host of smaller, agile combatants. Ten new boomers—nuclear-tipped ballistic-missile submarines—and eleven nuclear-powered attack subs had also been constructed and undergone successful sea trials. At a third or less than the cost of one nuclear-powered sub, Moscow had been turning out far quieter diesel-electric boats that were as well suited for the lucrative export market as they were for operating in the relatively shallow waters of the Baltic and North Seas.

Still, the Russian Federation's military was a shadow of its communist predecessor's armed forces. In nearly all categories of weaponry, even with oil prices back at their pre-2014 levels, Moscow could not afford the expense of a robust conventional force. It was not a superpower and could not bring armed might to bear except on its borders. It could not keep forces in the field in a prolonged conflict. But Russia had maintained and modernized a powerful nuclear arsenal of hundreds of weapons that could be launched from land-based aircraft, silos, and submarines.

The United States, still the dominant global power in 2025, was less so compared to ten or fifteen years earlier. As the federal debt reached $24 trillion, politicians had failed to staunch the borrowing or limit the growth of entitlement programs. Debt service and spending that the law required tightened their choke hold on the defense budget.

The portion of the budget that the Navy devoted to shipbuilding had been preserved, not increased. But the foreseeable expenses of replacing a fleet built during the Reagan era had shredded the admirals' sober long-range shipbuilding plans and left them in tatters.

For example, the first of the *Ohio*-class nuclear-powered ballistic-missile submarines (SSBNs) had been commissioned forty-five years earlier. American military planners held fast to the idea that powerful, quick response and/or undetectable nuclear weapons would help discourage an enemy from launching a first strike. So land-based intercontinental ballistic missiles, land-based long-range bombers, and boomers remained the triad that, it was hoped, would deter an enemy from launching a nuclear attack against the United States.

The new SSBNs cost more than $7 billion each, more than half the cost of an aircraft carrier, but not by much. Arguing that ballistic missile–carrying subs performed a national mission rather than a seapower one, the Navy had tried to persuade the administration and Congress that additional money should be appropriated to build the new boats—without success. Other programs were slowed or cancelled during the decades it would take to replace the fourteen aged SSBNs with twelve new ones. Congress passed legislation that allowed the number of aircraft carriers to drop from eleven to eight. It accepted the Navy's proposal to stop buying two new attack subs each year to replace the aging *Los Angeles*–class boats. By 2025, the U.S. attack sub force had shrunk in a single decade from fifty-three boats to fewer than forty.

Only one carrier was built during the decades it took to modernize the boomers. The refueling of others was delayed as they were tied up dockside. The United States, at least for the indefinite future, could keep only two aircraft carriers at sea on sporadic patrols. The same cost-cutting measures were applied to the attack submarine force, with parallel results. Only thirteen attack boats could be put to sea.

America's combatant commanders were nervous. Four-star admirals or generals, they commanded the air, sea, and ground forces that were deployed around the world to keep conflict away from the borders of the United States, defend vital American interests, and protect allies. China's navy had not only surpassed

America's in numbers of ships but had also become a
global presence, with constant patrols in the western
reaches of the Indian Ocean, the Mediterranean, and the
entire length of the Western Hemisphere's Pacific coast.
The few ships that remained in the U.S. 6th Fleet in the
Mediterranean had been recalled home when its handful
of ballistic-missile defense ships were judged redundant,
once defenses against Iran's nuclear-tipped medium- and
intercontinental-range missiles became operational in
Romania. This made sense to budget cutters only. Ships
at sea are harder to target than fixed land-based missile
batteries.

The diminished U.S. Pacific Command was able to
keep a single aircraft carrier battle group in the Western
Pacific. While serviceable in peacetime, a lone U.S. carrier
would have very limited usefulness if an incident between
China and Taiwan or Japan turned nasty. Long-standing
allies cast about for other ways to protect themselves.
In Taiwan, one political party was actively engaged in
reunification talks with the mainland. China had secretly
offered to ensure South Korea's security if Seoul would
send the American military packing, and the Blue House
was thinking it over. Japanese politicians were divided
between those who wanted to improve relations with
China and others who sought to nullify the constitution's
Article 9, which outlawed war as a means of resolving
international disputes.

Vladimir Putin had just turned seventy-three; just a
few years older than Nikita Khrushchev when he placed
medium-range nuclear missiles in Cuba, and three years
younger than Leonid Brezhnev when he was gathered to
his fathers. Putin remained firmly in command and had
taken to sky-diving, which impressed his countrymen. All

of Ukraine had long since been absorbed into Russia. So had bordering Transnistria, the slender belt—a bit larger than Rhode Island—inhabited by Russophiles, which once separated Moldova from Ukraine. In each case, the West objected strenuously, as it had when Russia invaded Crimea. Sanctions were applied, but always ended up leaking, then bursting. European dependence on Russian oil and natural gas overcame other concerns.

NATO, however, had strengthened its military presence in the Baltic States and Central Europe. After the Obama administration's 2009 tergiversation, Polish and Czech leaders would not risk political capital to argue publicly for acceptance of defenses against Russian ballistic missiles on their territory. But Romania would—and did. NATO conducted annual exercises from the Baltic Sea to the Black Sea.

The other side of the ledger was darker. Despite promises, only one of the Western European alliance members lived up to their NATO defense spending obligations, the U.K. But Britain had long since abandoned its alliance gold standard, the ability to deploy an entire expeditionary division. The Royal Navy was down to a few attack subs and fewer ballistic-missile boats. The surface fleet had nine ships available to patrol the Channel and parts of the North Sea. Two carriers built only a decade earlier had been mothballed.

Putin knew the time was right to crack NATO's atrophied spine. He did not have to cast about for an achievement to crown his twenty-five-year reign as Russia's supreme leader. NATO's demise would allow gains in Ukraine, Belarus, Georgia, the Balkans, and Transnistria to be extended. The excuse for invading Ukraine applied equally to the Baltic States: the million or so ethnic

Russians who lived in Estonia, Latvia, and Lithuania must be protected. Returning the Baltic States to Russian control would shatter NATO and make smooth the highway to recreating an imperium in Europe. Except that this time, it might reach the Atlantic, an accomplishment that would dwarf Stalin's seizure of Eastern Europe at the end of World War II.

In mid-2024, Russian foreign intelligence agents began to contact pro-Russian intellectuals and writers in the Baltic States, and small think tanks sprang up in Tallinn, Riga, and Vilnius. Staffs were hired. They turned out articles that explained the "facts" of growing discrimination against ethnic Russians. Friendly reporters repeated the untruths in their journals. Other sympathizers whose pro-Russian credentials had been validated years earlier began to press for solidarity among ethnic Russians in the Baltic States' trade unions. Websites appeared with fabricated stories of mistreatment, arrests, and harassment directed against ethnic Russians. Moscow contacted ethnic Russians and offered them Russian passports, citizenship, and higher pensions than those that the Baltic States offered.

Russian agents initiated a low-level bombing campaign against ethnic Russian–owned small businesses that heated up the political warfare. The bombings "proved" the dangers that ethnic Russians faced. Other crimes, such as kidnappings and the occasional murder, received international attention. From Moscow to Vilnius, the pro-Russian social media called for "measures" to protect ethnic Russians in the Baltic States. Members of the Duma howled, and eventually Vladimir Putin felt obliged to weigh in.

Putin warned the Baltic leaders to stop what he termed

provocations or face the consequences. At the same
time, he put the Baltic Sea Fleet on a heightened alert
status, mobilized three infantry brigades, and moved
one Spetsnaz battalion with helicopter transports and an
armored division into the Pskov oblast near the Estonian
border.

The U.S. State Department and foreign ministries
in London, Paris, and Warsaw issued démarches, and
NATO's general secretary called an emergency meeting.
His public statement surprised the foreign policy estab-
lishments of most alliance members by reminding Putin
that Article 5 of the North Atlantic Treaty required all
members to assist one who had been attacked.

Putin corrected this—privately. He told his close advis-
ers that Article 5 actually says that an attack against one
member, and here he quoted from memory, "shall be
considered an attack against them all." "What does *that*
mean?" he asked contemptuously. The Russian president
noted that the United Kingdom had told the Polish government in March 1939 that it would "feel" itself "bound"
to help Poland if the Nazis attacked. Five months later
the Chamberlain government dropped tons of leaflets
over Germany after Hitler invaded Poland. "Some feel-
ing," Putin snorted. "Some binding," he added. "Treaties," he declared, "are not handcuffs. They're like shirts.
You wear one when it suits you.

"The Americans," he continued, "are stretched between their Arctic Fleet, the Mexican civil war, their
peacekeeping operations in Kashmir, and stopping the
Sunnis and Shiites from a second nuclear volley." Putin
was referring to the concentration of jockeying international naval vessels in the nearly ice-free Arctic, the
anarchy of Mexico's armed struggle between drug lords

and the government, the aftermath of war between India and a jihadist Pakistan in which both sides had launched nuclear weapons, and a brief nuclear exchange between the Gulf States and Iran that had driven the international price of oil to just over $300 a barrel.

The Supreme Allied Commander Europe (SACEUR) responsible for all NATO forces, U.S. Admiral Alec Krone, ordered a squadron of F-35s to move from Timisoara, where they were stationed in Romania, to the Amari air base in northwestern Estonia. U.S. President Algodón started calling the leaders of NATO member states. They were reluctant to admit that the hopes for peace that their defense budgets over the previous two decades reflected might have come a cropper. But for the most part, they agreed that a successful Russian military takeover in the Baltics risked the entire continent and would doom the alliance.

All of Europe's NATO members maintained ground forces of one kind or another. They started to flow into the Baltic States. Not all the European states possessed major naval combatants. For its part, the United States had bet that the next half century would be pretty much like the previous fifty years: emergencies and the occasional crisis, but nothing more. Under increased budgetary pressure, the U.S. Navy had changed the thirty-year naval shipbuilding plan into a fifty-year plan. The number of ships that were to have been built in three decades would now be constructed in five decades. As a result, the U.S. fleet was short in every category of major combatant: amphibious, attack submarines, ballistic-missile submarines, aircraft carriers, the planes carried on their decks, frigates, destroyers, and the logistics ships that kept the fighters supplied. New technology that might have helped remedy deficiencies—for example, small drone submarines—had been developed but was not deployed in significant enough numbers to make a positive difference.

Russia had been busy building up its navy while the Western powers were dismantling theirs. Moscow had far surpassed the goal it set in 2010 of modernizing 70 percent of its fleet by 2020. The $600 billion it spent during that decade had proved a good investment, especially the supercarrier, *Yekaterina Velikaya*, with its hundred-plane capacity and electromagnetic launch catapults. Russia had replaced the United States as the dominant naval force in the Mediterranean eight years earlier, and *Yekaterina* was patrolling the Med during the second week of June 2025 when Putin began to flood the Baltic Sea with amphibious vessels, attack subs, and large surface ships bristling with anti-surface and anti-aircraft missiles.

A debate erupted within the U.S. intelligence community over whether Putin intended to go to war when *Yekaterina Velikaya* exited the Straits of Gibraltar and sailed north to join the gathering Russian armada in the Baltic Sea. Smaller vessels and ground-based naval aviation would assist her in hunting for NATO submarines.

At the president's request, Admiral Krone flew back to Washington from Estonia's Amari air base, where he had established an allied joint force command headquarters. After a lunch of canned sardines, yogurt, and a kombucha—the admiral was a SEAL officer and remained in excellent physical condition—Krone went over his briefing papers and current intelligence reports. Done, he napped for twenty minutes, awakened, and finished the third chapter of *Finnegans Wake*. It was his second read of the impossible novel. After touching down at Andrews in

mid-afternoon on Sunday, June 29, the admiral was fer-
ried by helicopter to land on the White House South
Lawn. He began to brief the president and Chairman of
the Joint Chiefs General Thomas Zrebiec less than thirty-
five minutes after landing at Andrews.

The essentials were straightforward. NATO fielded
more powerful conventional ground and air forces than
Moscow. Putin had an important, perhaps decisive, advantage in combat ships—unless the United States were
to swing naval forces from the Persian Gulf and West Pacific to the Baltic Sea. This would take at least six weeks.
It would also risk additional fighting between the Gulf
States and Iran and another even more devastating spike
in international oil prices, while encouraging Chinese or
North Korean adventures in East Asia.

Then there was the nuclear unknown. Putin had
hinted for years that one mission of his nuclear forces was
to backstop any conventional weakness. "The military
balance between Russia and the West," Admiral Krone
told the president, "is exactly opposite the one we faced
in the Cold War." He meant that, while the Soviets had
held the upper hand in conventional forces, the U.S.
nuclear umbrella was understood during the Cold War
to have protected Europe against being overrun should
the Red Army start to push alliance forces west.

"Today," Admiral Krone observed, "if it comes to
war, we can stop them from taking the Baltic States with
conventional forces. But Putin is a risk-taker. There is no
telling whether he would use nuclear weapons if he feels
he is losing." The president did not have to be told that
Putin's entire calculation was that, while NATO might
move forces into position to defend the Baltics, the Europeans and Americans would in the end find some excuse

82

not to act—as they had when all of Ukraine fell eight years earlier.

The president raised an eyebrow and threw a glance in the direction of General Zrebiec. "Do you have everything you need?" asked President Algodón.

Admiral Krone hesitated, coughed slightly, and said, "Yes, militarily."

"But, what?" asked Algodón.

"Sir, our ground and air forces can handle the Russians. As you've probably seen from the intelligence reports, the Russian high command knows it is outgunned on land. We're at a large disadvantage at sea. The Russians will fail if they try forcing their way from sea. They don't have enough close air support to conduct an opposed landing, and they have no experience with these operations. But they can harry NATO's ground operations if the Russians invade Estonia. I am confident that our ballistic-missile defenses can handle anything Putin throws at us. But . . ." Here the admiral hesitated again.

"But what?" the president repeated.

"Aside from Poland, the Czechs, and the Romanians, I don't think that the Europeans have their hearts in this. I mean I think that Putin is making a good bet. He expects the big NATO states to fold if he actually invades."

The president nodded. "Yes," he said. "We led them into Afghanistan and Iraq, and they lost their nerve. Hell, we lost ours. Look, I'll invite them to Washington on Thursday and remind them what's at stake for the alliance. I want you there to brief them on the military situation."

"Sir," answered the admiral.

"Anything else?" asked the president.

"Yes, sir. If the Russians invade Estonia, I need much more naval support."

The president, a former Army Ranger, asked SACEUR to explain.

"Sir, a carrier's air wing; ships and subs equipped with cruise missiles; even destroyers with their electromagnetic rail guns, which can reach a target a hundred miles away, could rip up Russia's northern naval bases and cut the supply lines their ground forces would depend on in Estonia. I don't have enough ground-based air now to execute those missions *and*"—the admiral emphasized—"check the naval forces Putin is collecting in the Baltic. Sir, I need the Navy."

"Ok," said the president. "I'll talk with General Zrebiec here about getting some more ships up there." The chairman made a note on his yellow pad.

"Sir." The admiral's helicopter's engines were still warm when he climbed back aboard it on the White House South Lawn. Krone was airborne for Estonia two hours after landing at Andrews.

One hour into SACEUR's eastbound flight, as the C-37A flew over Cape Cod, heading northeast toward the open Atlantic, a pair of Russian multipurpose Sukhoi T-50s lifted off from Pskov and met up with an Ilyushin Il-78 tanker over central Estonia. The summer solstice had occurred a week earlier. At 59+ degrees latitude the northern horizon stayed a blue-gold hue from sunset to dawn. All three planes flew through the quasi-night with their transponders off.

The crews of two C-17 USAF transport planes rising up from Amari on a return flight to Dover Air Force Base in Delaware were settling in for the nine-hour haul back home. Besides the C-17, the traffic controllers at Amari were also monitoring an inbound flight of American F-35s from Frankfurt. The controllers directed the in- and outbound flights safely past one another.

But air traffic control did not know that the Russian stealth tactical fighters were in the vicinity. Both the American and Russian planes were equipped with stealth technology. The F-35 and Sukhoi pilots finally saw one another at an approach speed of Mach 1.89 when they were less than a mile apart. All four pilots turned on their targeting radars and jinked to avoid collision. The evasive action saved one American and one Russian plane. The other two were less fortunate. Their wings brushed each other, severely damaging both aircraft and rendering them uncontrollable. The Russian pilot's ejection seat failed. He died when his plane crashed. The American was luckier. He parachuted safely, walked away out of the potato field where he'd landed, and hitchhiked to the nearest village.

Russian national security advisor Dmitri Bogdanov awakened Putin at 0400, a half-hour after the sun rose in Moscow. He told the Russian president that a Russian fighter had been downed over Estonia; that the NATO planes had their targeting radars on when the Sukhoi went down; and that the Russian pilot was presumed to have been killed. The second Russian pilot had returned to his base unharmed and was still being debriefed. Bogdanov could not answer whether the Russian plane had been shot down. Putin didn't care.

He dressed and strolled to the presidential briefing room in the Kremlin, thinking. The surviving Russian pilot had seen his wingman's plane on fire after the collision and had told briefers that the American pilots had "painted" the Russian jets, that is, turned on their targeting radars. He described how the Russian and American planes had had visual contact prior to the incident. He did not know that his wingman's plane had collided with the F-35. Putin called for his chief of staff, defense minister, and intelligence head.

Admiral Krone received word of the incident aboard his flight to Estonia. On arrival at Amari, he was driven to his command center, where the reports started to come in. So did the two American pilots who had survived the encounter. Krone ordered an uptick in NATO's defense readiness condition and sent a draft press release to the Pentagon.

> Two NATO F-35s piloted by United States Air Force officers encountered two Russian Sukhoi T-50 fighters over Estonian airspace at approximately 0315 local time this morning. The Russian fighters were overflying a NATO member's airspace without Estonian approval with their transponders turned off. The NATO pilots were on a standard patrol mission. They and the Russian pilots became aware of each other visually at a distance of less than one mile. They took action to avoid collision. One NATO and one Russian plane avoided each other. The other Russian fighter's wing collided with the F-35's wing. Both planes were seriously damaged. The U.S. pilot ejected. He is safe. There is no evidence that the Russian pilot ejected. NATO investigators have located the site of the crash and are making every effort to find the missing pilot. There are no reports of ground fatalities or injuries related to the collision.

After Washington approved the draft, it was sent for information purposes to the NATO ambassadors of all the alliance members. The statement was issued to the media at noon local time in Tallinn.

Before NATO's first public comment, Putin had gone on state-run television to accuse NATO of "provoking Russia." He angrily denounced NATO for targeting the Russian planes with their radar, which he said was proof of "hostile intent." "Ethnic Russians who live in the Baltic States," said Putin, fixing his hooded eyes on the camera, "have been the subjects of repression and aggression by the governments of Estonia, Latvia, and Lithuania. Now, NATO has joined these criminal states."

The accusation was Putin's idea. His meeting with Defense Minister Vissarionovich and Intelligence Chief Ulyanov yielded another. Russia initiated bot attacks—Web robots that transformed selected Estonian computers into virtual zombies. The attacks allowed Moscow to control the little Baltic state's interior ministry's command and control center. From this center in Tallinn went orders to local police around the country to start rounding up leaders of the ethnic Russian business and civic communities. Once in police custody, they were to be interrogated about subversive activities.

Other bot attacks targeted the Estonian prime minister and his defense, foreign, interior, and finance ministers, as well as their deputies, who learned that their bank accounts, equity, and bond holdings had been either zeroed or reduced by 75 percent.

The alarming reports of personal financial ruin distracted the government's chief ministers from the arrest of ethnic Russians in Tallinn, Tartu, Narva, and the country's other population centers, large and small. The government learned of them when the Russian state media broadcast Vladimir Putin's stormy declaration that "I will not stand by and allow ethnic Russians to be treated like dogs." By the time of Putin's broadcast, the Estonian government had already stopped the roundup. Its prime minister went on national television and explained the cyber attack. For naught.

At dawn the following day, Tuesday, July 1, the Kremlin issued the warning order that confirmed military objectives and command relationships prior to combat operations. Russian tanks and mechanized units that had been training for six months made their final preparations. So did the infantry and helicopter gunship units that would assist in capturing airfields at towns west of the border with Russia.

Estonia is a small, low-lying country dotted with marshland and lakes. Unlike central Germany, it lacks an abundance of broad plains suited to large-scale armored battles. Estonia has no easy invasion routes from Russia. The center of the dividing line between the two states runs down the middle of Lake Peipus. Through the long lake's vertical axis passes about 120 kilometers of the 294-kilometer-long border. Lake Peipus empties into the Baltic Sea through the north-flowing Narva River.

Russian forces went into action at 0300 on July 2. They established bridgeheads along the Narva River and began rolling west to encircle Narva, Estonia's third-largest city.

The invasion route was well trodden. Russia's military under Peter the Great had used it twice at the beginning of the eighteenth century. More recently—in the first half of 1944—Soviet General Leonid Govorov, commanding the Leningrad Front, drove west with the immediate object of seizing Estonia from Nazi control. The three armies under his command invaded across the Narva River. This time, the field commander of Russian forces would be a veteran of the 2014 invasion of Crimea, General Alexander Lentsov.

President Algodón had spoken with the other NATO member chiefs of state. He persuaded them that, as Putin had not stopped in Ukraine or Moldova, he would not stop if he could swallow the Baltic States. He reminded them of what European defense would look like if American voters decided that the Europeans were unreliable allies and forced the United States to withdraw from NATO.

Article 5 was invoked. The Russian invasion of Estonia would be regarded as an attack on all the NATO member states. The essence of Putin's gamble failed. NATO had gone to its highest alert status twelve hours earlier. The Pentagon elevated its level of readiness from DEFCON 4 to DEFCON 2. The last time U.S. forces had been placed on a DEFCON 2 status was during the Cuban Missile Crisis. Now it was up to Admiral Krone to turn back the Russians' advance.

Admiral Krone deployed NATO armor and mechanized units back from the border, taking advantage of lakes and marshes that the invading force must circumnavigate. He meant to force Russian ground forces into killing zones, where combined tank and close air support could destroy them. Other tactical aircraft would contest Russian fighters at higher altitudes.

The struggle to control airspace above the battlefield was critical to the outcome below. NATO and the Russian air forces were roughly equal in numbers, although the West enjoyed a technological edge in fighter capability. And here, the admiral cursed. He'd told the president that he needed more naval support, but the conflict had exploded before any ships could arrive—even if a carrier could be dispatched from the Persian Gulf to the Baltic Sea. And he'd told his flag aide, a young SEAL lieutenant, "This is what happens when budgets make strategy. U.S. security policy gets tunnel vision and forgets Europe."

The aircraft carrier USS *Theodore Roosevelt* was currently on station in the Persian Gulf. Her seventy F-35C fighter-bombers would have given NATO's air forces an advantage, clearing the skies of Russian aircraft and then striking Russian columns to stop them from moving deeper into Estonia. Any aircraft carrier in the U.S. inventory would have done so. The USS *Carl Vinson* was currently in intermediate maintenance in Norfolk. She would be pulled out and ordered to the Baltic, but it would be at least seven weeks before she could go into action. There were no other carriers that could arrive sooner. The United States had one other deployed carrier, halfway around the world—in the West Pacific.

The consequence, as Krone had earlier warned the Joint Chiefs, was that the ground campaign would be longer and bloodier. It was. Instead of confronting the Russians with ground forces on the Narva River's east bank, Krone attacked them as they crossed, smote them as they maneuvered to avoid lakes and marshes, and arrayed his forces west of the river, where the enemy was stopped with U.S. allied units to their west and the river behind them. Estonia's superbly trained special operations forces nipped at the heels of the invaders and demoralized them.

Krone's plans accomplished their objective. They crumpled the Russian offensive and brought it to a halt.

Putin could not turn back politically. Tactically, the Narva complicated his generals' escape route back into Russia.

Putin had bet that NATO would cave. He lost. A military defeat would now shatter his accomplishments of the past twenty-five years: the subjugation of Georgia, Moldova, and Ukraine, the withdrawal of Bosnian Serbs from the Dayton Accords, a permanent Russian presence in the East Mediterranean, rising dissension within the NATO alliance, a stranglehold on Europe's supply of energy, and the revitalization of the Russian empire. Worst of all, military defeat would splinter Putin's grip on power and destroy his legacy as the most successful Russian strongman since Peter the Great.

NATO's ground-based aviation held at bay the naval air power that arrived with the Russian aircraft carrier. But the Russian fleet stayed in place off the Estonian coast. The U.S. Joint Chiefs had ordered ships that were not fully combat ready out of Norfolk and sent what they felt they could spare from other parts of the world.

Putin doubled down on his bet. The reserves that had been mobilized earlier in the spring were ordered to join the forces already engaged. Divisions from the Chinese border were moved west. But Krone was grinding up the Russians in the pocket between the Narva River and the leading edge of NATO ground forces at an accelerating pace. NATO had performed according to plan. The Russian ground offensive teetered on its hind foot.

Putin called a war council. His chief of staff, General Malenkov, agreed with the commander of Russian forces in Estonia, General Lentsov, that Russia was losing the ground campaign and that the reinforcements that had been called up would increase the density of troops in the

Narva pocket without adding to their strength. The additional units, as Lentsov put it, will "make richer targets for the NATO air war."

Putin questioned Malenkov. "What targets within Estonia," he asked, "could be destroyed by a tactical nuclear weapon and would halt NATO's progress?" Malenkov looked down at his shoes and gripped his pen as though he was holding a stirrup on an out-of-control subway.

"Mr. President," he said slowly, "our army has shifted its position to the West. A large part of it is concentrated between here and the Baltic States. Do we want to risk its destruction in a nuclear war?"

"Who said anything about a nuclear war?" snapped Putin. "I'm not thinking about attacking the United States or Germany. The Americans," he continued, "will get angry if they lose some tanks and ammunition. But the rest of NATO will be screaming when they realize that they are next on the nuclear target list. NATO will do what it did in Georgia, Ukraine, and Moldova. They'll think it over and call it off."

No one in the room dared point out that Putin had been wrong when he said that NATO would never use force to repel a Russian invasion of Estonia.

General Lentsov said that he would need anti–ballistic-missile defenses if he was being ordered to use tactical nuclear weapons. Putin responded that Moscow's ballistic-missile defenses could not be spared. He looked at General Malenkov and said that additional anti-missile defenses—the S-400—would be sent.

Admiral Beria, chief of staff of the Russian navy, rocked on the two back legs of his chair. He pulled out a cigarette and almost lit the filter end before catching himself. He cleared his throat.

"Mr. President," he said, looking somewhere to the left of Putin's bald head, "we have our largest carrier, two landing ships, two large battle cruisers," and here he looked up at the ceiling as though the list was written there, "four attack subs, three destroyers, and two frigates plus three logistics ships patrolling in the Baltic."

"Yes?" replied Putin, as though asking a question.

"They have defended themselves valiantly from the enemy's air attacks," answered the admiral.

NATO's land-based air had been targeting the Russian combatants with losses on both sides. One Russian frigate had been put out of commission and a destroyer sunk. But the fighting had not been decisive nor had it influenced land operations. Like the Battle of Jutland, fought over a century earlier on the western side of the Danish peninsula, the naval conflict had yielded mixed results.

Another inquisitorial "yes?" from Putin.

"If there is going to be an exchange of nuclear weapons . . ."

Putin cut him off. "I said that there would be no such exchange."

"But, if," said the admiral, who wanted more missile defense–equipped ships to join the Baltic flotilla.

"If, if, if." Putin interrupted him and got red in the face. "If you feel that you cannot defend the fleet, I will find another officer who can."

Three days later, a wooden glider was released at night 70 miles south of the Narva pocket. It descended slowly in the dark and landed in a fallow hay meadow belonging to an Estonian whose great-grandfather had left Russia in 1917. No NATO radars noticed. A squad of Russian Spetsnaz troops, including two young women officers, met the glider and its cargo, a pair of tactical nuclear warheads. Specially trained, they loaded one weapon each into the trunks of a pair of old Skoda sedans.

The two women changed into farmworkers' togs and headed toward the Alexela Terminal of Tallinn's Paldiski South Harbor as daylight spread from the northeast. Arriving in the late morning, one of the women parked her clunker within 100 yards of the terminal's light oil and petrochemical storage facilities. By previous arrangement, her colleague and some helpers loaded the other nuclear device aboard a large fuel truck that was due to leave for the Amari air base the same afternoon. The operation had been timed so that both women could board the next ferry to St. Petersburg.

These tactical weapons were new in Russia's arsenal, one kiloton each, equal to 1,000 tons of TNT. They were timed to detonate at the same moment, 2230 hours local time on Monday, July 14.

The explosions ionized the cool night air above both targets, producing a brilliant red mushroom cloud. The blasts vaporized the fuel storage facilities and their contents at Alexela and Amari. The detonations killed about 1,700 people, and the fires spread to a few ammunition bunkers at Amari, destroying part of the port's loading infrastructure and killing another 450 stevedores.

Vladimir Putin accused Estonia and NATO of attacking the source of ethnic Russians' livelihood at the port of Tallinn and stonily insisted that Estonian ultra-nationalists had staged the attack at Amari to stir up the country against Russia.

Not even the most credulous Western press bought this.

As the workday ended, President Algodón was

receiving an intelligence briefing on Russian fleet dispositions in the Baltic when the director of Central Intelligence called with the news of the nuclear attack. A moment later, several Secret Service agents barged into the Oval Office and hurried the president to the White House underground shelter.

Putin denied Russian involvement and changed his story. He accused NATO of lighting off the weapons as an excuse for a nuclear attack on the Russian homeland. The charge was transparent nonsense. But the third use of nuclear weapons in eighty years was not a time to take chances. The U.S. military went to DEFCON 1, and a helicopter arrived at the White House several minutes later to take the president and his family to a location safely northwest of the city.

Other cabinet members, the U.S. high command, and congressional leaders were also flown to sites well outside the capital.

Two hours later, the president met with the National Security Council by secure video hookup.

"Is there any indication that a larger attack is imminent?" asked Algodón. Before anyone could answer, he added, "Are our forces ready to respond if the United States is attacked?" The chairman of the Joint Chiefs said that reports were still flowing in, but that real-time satellite imagery offered no evidence of unusual activity at any Russian airfield or intercontinental ballistic missile silo. The Defense Intelligence Agency and the CIA agreed that intelligence showed neither indications nor warning that an attack against the U.S. homeland was in the works.

The president asked for options. Joint Chiefs Chairman Marine General Thomas Zrebiec outlined two. He pointed out that the reported casualties from the Russian attack appeared to be relatively low and suggested that this was most likely intentional. "We could use the same size weapon against similar Russian targets," he said.

"Which targets?" asked the president.

"A fuel dump and a major railhead: approximately 30 miles east of the border with Estonia," answered the chairman.

"You mean they're in Russia?"

"Yes, sir."

"What is the other option, General?"

"Sir, we could target one of their armored divisions that crossed into Estonia."

"How many casualties?" asked Algodón.

"At least 3,000," answered Zrebiec, "probably more."

"What about the Russian fleet?" asked the president, remembering what his briefer had told him a few hours earlier.

Chief of Naval Operations Admiral Moreland pointed out that nuclear weapons would not be needed to attack the Russian Baltic flotilla.

Grasping what his boss was getting at, the national security advisor, Alan Sunder, a former international law professor, suggested that the point was not so much to retaliate in kind as it was to defeat Putin and drive the Russians out of Estonia.

The president closed his eyes for a moment before speaking. "They've got one-fourth of their entire fleet in the Baltic," he noted. "Including their new aircraft carrier and a couple of large amphibious ships. How will Putin react if his Baltic fleet is sunk while his ground forces are on the defensive in Estonia?"

The question was not directed at any single person.

The former professor spoke up. "Putin used the tactical nukes *because* he's losing on the ground. It was a measured escalation intended to split NATO or force it to sue for peace. The rest of NATO is much more likely to stay with us if a conventional response can accomplish the same objective as a nuclear one. A fleet action takes out one of Putin's prize pieces, keeps the alliance in one piece, and will allow us to concentrate all NATO's air forces on defeating the Russians on the ground."

Secretary of Defense Ian Thrift coughed and looked down at a paper on the table in front of him, not the video monitor attached to his computer. He cleared his throat again and then glanced at the list.

"Forty years ago the Standing Naval Forces Atlantic group (STANAVFORLANT) had seven surface ships it could have sent to the Baltics. We would have flushed a couple of subs from the Med and probably a couple more from regular exercises off Norway's northern coast. Still, all of that would take time.

"Today," he continued, "there are a couple of U.S. frigates patrolling the Skagerrak. They can defend themselves but they cannot take on the Russian Baltic flotilla. *Vinson* along with her small number of escorts is patrolling the Greenland–Iceland–United Kingdom (GIUK) gap, which Russian combatants must pass to sortie into the North Atlantic. She would not reach the Baltics for another week and a half, and action is needed immediately to stop Putin. The Joint Chiefs will advise against putting *Vinson* into the enclosed area of the Baltics, and they will be right that this is an extremely bad moment to leave the GIUK gap unguarded. If the Baltic situation escalates, we do not want Russian ships swarming into the Atlantic."

"What about our attack subs?" Algodón said quietly.

"Couldn't we send a few of them close enough at least to target their carrier with cruise missiles?"

Thrift shook his head. "It's a good idea," he answered. "But the Russians and Chinese have so many boomers on patrol around the world that we're using up the lion's share of our attack subs to trail them. This would not be the right time to lose track of a single one."

"And the other NATO states?" asked the president. "They're right there. Couldn't they sink the Russian carrier?"

"Britain has a total surface ship force of nine combatants. She can send one frigate. France has offered to send a destroyer. Both need air cover to supplement their air defenses. This will only become available when *Vinson* arrives," said General Zrebiec gloomily.

It was left to the national security advisor to state the obvious. "Two weeks is an unacceptably long time to respond to a nuclear attack. We do not want to create the impression that the Russians can get away with what they've done."

Sunder was right, and the president knew it. Pushing ahead with the ground campaign as though Russia had not crossed the nuclear threshold would sap the will of the other NATO member states. It would start political firestorms among their electorates, who feared a second, more lethal Russian nuclear attack, perhaps against a population center. Many Americans would be angered over the loss of U.S. servicemen's lives and demand action. Others would be in the streets, demanding that the United States pull out at once.

A powerful U.S. naval force—especially submarines—that was already in the area could have begun to sink or put out of commission the flagship of the Russian fleet and destroy many of the Russian navy's other ships immediately. Lacking such a force, the president would have to swing U.S. naval forces from East Asia or the Persian Gulf. They would not arrive for many weeks. More important, their departure from East Asia and the Persian Gulf would be the clearest signal to America's allies in both places that their security could not survive an unexpected crisis somewhere else in the world. The president was left with the option to launch tactical nuclear weapons against targets on Russian soil or in Estonia, which had already experienced two nuclear detonations.

FACT While America races to deplete its seapower, Russia and China are accelerating their efforts to build theirs. The consequences may not surface in the Baltics. But an imbalance such as is now under way must eventually have profound strategic consequences.

CHAPTER VI

SINEWS CHALLENGED: CHINA

Unlike Russia, China stands on much firmer economic ground. Its enterprising people manufacture electronics, textiles, cameras, machinery, and a variety of consumer products that fill the shelves of large retail stores around the world. The price of oil affects China's economy, but not nearly as much as it affects Russia, whose economic health depends significantly on the global price of hydrocarbons.

But where Russia is rich in energy reserves, China depends on oil from the Middle East, Africa, Southwest Asia, and, increasingly, Russia. Most of this oil arrives by ship. China's rulers know as well as anyone the straits and choke points through which seaborne oil must pass: the route around Africa's southern tip, the entrances to the Red Sea and Persian Gulf from the Indian Ocean, and the narrow passages through which ships bound for China must sail as they navigate the archipelagic regions of Southeast Asia. Secure sea lines of communication (SLOCs) are just as necessary to export the Chinese manufactures on which their productive economy depends. Absent a healthy economy, a large part of the legitimacy of the rulers in Beijing vanishes. A navy ensures the safety of these SLOCs and also provides a fallback position for Chinese rulers as defenders of the nation if the economy falters.

Navies are flexible tools. Besides protecting SLOCs, they can project power, deny other navies access to vital areas, and interrupt communications—for example, those between the United States and its treaty allies in the West Pacific: Australia, New Zealand, Japan, the Philippines, Thailand, and South Korea.

Again, the issue of the legitimacy of China's rulers surfaces. As nationalism, encouraged by the Chinese Communist Party (CCP), grows, the ability to prevail in such disputes as are raised by China's territorial claims in the South and East China Seas supports the CCP's legitimacy. The party's unchallenged and supreme rule subsumes all else in the calculations of China's rulers. A powerful navy can hope to keep SLOCs open and oil and exports flowing. It is an important element in asserting territorial and mineral rights in nearby international waters.

The ability of the People's Liberation Army Navy (PLAN) to project power would be key if Beijing decides to slice communications between the United States and its West Pacific allies. China's intimidation of its neighbors, all of whom rely significantly on the South China Sea for commercial enterprise, raises questions about the commitment of the United States to remain an effective alliance partner and defender of international oceanic space. If the United States is found lacking, friends and allies will rearrange their defenses and alliances.

Protecting key SLOCs and asserting control over relatively nearby international waters are costly goals; however, China has the money. Its defense budgets have been
characterized by double-digit annual increases for two decades. As one expert on China's military has noted:

Whatever the true numbers may be, the Chinese military
has much more money to spend on fewer troops than it
did 15 years ago. At the same time, personnel, equipment,
and training costs for a more modern, technologically advanced military are significantly higher than in previous
decades. . . . If need be, the government could increase
defense spending even faster.[1]

The increases in China's military spending are impressive enough as things stand. The country allotted about
$15 billion in U.S. dollars to defense in 2000. By 2015, Chi-
na's defense budget had increased by a little more than
nine times, to just over $140 billion. These official statis-
tics may be true, or, in a regime where transparency is not
prized, they could be inexact.

More tangible are the products of whatever China is actually spending on the military. In 1999, the PLAN fleet
consisted of 50 land-based fighter planes, 14 surface ships,
and 10 submarines. These provided no significant ability
to deny access to the U.S. Navy in the West Pacific.

By 2016, the PLAN's naval aviation fighter force had
grown to 900 planes. Its surface fleet had increased to
88 combatants as well as a single aircraft carrier. Its attack submarine force numbered 60 boats. The range at
which the PLAN could contest, if not control, the access

of other navies' ships reached just over 900 miles from China's coast.

Official and unclassified U.S. sources anticipate that by 2020 China will have two carriers, although this estimate appeared before subsequent official reports in the Chinese media that "the Chinese Navy is expected to own a third aircraft carrier battle group."[2] By 2020, the number of surface combatants and attack subs is likely roughly to equal the 2016 figure, supported by 375 ballistic missiles, which will expand China's area denial capability to slightly less than 2,200 miles. Estimates vary, but all point to a growing PLAN with increasing capability and reach. In its 2014 report to Congress, the U.S.-China Economic and Security Review Commission, an independent panel of experts, reported that "by 2020, China could have as many as 351 submarines and missile-equipped surface ships in the Asia Pacific."[3]

Adding new combatants to the U.S. fleet takes time. Even with President Trump's full support, large increases in American seapower will not be immediate. From 1999 to 2020, the United States presence in the region is likely to remain at about its current level of a single aircraft carrier, 175 combat aircraft, and 12 surface combatants. U.S. submarines will probably increase from 4 attack subs in 1999 to 10 attack subs in 2020.

Beijing's military buildup is a byproduct of the nation's work ethic and resourcefulness. China's people are also thrifty with the wealth they have accumulated. Where Chinese citizens' savings as a fraction of GDP amount to one-half—the highest of the world's large nations—the same figure for the United States is about 18 percent, compared to a world average of 22 percent.[4] This partially ex-plains why China loans trillions to other nations while the United States borrows trillions.[5] Chinese banks have more to loan.

Beijing can pay for the military armament program it began decades ago, to which no end is in sight. The most often-heard explanation for China's aims is that it seeks the regional dominance that would secure its seaborne access to the rest of the globe. Addressing the possibility that China would move toward controlling air space over the international waters of the South China Sea, Professor Andrew Erickson, a highly respected authority at the Naval War College, told Congress in 2015 that:

> China's record on maritime sovereignty fuels this concern [i.e., the concern about the rights of other states' aircraft to overfly the South China Sea]. The *vast* majority of nations agree that under international law a country with a coast-line controls *only* economic resources in waters 12 to 200 miles out—and even less if facing a neighbor's coast less than 400 nm away. But China additionally claims rights to control military activities in that "Exclusive Economic Zone," as well as, apparently, in the airspace above it.[6]

In other words, China is building islands in the South China Sea to establish economic zones that it has chosen to regard as military ones: the islands establish what Beijing regards as sovereign rights that it may use armed force to defend.

Another highly regarded expert on Asia is former naval officer Paul Giarra, who sees China's effort to control the South China Sea as predicated on a large regional objective: domination of all the international waters within the "first island chain." The first island chain begins with Russia's Kurile Islands, which separate the Sea of Okhotsk from the North Pacific. It passes through Japan, which divides the Sea of Japan from the North Pacific. It reaches along the small Japanese islands that stretch to Taiwan and set off the East China Sea from the Pacific.

Taiwan is the center and hinge of the island chain. From Taiwan, the Philippines and a portion of Malaysia stand in the way of China's direct access to the Pacific. It is not a true chain, because its links are not connected and large open passageways exist from the South and East China Seas into the Pacific. But it is an important strategic chain, because all of its land masses, larger islands, and dots are positioned to contest access—by air, sea, or both—to and from the Asian mainland. The United States has security agreements and treaties with Taiwan, Japan, and the Philippines.

Giarra correctly sees the advantages of China's manmade islands in dominating the South China Sea and laying the foundation for stretching out a vambraced and gauntleted arm to grasp the first island chain.[7] The reefs and shoals that China has dredged into islands can be used as airfields and small naval bases for either defending or projecting power into the surrounding sea. Although limited by size, the islands increase the military or naval task of rolling back Chinese control. Notwithstanding law and internationally acknowledged maritime usage, the armed force that China can place on the islands underscores their unfounded sovereign claims.

Reaching south and east into the South China Sea, the

man-made islands extend the operational grasp of China's land-based naval and military aviation—just as the Ottoman capture of Venetian-held islands in the western Aegean could have been used to extend the sultans' naval power in the late fifteenth century. They weren't. The Ottomans raided, plundered, raped, murdered, and vanished. They didn't often think strategically. China's rulers do. Their man-made islands can also be used to deny regional access to U.S. and allied naval and air forces.

The second island chain is made up of very small islands that belong to Japan as well as the Mariana chain, which is U.S.-held territory. Shaped like the outline of a seated human facing east, it begins south of the center of Honshu, the large Japanese island, and ends at Papua New Guinea. It is geographically more permeable than the first island chain to the west, but contains the armed camp of Guam, which is the U.S. repository for naval, Marine, and air forces as well as army air defenses in the West Pacific. Guam also hosts a large ammunition and fuel logistic supply center, along with repair and maintenance facilities.

In 2014 a People's Liberation Army analyst commented on Guam's military importance:

> Owing to its proximity to the Asian continent, it is very convenient for aircraft of the U.S. Air Force and warships of the U.S. Navy to launch from [Guam]. For instance, B-52 bombers can fly directly to the Asian continent to execute missions without aerial refueling if they take off from here; F-35 and F-22 fighters can also reach the Asian continent with aerial refueling; aircraft carriers and nuclear-powered submarines can get replenishment and maintenance here.[8]

The PLA has created more than a cottage industry of intermediate-range ballistic missiles (IRBMs), anti-ship ballistic missiles, air-launched land-attack cruise missiles, air- and sea-launched anti-ship cruise missiles, and sea-launched land-attack cruise missiles that can reach Guam. Some of these are limited by the current ease of detecting Chinese aircraft, surface ships, and submarines. But in sufficient numbers, especially with large barrages of IRBMs, Chinese military planners are patiently building a genuine threat to the largest single U.S. military base in the Western Pacific.

The question of Chinese military reach goes far beyond the South China Sea and the second island chain: Guam is about 1,800 miles from the nearest point on the Chinese mainland. It would be a mistake to assume that China's military ambitions cease at the "nine-dash line," the tongue-shaped swath that China has drawn to include most of the South China Sea's international waters. Events over the past several years show that the field of vision of China's rulers is far broader than the waters of the Asian littoral.

The PLAN deployed ships for exercises with Russia's navy as far away as the Mediterranean in 2015. China's naval contingent included two new frigates. Naval vessels of both countries completed underway replenishment exercises and escorting missions as well as live-fire exercises.[9] In an underway replenishment, matériel is transferred between two ships as they sail alongside each other. This is a relatively sophisticated naval maneuver. Small mistakes in steering can pull one ship into the draft created by the other, with serious consequences. Or the lines that connect the logistics vessel with the one being refueled can snap.

The PLAN and Russian navies' live-fire exercises are a pellucid demonstration that the naval power that the United States and NATO once wielded in the Mediterranean is being challenged.

China now maintains a permanent naval presence in the Gulf of Aden. Its three combatants protect Chinese merchant ships from piracy, but the experience gained expands the PLAN's ability to keep ships on patrol at great distances. In 2015, a three-ship contingent of the PLAN completed a round-the-world tour, calling at ports in Europe, Central America, and the United States.[10]

Also in 2015, the PLAN sent several surface combatants to the Bering Sea. They were detected the same week that Barack Obama became the first serving U.S. president to visit the portion of Alaska above the Arctic Circle. The timing of these two events, while unpropitious, is less important than the demonstration of the PLAN's ability to deploy and supply naval combatants at increasing distances from China.

Farther from home—about 4,300 miles away—a Chinese Song-class, conventionally powered attack submarine and support ship docked at the Chinese-run Colombo International Container Terminal in Sri Lanka in September 2014.[11]

In simple terms, the PLAN's deployments, exercises, and ability to supply warships qualify it as a nascent global, transoceanic navy. China's navy is shorter today than the U.S. Navy on numbers, firepower, technology, and experience, but it has come a long way quickly. There is no reason to believe that China will stop modernizing and advancing both its naval capability and capacity.

As essential as ships are to a powerful global navy, more is required. The United States has basing agreements and rights in Cuba, Spain, Italy, Greece, Bahrain, Diego Garcia (in the Indian Ocean), Japan, and South Korea, to name but a few. These allow our navy to resupply, repair, maintain, and train. Some of the bases serve as launch points for ships that conduct combat operations, as Diego Garcia has for many years. This approach is unlike Britain's when it was a great seapower and incorporated whole states, a part of which served as bases in its expanding empire. The U.S. approach is similar to that of medieval and Renaissance Venice, which operated from a string of outposts that connected the great city-state to its trading partners in Constantinople and the Black Sea.

However, unlike Venice and China, U.S. naval bases combine American seapower with logistical support while also providing the host nation with security. U.S. bases in the Mediterranean and Asia are good examples. In contrast, China's recent attempt to establish a naval facility in neighboring Myanmar makes no pretense at mixing self-interest with that of the host state. Myanmar, like other nations bordering China, is sufficiently worried about the ambitions of its powerful neighbor to have canceled a proposed railroad that would have linked the two nations.[12]

For now, China is building a network of bases that largely coincides geographically with its increasing combat ship deployments. At the end of 2015, the China International Trust and Investment Corporation (CITIC), a state-owned company, won two bids to develop a special economic zone in the western Myanmar state of Rakhine. One of the contracts is to build a deep seaport at Kyaukpyu, a small city on the Bay of Bengal.[13] Myanmar shares a border with China's Yunnan province, and China already possesses a contract to receive oil by pipeline from Myanmar. The construction of a port at Kyaukpyu increases Beijing's ability to accept oil in quantity from the Middle East without having to ship it through the choke points of Southeast Asia's archipelagos. A Chinese-built port on the Bay of Bengal also helps allow the PLAN to project power into the seas on India's eastern border.

In mid-2016, China asked for 15,000 acres of land in the Hambantota district along Sri Lanka's south coast,[14] about 1,500 miles southwest of Kyaukpyu. The request follows by one year the Chinese state-owned China Communications Construction Company's proposal to construct new shipbuilding and repair facilities at Hambantota Port. If plans for the port transcend the vicissitudes of local politics, the port facility will, at 4,000 acres, be South Asia's largest, with a capacity for thirty-three ships at once.[15] In the "string of pearls"—a term coined by an American consulting firm's reference to China's budding network of bases in the Indian Ocean—Hambantota Port would be a very large and lustrous gem.

Two thousand four hundred miles northwest of Hambantota is the Pakistani port of Gwadar, a large facility located in the restive province of Balochistan. Gwadar is near the Iranian border, at the Gulf of Oman's gaping mouth, and 350 miles from the Strait of Hormuz. China Overseas Ports Holding Company, Ltd., a state-owned company, assumed responsibility for developing the port in 2013. China and Pakistan are united, among other things, by their enmity for democratic India.

Under the agreement between China and Pakistan that governs Beijing's participation, the port will not only receive and service ships but also include oil pipelines, supporting transportation infrastructure, industrial zones, and electrical generating facilities that carry a price tag of almost $50 billion.[16] This iridescent Chinese pearl, which can easily be used as a base for PLAN ships to project power at the approaches to the Persian Gulf, is enclosed in a hard steel case. Fifteen thousand Pakistani troops protect the facility against any threat that might come from Balochistan separatists.[17]

Pakistan's navy provides security for China's naval facility at Gwadar from the sea. Shortly before control of the port passed to the Chinese holding company, the chief of staff of the Pakistani navy at the time, Admiral Mohammad Zakaullah, said that his navy would protect the port "against all asymmetric threats under the prevalent precarious internal and external security environment."[18]

To fill in the interstices and further its naval presence, China also tried, in 2015, to establish naval bases in the Maldives, a string of islands astride the Indian Ocean's shipping lanes, and at the seaport city of Chittagong, Bangladesh, a year later. Indian national security officials were not pleased. The plans fell through. However, there is little chance that these setbacks will stop China from looking for naval bases elsewhere in the region.

To expand its reach westward, China announced plans early in 2016 to build a naval facility at the Horn of Africa. The agreement was reached with Djibouti on the western side of the Bab el-Mandeb, the strait through which ships steam as they enter or exit the Red Sea. At the Red Sea's northern end lies the Gulf of Suez and the canal of the same name. In the first quarter of 2016, an average of 1,400 ships transited the Suez to Bab el-Mandeb passage each month.[19]

When complete, China's naval bases that girdle the subcontinent from Asia to Africa will give the PLAN the ability to supply, repair, and maintain combatant and logistics ships along a 7,700-mile route from the center of the Asian mainland's seacoast to the straits that control access to energy for Europe and a significant portion of the United States. China's ability to apply power at a distance does not approach that of the United States, but the balance of projected power between Beijing and Washington is demonstrably in flux.

Patrolling this vastness with modern combatants remains a challenge for the PLAN, which possesses more submarines, albeit less technologically advanced ones, than the United States. There is no reason to count on our superior technology as an indefinite protection. Remember that Sitting Bull and Crazy Horse's numerically superior Lakota Sioux, armed with a mélange of bows, spears, clubs, muzzleloaders, and some modern repeating rifles, handily defeated George Armstrong Custer's much smaller command armed with up-to-date and uniform weapons.

The Defense Department's undersecretary of Defense for acquisitions, technology, and logistics observed in 2014 that a problem exists with "the modernization rate of other powers, in particular of China, . . . [which has been] investing for a long time in a number of systems which are essentially focused on keeping the United States out of the part of the world that's closest to China."[20] The same article—published by the Defense Department—added that "the United States tends to rely on a small number of very expensive, but very capable, assets, . . . and that makes the military vulnerable once an enemy learns how to attack those assets, noting that no one has a monopoly on technology, warfighting power or doctrinal and operational concepts."[21]

China's technological prowess predates contemporary times by several millennia. Sophisticated Chinese technology, in the form of ceremonial containers, tools, and weapons carved out of jade, dates from four thousand years ago. Sixteen hundred years before the birth of Jesus, Chinese artisans were creating wine flasks, cooking utensils, and ritual vessels by crafting ceramic molds, into which bronze was poured. The results were objects of timeless grace and beauty, in which shape and proportion balanced with extraordinary intricacy. If China struggled with technology, the contests were self-generated and political, not, as Tolstoy put it in describing Russia, issues of inertia or dejection of spirit.

China today is neither dejected nor inert. In the forty years since Mao Zedong's death, the country has, while retaining single-party rule and the façade of communism, emerged from severe poverty to become the world's second-largest economy and number two in military spending.[22] The years during which foreign powers interfered in and carved up China are regarded as wellsprings of today's nationalism and spurs to Chinese international preeminence. Inasmuch as China looks upon itself as the hegemon of Asia prior to the nineteenth century, its current effort to reestablish and expand upon this position is similar to Russia's, except within a much longer span of time.

For China, technological innovation comes more readily than it does in Russia, although both countries are increasingly competent with military hardware. China's anti-ship ballistic missile, the DF-21, is a good example. The missile was designed to hit large ships—American aircraft carriers and/or large-deck amphibious ships. It is a ballistic missile with a maneuverable warhead that can alter its course in the final stages of flight to better find targets and evade their defenses. The DF-21 can be fired from a truck, so launch sites are as plentiful as positions along a very large system of roads. The missile uses a combination of sensors to make the kill. These include over-the-horizon radars, probably drones, and satellites. There is every reason to believe that several such missiles would be launched at once. If the software that integrates the sensors can be perfected, this system would be a serious threat to American carriers and large amphibious vessels.

The DF-21's approximately 1,000-mile range would make an American carrier commander rightfully concerned about taking his ship much closer than that to the Chinese coast. The planes aboard a carrier cannot fly 1,000 miles without being refueled, by either land- or carrier-based tankers. Our land bases in the region would be obvious targets in a conflict with China. Using other planes based on the same carrier as tankers is possible, but would severely limit the number of sorties that could be launched from a single ship.

According to a Taiwan newspaper, China tested the DF-21D, dubbed "carrier killer," in 2013. The target was a carrier-sized rectangle in the Gobi Desert whose location would likely have been known to the launch crew.[23] Because there is a large difference between hitting a stationary target at a known position and identifying and then penetrating the defenses of a moving target at sea, the results of such a test are inconclusive at best. Similarly unclear is the ability of the DF-26 missile—with an advertised range of 2,500 miles—to strike a moving naval target.

Still, the U.S. Navy regards the array of China's missile, submarine, and land-based naval aviation threats to carriers seriously. Three years before the Gobi Desert test, Admiral Robert Willard, then head of the U.S. Pacific Command, said that he believed China's anti-ship ballistic-missile system had reached "about the equivalent of a U.S. system that has achieved IOC [initial operational capability]."[24] IOC is an artful military term; it means that a weapons system has attained the minimum level of performance required for deployment in the field, but suggests that considerable work remains before the system is fully operational.

No less reason exists to look carefully at the PLAN's submarine building program. From 1995 to 2016, China built or purchased from Russia forty-one attack submarines. The United States today has fifty-two attack subs. This number will decrease as older boats are decommissioned and resources are diverted to replace the aging ballistic submarines that are the most stealthy leg of our nation's nuclear deterrent (the other two legs are land-based bombers and ICBMs). The U.S. Navy, in the Obama administration's final long-range naval plan, proposed that its future fleet possess forty-eight attack submarines—although not before it reaches a low of forty-one subs in 2029. The goal of a 48-boat attack submarine force, of course, is now open to revision as a result of the 2016 election. It is reasonable to expect President Trump to ask for larger numbers of attack subs, although it is equally reasonable to ask from where the money for additional subs will come. What can be stated with certainty is that China in the foreseeable future will continue to increase its submarine force, including ballistic-missile submarines: it will surpass the number, although not the quality, of U.S. subs within the next ten years.

A possible future numerical imbalance between U.S. and Chinese submarines does not tell the complete story. So long as China focuses its subsurface force on the South and East China Seas while the United States maintains naval commitments to NATO, the security of Middle Eastern sea lines of communication, and perhaps the Mediterranean, as well as reconnoitering the gap between the United Kingdom and Greenland for the passage of Russian combatants into the Atlantic, American seapower must be apportioned globally. China will enjoy an important numerical advantage in concentrating the preponderance of its submarine forces in the West Pacific. The PLAN already enjoys a significant edge over U.S. seapower in mines and mine-laying capacity.

To this advantage will be added an increasingly capable sound surveillance system (SOSUS). SOSUS is a network of sensing devices located on the sea floor and linked by cable to receiving posts ashore. After the United States developed the system in the early 1950s, it was put to use along the U.S. East Coast. Later, SOSUS was placed in the gap between Greenland and Iceland and between Iceland and the northern United Kingdom during the Cold War to monitor the passage of Soviet submarines in and out of the North Atlantic. Its performance was of strategic importance to the United States and NATO. With permeable island chains to its east that enclose the South China Sea, China needs no reminders that intelligence about the movement of potential enemies' subs is particularly valuable.

In 2013 *China Science Daily* published an article, "Here They Are Quietly Listening to the Ocean: The Whole Story of the Building of Our Country's First Deep Sea Ocean Floor Sensor Network Base." The article reported that Chinese undersea sensors had been tested in 2005 and subsequently placed at strategic points near the mainland's coast.[25] China is likely to have progressed substantially since then in developing its undersea listening posts. The reach of China's SOSUS—called "the undersea Great Wall"—may expand in congruence with the PLAN's ability to project power. This would include not only the immediate coast but "the near seas, the depths of the far seas, . . . as well as in strategic areas [choke points] and such areas."[26]

China faces its greatest naval threat from the advanced technology of U.S. submarines and the long experience of American crews in submarine operations. But surface ships make up a part of any effective defense or offense against subs. They are critical to a host of other combat missions, including projecting power, defending against missiles, destroying other surface vessels, supporting amphibious landings, and escorting aircraft carriers or convoys. In a war with China, U.S. surface vessels would assist in patrolling choke points, destroying the PLAN, and ensuring the safety of seaborne logistical support to our treaty allies, among other tasks.

Again, China is aware of this. The PLAN has built five classes of anti-ship cruise missiles in recent years and has purchased such missiles from Russia. Combined with the subs and surface ships from which these missiles can be launched, the net effect is to succor China's goal of dominating the region's seas and place at risk the power of the United States to deter and/or conduct conflict, along with our ability to supply and assist allies if hostilities were to occur. The hundreds of land-attack weapons, including short-range ballistic missiles, that China has been adding to its already large arsenal imperil U.S. and allied land bases in the region and thus increase Beijing's ability to achieve regional hegemony through its military.

In the caliginous world of intelligence, one thing is clear. It is as crucial to know a potential enemy's capability as it is to know his intent. China's military capabilities, which also include increasingly sophisticated cyber war and other sea-related competencies not described in this sketch, are known. China's rulers have not stated their intent. However, portions of it can be inferred from the naval capability they are building as well as from senior officials' statements and actions.

Islands, rocky outcroppings, reefs, shoals, and, by extension, huge swaths of the South China Sea are enclosed by the nine-dash line noted above. Basing its action on "historic rights," China began to claim these maritime excrescences after Japan vacated the area following its defeat in World War II. According to the U.N. Law of the Sea

Treaty, which Beijing has signed and ratified, ownership of the islands would establish economic rights to resources as distant as 200 miles from their shores.

China has sought to equate economic rights with sovereign rights. This would transform nearly 1.5 million square miles of international waters in the South China Sea into an immense Chinese bay. The United States has insisted that maritime rights must be based on recognized sovereignty over land. The islands closest to China on which it bases these expansive claims are the Paracel Islands, which lie more than 150 miles southeast of the Chinese island of Hainan. No international agreement, written or traditional, recognizes a state's sovereign claims to land or coral formations that jut from waters 150 miles distant.

In 2013, the Philippines asked the Permanent Court of Arbitration in The Hague to decide on a dispute between Manila and Beijing over Johnson South Reef, located in the South China Sea about 200 miles northwest of the Philippines. The dispute is one of many between China and other states on the same body of water that have led to military confrontation, diplomatic recriminations, threats, and the growing potential for serious accidents and escalation.

The distance from the Chinese mainland to the disputed reef is more than 600 miles. Two years after the request from the Philippines, the court agreed to hear the case. While it deliberated, Chinese dredgers continued to pump sediment, enlarging the reef. In July 2016, the international tribunal found no legal basis for China's claim of historic rights in the South China Sea. The court also found that China had broken international laws by causing "irreparable" harm to the environment as it meddled with Philippine commercial activity in the area. The decision is important because it invalidates China's claim to sovereignty within the very large area of the nine-dash line.

China's foreign ministry promptly announced that the international court's decision "is invalid and has no binding force. . . . China does not accept or recognize it."[27] According to the state-run *People's Daily*, China's President Xi Jinping repeated that China's sovereign claims in the South China Sea date to "ancient times."[28]

For the United States, China's reaction is even more important than the actual court decision. Since the Reagan administration, U.S. policy has sought to make China a stakeholder in the liberal international order. This means that China would have an interest in such characteristics of the current system as freedom of navigation in international waters as well as respect for international agreements it has ratified, for the rule of law, and for other states' sovereignty—to name a few. Senior-level officials from both countries have been meeting together since the Nixon administration to encourage Chinese rulers to identify their nation's own interest with that of the international order. With U.S. support, China joined the World Trade Organization in 2001. In 2016, the PLAN participated for the second time in the large naval exercise that the United States conducts with other Pacific Rim states. This list of U.S. overtures is long.

No joyful music has followed them. Quite the opposite, as China's response to the international tribunal demonstrates. Encapsulating China's view of its relations with other states, when the subject of China's claims in the

South China Sea was raised at a 2010 meeting in Hanoi, Beijing's foreign minister at the time, Yang Jiechi, told other Asian senior officials that "China is a big country and other countries are small countries, and that's just a fact."[29]

China's brand of exceptionalism reinforces Minister Yang's blunt assertion that might makes right. The qualification "with Chinese characteristics" has become a commonplace in international lingo. The press and scholarly publications have reported on "a global order with Chinese characteristics," "foreign aid with Chinese characteristics," "environmental law with Chinese characteristics," and "nuclear deals with Chinese characteristics." The list of accepted international practices "with Chinese characteristics" is lengthy. It shows that China's exceptionalism lies not in its adherence to principle, law, or accepted norms of international behavior but rather in its deflection from these.

U.S. policy toward China has failed spectacularly. China's actions show that it sees us as a strategic competitor that must be bested. An exceptionally thoughtful and highly respected Princeton professor, Aaron Friedberg, offers evidence in a full volume that deserves wide attention:

> Shi Yinhong, a scholar known for his sometimes controversial views, has suggested that Beijing should take advantage of the prevailing trends in the world today in order to establish a position of "superior or near superior political, military, diplomatic, and economic influence on China's periphery (especially in East Asia)."[30] Men Honghua, a strategic analyst affiliated with the Central Party

School,[31] goes even further. For him, regional preponderance is vitally important, but it is also the means to a larger end. Beijing's ultimate aim, he writes, should be to "gain global influence by becoming the dominant power in the Asia-Pacific region."[32] A book published in 2010 by Liu Mingfu of the National Defense University, who is a senior colonel in the People's Liberation Army, takes a similar line. China should abandon any pretense of restraint and "sprint to become world number one." Its "big goal in the 21st century" must be to become "the top power," displacing the United States. If it fails, then "inevitably it will become a straggler that is cast aside."[33]

The American foreign policy community largely ignores these warnings and those of like-minded experts, whether Chinese or American. We prefer to see China as a large market that can be cajoled into joining us as a defender of international security and economic stability. U.S. policy makers have been hoping that the large volume of trade between China and the United States and the accompanying economic progress in the former would remold Chinese rulers to look, think, and act more like us. The evidence does not support this roseate hope.

History teaches the opposite lesson. The Venetian Senate argued over whether to assist the Byzantines as the Ottomans tightened their grip on the Bosphorus and successfully besieged Constantinople in 1453. They shilly-shallied, and, although some naval assistance was sent, it arrived too late. Most of the nobles believed that possession of the Bosphorus would make no difference in Venice's trade or security. Others believed that a recent peace treaty with the Ottomans would preserve trading relations and protect Venice. They were mistaken. After taking Constantinople, the Ottomans contested Venetian commerce and challenged them at sea. The great city was forced to retreat from its position as the Mediterranean's premier naval power.

Prior to World War I, Britain and Germany were major trading partners. This had no discernible effect on the enmity that grew between the two states. British leaders regarded Germany's rise as a threat, while German leaders saw Britain as an obstacle to their ambitions. World War I cast a dim light on the argument that British writer and Labor MP Norman Angell made in his 1910 book, *The Great Illusion*. Angell insisted that trade between great economic powers made war pointless. World War I was pointless enough, but trade did nothing to stop it.

Contrary to some current literature, the United States and China are not destined to fight. Professor Graham Allison offers the conventional opinion that more candid discussions "about likely confrontations and flash points" would avoid a Peloponnesian War–like outcome between Washington and Beijing.[34] But the professor has not read Thucydides carefully. An upstart maritime power, Athens grew powerful and added allies as a deterrent to another Persian invasion. The slow-to-act ancient continental power, Sparta, feared for its position on the Peloponnese peninsula. The discussions between the two sides were ineluctably clear and frank.

As tensions rose between Athens and Sparta, a dispute broke out between two smaller powers, Corcyra and

Corinth. The latter city is located at the neck of land that joins the Peloponnese with the Attic peninsula. The former, an island known today as Corfu, lies just west of the modern border between Greece and Albania, and about 75 miles east of the south end of Italy's heel.

Corinth attacked Corcyra's fleet in the same place where the battles of Actium and Lepanto would be fought. Corcyra's fleet won a decisive victory. Despite Corinthian arguments to stay out, Athens formed a defensive alliance with Corcyra, largely on the strength of the latter's strategic position in the Ionian Sea along the trade routes to Sicily. This engaged and enraged Corinth. Another, less decisive, naval battle followed, in which both the Corinthians and their enemies, Corcyra and Athens, claimed victory.

As the Corinthians looked for ways to retaliate, the conflict jumped like a crown fire to the northwestern Aegean Sea, where the city of Potidaea, a Corinthian colony but a tributary ally of Athens, revolted against Athens. Potidaea's example inspired other nearby cities to revolt against Athens. Athens' leadership was understandably concerned: the region that had turned on it sat squarely along the land route that Persia had used twice in the previous sixty years to attack Greece. Corinth sent representatives to persuade its famously reluctant ally, Sparta, to join the fight and invade Athens' stronghold, Attica.

Athenian envoys urged Sparta to exercise restraint. They reminded their listeners of Athens' initiative and valor in defeating Persia. They sought "to show, if you are so ill-advised as to enter into a struggle with Athens, what sort of antagonist she is likely to prove."[35] They recalled the battle of Marathon, in which the Athenian general,

Miltiades, unassisted by Sparta, had turned back the first Persian invasion. Harkening back a half century, the Athenians pointed to the daring and innovative tactics of Themistocles, who had outwitted and outfought the Persian fleet at Salamis.

The Athenian representatives did not stop at warning Sparta that its cautious ways would be no match for Athens' superior naval force and willingness to accept risk for the purpose of holding together the alliance against Persia that was now threatening to dissolve. They concluded their speech with the warning that, if Sparta decided to intervene on the Corinthians' behalf in any way, Athens would fight.[36]

In Thucydides' account, neither Athens nor Sparta minced words. The "Thucydidean trap" of which Professor Allison writes did not snap because diplomatic language hid the two parties' true intent. The trap closed because of conflicting interests in which, according to Thucydides' famous description, fear and honor also formed opinion and shaped action.

More candor in American diplomacy would certainly benefit our interest in peace, stability, and democracy in Asia, just as it would advance the companion goal of preventing a Chinese hegemony. But the condition for candor in speech is resolution in policy. Dependence on trade volumes, the Obama administration's diffident policy of responding to China's array of provocations in the South and East China Seas, and the same administration's minimalist naval construction program have increased the possibility for conflict between the United States and China. These supine policies renew the faith of the Chinese lead-

ership that building and arming islands, provoking neighbors, and projecting global power will benefit them.

A resolute American policy would concentrate on
strengthening current alliances so that partners and friends
could increase their contribution to preserving the region's
security. American officials don't have a major task in persuading smaller states on and near the South China Sea
that Chinese domination would harm them. China's many
attempts to subjugate Vietnam, for example, go back two
millennia. The leaders in Hanoi need no lessons from us
on this subject. More effective policy would require the
United States to resume meaningful and regular military
assistance to Taiwan, including the aid in acquiring submarines that Taipei needs to defend itself from a Chinese
submarine-enforced blockade.

A more vigorous defense of U.S. interests would also
mean a large increase in freedom of navigation operations
(FONOPS) that the U.S. Navy and allies conduct in the
international waters of the South China Sea. In the first
seven months of 2016, three U.S. naval vessels carried out
"innocent passage" operations in the area. Innocent passage is a benign transit that, as its name suggests, does not
challenge the sovereign claims of another state to disputed
waters. Freedom of navigation operations, however, are a
more robust form of asserting the international character
of disputed international waters.

A persistent regular regimen of FONOPS would de-
serve more respect from China and help convince its rulers
of American will. So would a significant increase in U.S.
naval shipbuilding, especially attack submarines, a category of weapons in which our technological superiority to

Chinese submarines offers us an asymmetrical advantage. So would the dispatch of an aircraft carrier, rather than a much smaller destroyer, to emphasize the defense of freedom of navigation in international waters by the United States.

The objective in all of these policies is to secure the region's peace and stability. This is best accomplished by convincing China of our commitment. Beijing has abundantly demonstrated its lack of interest in the liberal international system, which Washington has been promoting for forty-five years. The region will be far better off if China understands that there is nothing to be gained from continued threats, military maneuvers, island building, and deliberately manufactured incidents. The policies advocated here will help persuade China of America's commitment to remaining a Pacific power, which—together with the cooperation of allies, partners, and friends—will assure Beijing that initiating a conflict or hoping to benefit from an accident or provocation is futile.

CHAPTER VII

OLD STRATEGY MEETS NEW FACTS

China Tests U.S. Seapower in the West Pacific

A Scenario In 2010, Zhang Liu started a small company that specialized in gourmet cutlery, cooking knives in particular. Located in a suburb of the boomtown Shenzhen, about 25 miles north of Hong Kong, Kindest Cut Manufacturing turned out high-quality cleavers, chopping knives, shears, sharpeners, and small paring knives that retailed in the United States and Western Europe at two-thirds the cost of fine Wüsthof knives made in Solingen, Germany.

Mr. Zhang started with fifteen workers, and, by 2025, Kindest Cut employed about seventy. He worked hard and plowed the firm's profits back into the business and into the stock market. The business flourished. The stock market galloped. In the fifteen years since he started investing, his portfolio had quintupled in value. Irrationally exuberant, as Federal Reserve chairman Alan Greenspan had described U.S. markets before the dot.com bubble burst in the 1990s, China's equity markets plunged ahead like a large truck that had lost its brakes descending a mountain road.

Betting that the steep climb would continue indefinitely, uneducated and uninformed first-time investors borrowed from brokers and rang up huge margin debts. Markets don't work that way. When real estate prices dipped sharply in the fall of 2026 as supply far exceeded demand, the equity markets in Shanghai and Shenzhen pulled back just enough so that investors who had bought on the margin had to cover their losses. They started selling stocks to do so. This was not a "correction." The stock market fell like a cell phone tossed from the roof of one of Shenzhen's new high-rises.

The capital gains tax first levied on foreign investors eleven years earlier had been extended to include Chinese citizens. Revenues from these taxes had helped support the massive section of China's economy that state-owned industries represented. The level of non-performing loans that China dished out to keep the state-owned industries afloat had reached 10 percent, just as it had in Spain and Italy over a decade earlier. Beijing's shell game of rolling over bad loans and issuing bonds to provide government banks with the appearance of financial solidity cracked, and the productive sector of the economy faltered as interest rates zoomed. Job losses in the private sector started creeping into the public one. The equity market imploded and wiped out the savings of the newly unemployed.

The Chinese Communist Party (CCP) leadership had been preparing for something like this for years. Their naval buildup, assertions of sovereignty over islands far from China's territorial waters, confrontations with neighboring states' ships and aircraft, and transforma-

tion of distant shoals and reefs into armed land dots in
the South and East China Seas generated the hoped-for
nationalism. Deprived of the justification for rule provided by a booming economy, the CCP succeeded in por-
traying itself to China's newly impoverished as defenders
against a resurgence of foreign colonialists.

This helped neither Mr. Zhang's business nor his bank
account. But he and his wife lived close to the coast and
felt some relief that if the government could not resolve
the burgeoning financial crisis it would at least protect
them.

Others of his countrymen were less forgiving of the
national government. Riots had broken out in large Chinese cities—Chengdu, Hangzhou, Nanjing, and Wuhan,
to name a few. Demonstrators called on the government
to provide immediate relief in the form of food, jobs,
lower taxes, and rent relief. The protests were spreading.

The Central Committee of China's Communist Party
ordered the People's Liberation Army Navy (PLAN) to
increase its naval presence in the East and South China
Seas. Corvettes, frigates, destroyers, and cruisers sal-
lied forth from the East Sea Fleet base at Ningbo and
the South Sea Fleet at Zhanjiang and fanned out along
the edges of the tongue-shaped area over which Beijing
claimed sovereign control. The tongue reached 1,000
miles south of China, deep into the South China Sea's
international waters.

The aircraft carrier *Liaoning* was ordered to take up station on the 15th parallel to patrol a large oval centered at
the midpoint between Olangapo in the Philippines and
Quang Ngai Township in Vietnam, a convenient spot
located within strike aircraft range of both Subic Bay
and Cam Ranh Bay. A tripartite agreement had resulted

in the recent return of the U.S. Navy—and its supporting facilities—to both bases. Land-based naval aviation
patrols increased in and around the Senkaku Islands, and
Japanese surface combatants in the area reported a large
uptick in Chinese submarine presence.

Tokyo and Hanoi put a total of three large amphibious
ships to sea with escorts. Japan also increased its fighter
aircraft sorties and maritime patrol aircraft surveillance in
the waters surrounding the disputed islands and placed
a pair of destroyers in position to defend the islands if
hostilities occurred. The Philippines dispatched several
coast guard cutters and an anti-aircraft warfare-equipped
frigate.

Chinese leaders were satisfied with shaking the naval
stick. But the financial crisis deepened as discontent in
the form of protests expanded. More distractions were
needed.

Demonstrating China's global reach, the official news
agency Xinhua and the large government-run *People's Daily*
started reporting extensively on the long-awaited opening of a Chinese-designed and -financed canal through
Nicaragua that linked the Atlantic to the Pacific. Wider,
longer, and more impressive than the Panama Canal,
the Nicaraguan route would open with lavish ceremo-
nies in two months. The media reminded its audience of
the opening ceremony three years earlier for the Winter
Olympics in Beijing and Zhangjiakou. Ten thousand
drones with lights flashing the word "peace" in most of
the world's languages had buzzed overhead in a huge
airborne formation that was a stylized representation of
the Mandarin character for "love." The 85,000 spectators
had sat in warmed bleachers at the site of the downhill,
slalom, and ski-jumping events and gazed skyward in awe

and delight. Communist Party leaders decided that the canal opening offered similar possibilities. Xinhua told its audience to expect the inauguration of the Nicaraguan Canal to outdo the recent Olympic spectacle.

The PLAN would sail a mighty flotilla across the Pacific and participate at both the Atlantic and Pacific entrances of the new canal. The announcement had a minor calming effect in Asia. If Beijing was dispatching major naval power to Central America, perhaps its movements in the South China Sea did not represent a prelude to something ominous.

Two of China's very large carriers, the *Zheng He* and *Tianming*, were readied to sail. So were two large amphibious ships with space for helicopters, tanks, and marines. Japanese and Taiwanese intelligence confirmed that both carriers and amphibs would carry a full complement of combat equipment, including ammunition.

Meanwhile, China's ground-based naval reconnaissance and fighter planes continued to orbit over the contested Spratly Islands throughout the day and for most of the night, straying deliberately and routinely into Philippine and Vietnamese airspace. Escorted by one submarine, one destroyer, and two frigates, a large-deck amphibious ship—outfitted with eight helicopters, half as many hovercraft, and a thousand marines—appeared off the coast of the Senkaku Islands and maintained a position where it could descend upon the islands or sail southwest to join a larger force that was heading from the amphibious fleet's headquarters at Zhanjiang toward Taiwan.

Diplomatic activity between the United States and its allies and friends in the region spiked. During his 2014 spring visit to Tokyo, President Obama had assured

Japan's Prime Minister Shinzo Abe that the United States would assist Japan in a conflict over the disputed Senkaku Islands. Subsequent U.S. presidents had offered similar assurances to other treaty allies, for example, the Philippines. The defense treaty that the United States signed with Vietnam in 2021 included a specific provision for Washington to assist Hanoi in the event of hostilities within the waters of Vietnam's exclusive economic zone.

This was not an academic exercise. China had towed an oil rig to the waters off Vietnam's coast in 2014 and begun exploring for oil and natural gas. In 2012, Beijing occupied the Scarborough Shoal, which sits inside the Philippines' exclusive economic zone. As China's financial woes sharpened in 2025, the PLA stepped up its transformation of distant reefs into armed islands. The increased chances for conflict, China's rulers figured, were critical as part of their current effort to divert attention from an ailing domestic economy.

China's redoubled policy of extending its sovereignty hundreds of miles from its coast by dubious means and its aggressive and widespread naval deployments surprised many in Washington. Since the beginning of the twenty-first century, Beijing had insisted that China's rise would be peaceful. An unending series of incidents with its neighbors over disputed islands in the South and East China Seas, as well as an armed confrontation with India over the Aksai Chin border area in 2022, had generated skepticism in Washington's official circles. But the position maintained by both American political parties was that the mostly eastbound trade flows between China and the United States, along with China's massive holdings and continued purchases of U.S. treasury bills, would keep the peace. Thirty-five years earlier, President

George H. W. Bush's administration aimed to use trade, inclusion, diplomacy, and time to make China a "stakeholder" in the international order. This policy had not changed in one-third of a century.

As a partial result of China's confrontations with its neighbors and the United States in international waters, many shadows had darkened the assumptions of this long-held policy since 1990. A particularly ominous shadow took shape when Farnsworth Doolittle, the director of the Central Intelligence Agency, called President Algodón at noon on October 31 and asked for a meeting that day.

He arrived two hours later to report that, over the preceding month, China had nearly doubled the number of ballistic missiles it annually placed on the mainland immediately across from Taiwan. In 2024, China had added 150 missiles to its array aimed at key infrastructure, command and control, communications, military, and financial targets on Taiwan. Since the beginning of October, 293 ballistic-missile mobile launchers had been moved into position across the Taiwan Strait. The director of the CIA also reported that PLAN amphibious vessels from the North Sea Fleet at Qingdao and the South Sea Fleet at Zhanjiang were converging at the East Sea Fleet port of Ningbo, closest in sailing distance to Taipei. Doolittle told the president that he believed China's public statements that the amphibious fleet was preparing to conduct training exercises. He dismissed as "alarmist" the minority opinion within the intelligence community that China was preparing to attack Taiwan.

The president knew that Central Intelligence had bought Saddam Hussein's argument that the Iraqi ground forces called up to the Kuwaiti border in 1989 prior to invasion were being mobilized for an exercise. He had heard aging members of Congress privately describe the CIA's Iraq expert at the time as a publicist for the Iraqi regime. He had been told that the CIA insisted up to the morning of the Iraqi invasion that Saddam was merely conducting training. But Algodón said nothing, at least for now. He asked other questions.

"You've had a lot to say over the past few days about Chinese naval activity in the South China Sea. Are there any other significant PLAN movements in the region, or globally?"

Doolittle, a holdover from the previous administration while the Senate deliberated on the new president's choice as DNI, cleared his throat.

"Well, Mr. President, you're aware, of course, of the aircraft carriers and amphibious ship group that China is preparing to send to the opening of the Nicaraguan Canal."

"Yes," said Algodón. "Any other ships accompanying?"

"Yes, it seems like quite a show they're putting on. They're also sending a couple of attack subs, two logistics ships, and several cruisers and destroyers. Not sure of the numbers of surface ships yet. But I'll get back to you on that."

"Mr. Doolittle, this seems like a rather large task group. Anything else going on here? What are the Japanese saying? Have the Vietnamese or Filipinos increased their readiness? Are the South Koreans saying anything among themselves? Is Canberra doing anything unusual in anticipation?"

"Mr. President, the Chinese like shows. Remember their two Olympics openings? Real shindigs, didn't you think? The Nicaraguan Canal is a big deal. They planned it. They paid for it. They built it. If we're not able to widen the Panama Canal and increase its throughput (this was a little dig at Algodón, who was battling with members of his own party about the White House's request for appropriations to do exactly this), the world's shipping will be using China's canal to move back and forth between the Atlantic and the Pacific."

President Algodón ignored the jab.

"I'm aware of the stakes here. But could you answer my question? What are our Asian allies and friends doing about the naval/amphibious task group that China says is preparing to cross the Pacific?"

"They're not happy."

"Not happy?"

"Well, the Japanese prime minister, intelligence chief, and chief of staff are arguing over taking preemptive action to defend the Senkakus. Hanoi will probably tell China sometime next week to stop violating Vietnamese airspace or accept the consequences. The Filipinos are planning to announce a full mobilization of their reserves in ten days."

"And the Taiwanese? You told me a couple of days ago that they were putting all their submarines to sea and practicing civilian air raid drills. Anything else since?"

"Well, sort of."

The president leaned forward and twirled a pen with his fingers.

"Sort of?"

"Yes. The Chinese moved six naval special operations units onto Hainan Island last night. They're holed up in a container storage warehouse owned by the PLAN along with rubber inflatable boats. The boats can rendezvous with almost any Chinese sub, which could transport them to within a few miles of their destination."

"Is this another drill, Mr. Doolittle?"

For the first time, the DCIA squirmed.

"I have a meeting later this morning with the DIA director. We're going to discuss."

"Please keep me informed," said the president, ending the meeting.

The president had known the Defense Intelligence Agency director, General Simon, since both men were lieutenants. Algodón asked his secretary to put the call through.

"'Morning, Mr. President," said the general.

"Jake," said the president, "I just had a meeting with the DCIA. It looks to me as though things are going south in Asia very quickly. Doolittle has an explanation for almost everything. What's happening?"

"Sir, Doolittle and I don't agree. The Chinese have mobilized reserves, increased their provocations from Japan to the southern end of the South China Sea, and turned the coast of Fujian Province into an armed camp—all in the past two months. There's a 50-50 chance they're planning to attack Taiwan. Doolittle and I are supposed to talk about their special operations movements in an hour."

"Have we told Taipei's intelligence people about this?

"I think they already know. But that's item number one on the agenda this morning. Doolittle will resist, because he doesn't want to risk letting the Taiwanese know that we know. The usual business about protecting sources."

"Ok, Jake. Give me a ring when you finish talking with him."

"Sir."

A meeting of the National Security Council that evening overruled the DCIA's objections to sharing with the Taiwanese government intelligence that a large contingent of naval special operations forces had assembled on the Dongchong Bandao Peninsula.

Too late. That morning, November 1, China closed its banks to depositors who had lined up around the country to withdraw their savings. Late that night, Chinese naval special operations units, borne to their destinations by submarine, landed on Taiwan and began to strike submarine logistics, repair, and command and control nodes.

Taiwan, after decades of trying, without success, to enlist U.S. help in building submarines, had designed and constructed its own air-independent propulsion submarines. They had built 12 in addition to a dozen small unmanned submersibles, and they were good. The submarines had already put to sea and formed an arc through which Taipei's high command expected PLAN amphibious vessels to pass on their way to conducting an opposed landing on Taiwan. When the Taiwanese government accused China of violent aggression, Xinhua justified the special operations attacks by claiming that they were only preempting Taiwan's plans to conduct submarine warfare against China's commerce. No evidence was offered to support these accusations.

Taipei invoked the Taiwan Relations Act, passed by the U.S. Congress in 1979, which required the United States to assist Taiwan if it was attacked. The U.S. Pacific Command declined to send a large aircraft carrier so close to where China's anti-ship ballistic and cruise missiles could threaten her. But, as tensions in East Asia had heightened in recent months, two nuclear-powered *Virginia*-class attack submarines had been diverted from their patrols in the Western Pacific, and another two had been dispatched from Guam and Japan. The decision was not easy. Part of the strapped U.S. Navy's West Pacific attack sub force was needed to keep tabs on China's ballistic-missile subs. Diverting subs elsewhere pressured a force that was already tasked with more than it could fully handle.

Each of the American boats had been back-fitted with dozens of underwater drones that expanded the mother ships' surveillance as well as its ability to launch underwater attacks many scores of miles away. As China initiated limited missile attacks against military and industrial targets on Taiwan, the Pacific Command's rules of engagement to its submarine commanders were straightforward: "attack and destroy all Chinese amphibious vessels making for Taiwan."

China and Taiwan were at war. As diplomats in Beijing and Washington tried to prevent hostilities, neither state chose to go on record about the possible naval confrontation between the two. This situation lasted for a week and ended with a short, intense battle in the Taiwan Strait as U.S. and Taiwanese submarines and Taiwan-based naval aviation attacked the first echelon of a Chinese amphibious assault.

Several of Taiwan's unmanned subs were sunk in the melee. A near miss from China's new Yu-8 torpedo took one of the U.S. *Virginia*-class attack boats out of the fight and sent it limping back to Japan for repairs. The Chinese squadron lost an 18,000-ton *Yuzhao*-class amphibious transport, and the remaining ships hesitated, waiting for reinforcement. China's missile barrage intensified and assisted the amphibious forces that had gained a beachhead on Taiwan's north coast. Beijing accused Washington of interfering in a strictly internal matter and stopped its purchase of U.S. treasury bills.

When a dozen Halberd cruise missiles (the Tomahawk's successor could not be named after an Indian weapon or tribe) struck military command and control centers at China's three fleet centers, Beijing closed its embassy in Washington, fired a salvo of ballistic missiles armed with conventional warheads at fuel and ammunition dumps on Guam, and warned of "more dire consequences" if U.S. forces were not withdrawn from the Taiwan Strait at once. Algodón didn't back down. A single enemy missile reached its target, one of the Apra Harbor fuel storage facilities. U.S. Army-launched antiballistic missiles destroyed the rest of the Chinese salvo.

The White House and U.S. high command were about to learn of more dire consequences. As the adversaries in the Taiwan Strait fought, a combination of satellite imagery, a pair of attack submarines, and P-8 Poseidon maritime patrol planes continued to monitor the *Zheng He* and *Tianming* aircraft carriers along with two accompanying large-deck amphibious ships as they progressed eastward in the Pacific toward the Nicaraguan port of Corinto, ignoring the confrontation with Taiwan. They had been navigating a great circle route since taking leave of the port of Ningbo's exuberant sendoff.

On the morning of December 1, the DCIA called the White House and asked to see the president that same hour. Fifty minutes later, Farnsworth Doolittle walked into the Oval Office with a large sealed envelope marked "ULTRA." He laid it on the president's desk and pulled out a single photograph. The picture, taken from 23,000 miles in space, showed a large formation of ships whose wakes showed that they had swung to starboard.

"What," asked President Algodón, "is this?"

"The Chinese flotilla that was sailing for Nicaragua," replied Doolittle, "is now heading south. They are sailing directly for Hawaii, Pearl Harbor to be specific. The satellite imagery shows their change in course. Our attack subs and P-8s confirm that, if they continue on this course at this speed, they could reach a point where they can launch aircraft for Hawaii in two days."

Algodón clicked his computer and spoke into the receiver on his desk.

"Rose, could you call Jake Simon and put him on the speaker phone?"

"Good morning, Mr. President."

"'Morning, Jake. I have Farnsworth here with me. I assume you know the subject."

"Yes, sir."

"What's your read, Jake?"

"It's a mess. We have no carriers at Pearl. The Chinese amphibs are prepared to conduct an opposed landing. Besides taking out our base at Pearl, we have to assume that's what they're up to."

The president called his chief of staff to schedule a meeting of the National Security Council at noon.

Hawaii remains of vital strategic importance to the United States, but for different reasons than when the Imperial Japanese Fleet attacked it in 1941. Then it was the repository for the U.S. Navy's Pacific Fleet. In 2025, the same fleet had been spread out from Hawaii to Japan to a restored presence in the Philippines, major military installations at Guam, a reconstructed naval base at Cam Ranh Bay in Vietnam, a Marine unit on the north Australian coast, and a much smaller one in Singapore. Hawaii possessed ship repair facilities, docks, ammunition and fuel storage, runways, military aviation support, and other vital logistics. Its strategic value lay in its proximity to the U.S. mainland and the potential it offered China to control the entire West Pacific as it boxed in America's Asian allies from the east.

President Algodón opened the NSC meeting with a correct observation.

"Whatever happens, there can be no question of a surprise attack. Where are our carriers?"

Marine General and Chairman of the Joint Chiefs Tom Zrebiec answered. "Sir, the *Washington* is en route Subic Bay from Yokosuka. As you know, *Enterprise* entered service at the beginning of this year and is on her first deployment, in the Persian Gulf. *Reagan* is conducting pre-deployment workups off the southern California coast, and *Roosevelt* is in intermediate maintenance at Puget Sound."

"How soon can *Roosevelt* be deployed?" asked the president.

"Sir, *Roosevelt* can be pulled out of the yards and be sea-ready within three weeks. Only then can her air wing begin their pre-deployment training. The earliest she could make Pearl Harbor is two months from now."

The president did not have to be told the details. He had campaigned on strengthening the U.S. military. When he took office, the Navy had been reduced from its 2016 level of eleven carriers to eight. At the absolute minimum, three carriers were needed to keep one on permanent station. This meant that the United States could stretch and maintain one carrier each in the West Pacific and the Persian Gulf, with, under the best conditions, a single combat ready carrier in reserve.

Another three carriers could be pulled from their predeployment workups and dispatched unprepared for combat. This would take months. The remaining two were either undergoing extensive maintenance or having their reactors replaced. The soonest any of these two could leave port was eleven months. Unlike in Desert Storm, when the United States sent four carrier battle groups to the Persian Gulf in advance of the military operations that drove Saddam Hussein's forces from Kuwait, there was no possibility of massing carriers for large-scale strike operations except to wait for months or vacate carrier patrols elsewhere. Hope there might be, but it was far beyond the horizon.

Funds needed to replace the aging *Ohio*-class ballistic-missile submarine had reduced the Navy's ability to buy surface ships, including carriers, and the unseen but indispensable supply ships that replenished a carrier strike group's aviation fuel and ammunition. In every category of combatant, the Navy had continued the shrinkage that had been under way since its high-water mark of 590 ships almost forty years earlier. The entire U.S. combat fleet now stood at 233 ships.

More important, the Navy was still years away from completing the shipbuilding program that would place sea control on an equal footing with its post–Cold War emphasis on projecting naval power from ship to shore. President Algodón had succeeded in substantially increasing the defense budget and was personally overseeing a long-overdue reform of the Pentagon's business practices. But even with streamlined procurement, new ships took years to build and put to sea.

The president turned to face the chairman directly.

"What are the options?"

"Sir, the Joint Chiefs recommend three objectives. First, protect Hawaii; second, honor our defense treaties and cripple China's economy; third, sink its fleet."

"Please continue."

"Sir. The first objective is self-evident. The U.S. homeland must be protected above all else. Next, our defensive treaties and agreements with Japan and Taiwan must be honored, or the United States risks all its close security relations along with our commerce in East Asia. On a parallel point, we cannot cripple the Chinese economy in one blow. But a campaign aimed at cutting off China's export of goods and import of oil may convince Beijing that whipping up nationalism at the cost of an even worse economy is not in their interest. Third, sinking China's combat fleet endangers the supply lines their economy depends on at the same time that it threatens to make the ocean safer for projecting our own power."

Secretary of State Halley noted that the missiles China had launched at Guam already constituted an attack against U.S. territory.

"If China attacks Hawaii," she asked, "why aren't we hitting the Chinese mainland?"

Algodón looked at General Zrebiec, who spoke up. "A successful attack, to say nothing of a landing on Hawaii, leads to exactly that. But our goal should be to prevent escalation without letting China get away with what they've already done so far. A large attack on the Chinese mainland would be an enormous escalation.

The Chinese leadership's distinction between conventional and nuclear weapons is different and less defined than ours. I'm not saying that they would respond with nuclear weapons to a conventional attack on the mainland. But such a response is definitely on the table as far as they're concerned. We do, however, want them to believe that continued hostilities carry the *threat* of a conventional response against military targets on the mainland."

"Returning to your point about targeting their commerce and combat fleet," said the president. "When we put Japan in an economic corner, they didn't respond very well." He was referring to the Imperial Navy's attacks on Pearl Harbor, the Philippines, and Southeast Asian targets eighty-four years earlier.

"Yes, sir. But President Roosevelt's economic sanctions against Japan were imposed two years before Pearl Harbor. The military objectives that we recommend in response to a very serious Chinese provocation can be ended immediately and the economic threats they carry lifted overnight."

Reversing the practice of his recent predecessor, the president had invited all the members of the Joint Chiefs—not just the Chairman—to attend National Security Council meetings. "Maybe the chief of staff of the Army knows more about tanks than the chief of naval operations," he said when a *Wall Street Journal* reporter asked him about the change.

Now he turned to Chief of Naval Operations Admiral Moreland and asked for an assessment of Hawaii's defense.

"Sir, the two subs we dispatched from Pearl to shadow the Chinese group are the first line of defense. But the

Chinese have attack subs as part of the flotilla's defenses and they're doing surprisingly well in keeping out boats on the defensive. If this turns kinetic, the Chinese boats will not sit around and let our guys sink the carriers and amphibs."

Here, the chairman broke in. "With your permission, sir, we'd like to deploy all four of the 12th Air Force's active duty wings from Davis-Monthan (in Arizona) to Hickam Field at Pearl today. The 15th air wing based at Hickam has an F-22 wing and enough logistics to support the added planes."

"Do it."

"They're not equipped," added the chairman, "or trained to attack ships, but our planes can go after the Chinese planes minutes after the latter leave their carriers."

Admiral Moreland urged engaging the Chinese flotilla immediately. "They've changed course for Hawaii and stopped all radio transmissions. Is there any doubt about their intent? Do we want to wait until they've actually launched planes before taking them down?"

"So," asked the president, "we have no carriers in the neighborhood; this means that our only defense for Hawaii is those two subs and the hope that the Air Force can stop the Chinese planes before they start hitting targets at Pearl?"

The CNO broke in before the chairman had a chance to answer. "PACOM (the U.S. Pacific Command) has one cruiser, two destroyers, and a frigate at Pearl. They're ready to go and they're well suited for sub-hunting and have anti-surface missiles as well as counter–air defense. They can coordinate with our subs in stopping the Chinese group."

"How long until they can strike the Chinese task group?" Algodón asked.

"Forty-eight hours from warning order, sir."

"Go ahead," said the president, "but I want to see if it's possible to get the Chinese to back off. Escalating this is in no one's interest. I want those ships in position and ready. But the order should be written to wait for final authority to engage."

"Sir."

"Ok, last item on the agenda for now: what needs to be done to close off China's sea-lanes and sink its navy?" asked Algodón.

General Zrebiec leaned back in his chair and drew an audible breath.

"Sir, as I mentioned earlier, *Washington* is en route Subic from Yokosuka. The carrier's course puts her in range of China's anti-ship ballistic missiles. But her planes would be very useful in chewing up the PLAN and keeping it from assaulting Taiwan. She is steaming with a full complement of surface ships and a sub. We have developed and refined carrier strike group operations for seventy-five years. The *Washington* strike group is the most powerful naval instrument in the world."

President Algodón looked at the CNO. Admiral Moreland squinted.

"It's a risk," he said. "But we don't have other good options. And it's likely that the carrier critics in Congress will object. But," he added, "Carrier critics have come and gone since World War II. The conventional wisdom before Desert Shield was that it was too risky to put a carrier strike group in the Persian Gulf. We've had carriers in the Gulf for the past thirty years."

The chairman continued. "We recommend that

Washington be diverted to the South China Sea to conduct anti-surface and anti-submarine operations against the PLAN. If China attacks our fighter-bombers at bases in Japan and elsewhere throughout the first island chain we may have few other options than carrier planes to hit the PLAN. If China's navy stays in port, all the better."

"What else has to be done?"

Again, the chairman: "We want to flush all surface ships and subs from Yokosuka, Guam, Subic, and Cam Ranh Bay. The PLAN has put most of its ships into the waters behind the first island chain. Our combatants will have the same orders as the *Washington* strike group: find and destroy China's naval combatants. The objective is to avoid the escalation of attacking the mainland and to cut off China's ability to import or export anything by sea."

"Anything else?"

"Yes, sir. We need to close off the sea-lanes between China and the Middle East. Dry up their energy supplies at the same time we cut off their commerce. The Joint Chiefs recommend moving *Enterprise* out of the Persian Gulf and into position equidistant from the straits that connect East Asia with the Middle East. *Enterprise* with her escorts will enforce a blockade of ships to and from Chinese ports. We'll seize them and take them into Singapore, pending cessation of hostilities. The *Enterprise* strike force outguns China's Indian Ocean carrier group, so a confrontation is not likely, but there's no point in taking chances, and the entire campaign depends on cutting China's imports and exports without having to attack the mainland."

"What happens to the Persian Gulf?" the president wanted to know.

Both Iran and the Gulf States had built or bought a mid-sized arsenal of nuclear weapons, and the Iranians had been building their navy since sanctions were lifted in 2015.

"Sir, *Enterprise* will sail without all her escorts. They will remain in the Gulf and be augmented by ships from the Med. We recommend pulling a couple of destroyers and three frigates out of their scheduled rotation and sending them from the East Coast to beef up what's left of the *Enterprise* strike group."

"Spreading ourselves a bit thin," noted Algodón.

"Yes, sir. Our options are limited."

"Ok," said the president. "But, same here as with the Hawaii situation. Give me a couple of days to see if there's any way of getting the Chinese to stand down. I'll also talk with our Australian and Asian allies, and I want to speak to the Indian prime minister after this meeting adjourns. If China wins this one, they'll all be toast sooner or later. I want them in."

That day the New York Stock Exchange added another 2 percent loss to the 5 percent it had fallen over the previous three trading sessions. It had been a bloody run, but much less sanguinary than the Chinese equity markets, which had lost nearly a third of their value since the beginning of the economic crisis that had helped precipitate the present security crisis.

President Algodón went on national television to reassure Americans that the U.S. economy was fundamentally sound—although he admitted that entitlement programs and servicing a debt of $28 trillion left no choice but to raise taxes for rebuilding America's defenses. He repeated his confidence that the United States would prevail in the armed conflict with China and warned that sacrifices would be required of civilians as well as the military.

Secretary of Defense Taylor stayed at his office that night using third-party go-betweens in Asia to communicate with the Chinese leadership. They were adamant. The United States must stop aiding the Taiwanese and withdraw its naval presence entirely from the South China Sea, whose waters Beijing claimed as sovereign. China rejected the secretary's offer to suspend hostilities and return all military forces to their positions before the conflict while talks began. It rejected the suggestion to begin talks without condition. The Chinese leaders repeated that no progress toward peace could be made until and unless the United States ended its combat operations in support of Taiwan. The secretary warned China's leaders that, if the PLAN flotilla continued to sail toward Hawaii, there would be consequences.

"There will," he said, "be no second Pearl Harbor."

The answer back from Beijing was that it would reverse its flotilla's direction if the United States would suspend combat operations in the Taiwan Strait.

Observing that Taiwan was a sovereign state with which the United States had an alliance obligation, whereas Hawaii was an American state, Algodón declined.

USAF fighters completed the three-hour flight from the mainland and augmented those already based at Hickam Field. When the Chinese carrier *Zheng He* passed a line 200 miles south of its aircraft launch point for the Hawaiian Islands, the USS *New Mexico* and USS *California Virginia*-class attack subs went into action. Both had been back-fitted on their after-decks with large pods that each carried a pair of unmanned underwater vehicles (UUVs).

The two subs had shadowed the Chinese flotilla at a distance of 75 miles, where the little noise they emitted was undetectable in the cavitation and other thrumming sounds from engine systems that the advancing Chinese ships put into the water. New technology that monitored disturbances to tiny marine life made by the Chinese ships' propellers also helped the U.S. subs keep a safe distance astern. The PLAN flotilla commander did not know that he was being followed.

New Mexico and *California*'s pods filled with seawater. The three-ton doors opened, and the self-guided UUVs glided into the Pacific's blueness. One of them hunted the *Zheng He*, the other, the *Tianming*. When the UUVs fired a pair of Mark 48 Mod 10 torpedoes at each carrier, their mother ships were already developing target solutions for the escorting PLAN subs.

Two hours later, the two Mark 48s slammed into the *Zheng He* 25 feet below her waterline and halfway between amidships and her screws. The force of the blow vibrated the carrier like a mammoth sledgehammer striking an oversize bourdon. The first explosion melted the propulsion system's turbines and broke the big ship's keel. The second tore into the aft magazine, whose instant vaporization knocked men off their feet six decks above and 500 feet away. The big ship vanished within seven minutes.

The *Tianming* fared better. One torpedo narrowly missed. The other barreled into the rudder post, opening a large hole in the ship's stern, completely destroying her steering ability, and rendering her propellers useless. Damage controllers extinguished the fires, but the ship listed to port. She would not be launching aircraft anytime soon.

President Algodón had been correct in his prediction that there would be no second Pearl Harbor. This also meant that the United States would not have to fight in the middle of the Pacific and in the West Pacific simultaneously. The PLAN's large amphibious ships could not land troops on Hawaii without close air support, and the helicopters on their large flat decks could not defend against even a small number of U.S. surface ships, whose anti-aircraft missiles had no targets, but whose recently arrived anti-surface missiles represented a mortal threat to the big PLAN amphibious ships. The Chinese high command aborted the mission, and the Central Military Commission deliberated over whether to launch a ballistic-missile attack against Hawaii.

They ordered *Tianming* to be towed back toward the mainland and considered how to employ the flotilla's amphibious ships for the planned Taiwan invasion. All the surviving Chinese ships except a destroyer, left behind to tow *Tianming*, sped westward. To little avail. The U.S. subs that had shadowed the Chinese flotilla, together with U.S. naval combatants from Pearl, closed the distance and commenced a naval battle similar in size to the 1942 Battle of Sunda Strait, where two large and one smaller allied surface ships faced a larger Japanese force made up of a light carrier and seaplane carrier plus twelve destroyers and five cruisers. The Battle of Sunda Strait was a disaster for the allies. The Battle of Johnson Atoll, for this was where the American squadron caught up with the fleeing Chinese, was a U.S. victory.

The battle for Taiwan did not go as well. It spread when the Chinese landed on the little Senkaku Islands, whose Japanese sovereignty the United States recognized and had pledged to defend if attacked.

Japanese marines, land-based aviation, and surface ships as well as submarines were in position when China attacked. If the Chinese political leadership had doubts about their military progress, they were entirely satisfied that the renewed—that is, since World War II—struggle against Japan had distracted the population's attention from a still cratering economy. Riots in China's large cities had been replaced by huge demonstrations against Japan. Beijing turned out truckloads of posters with photos from Japan's brutal 1937 attack on Nanjing with the slogan "never again." Young men and women lined up to enlist in the military.

Washington and its escorts took up a position just east of the little islands to Okinawa's southwest. Shielded by recently implanted missile batteries, the carrier strike group sailed just beyond the reach of land-based long-range anti-ship cruise missiles, but well within range of China's ballistic missiles, which could strike ships as far as 1,200 miles away.

Washington's planes, together with U.S. and Japanese maritime patrol aircraft based at Iwakuni Marine Corps Air Station, hunted Chinese subs in the waters around Taiwan. The mission was quite dangerous. China's numerical superiority in missiles and aircraft had rattled American allies in East Asia. Now China exploited it. Asians who feared Chinese hegemony were not surprised. Quietly at first, and then directly, they had asked successive American administrations how they planned to counter the greater number and, more important, greater range of China's anti-ship missiles.

American secretaries of defense and state had answered with charts and budgets that described future directed energy weapons (lasers), future deployment of rail guns aboard Navy ships, and plans for both longer- and shorter-range, less expensive anti-ship missiles. The plans were good, but they had not comforted Asians who wanted to know what would happen if a conflict preceded the anticipated improvements. Now they would find out.

Legislative compromises had blocked the most draconian effects of the deep defense cuts, known as sequestration, made in 2014 and the following year. The cuts were suspended until 2022 and 2023. But there had been no appetite for making procrastination a policy. Americans were divided between unease at seeing the nation's international power ebb and their distaste for another war—anywhere. Democrats united to oppose international engagement. Republicans divided over their party's post–World War II support for robust defense budgets. The U.S. military shrank in some places and increased anemically in others.

Little had been done to keep pace with either China's expanding missile arsenal or its fighter-bombers that could carry whole quivers of missiles. U.S. naval and land-based missiles rose up to hit anything that threatened at a distance. When *Washington*, together with its escort of large surface combatants and land-based missiles, had splashed clouds of long-range and some very fast-moving cruise missiles, China's naval aviation and air forces had plenty left. The problem of reloading American naval combatants with missiles at sea had been the subject of much discussion and no action—for decades.

U.S. Pacific Command commanders had warned for years that the failure to arm small U.S. surface combatants, like frigates and converted littoral combat ships, with effective defenses against air threats would divert large combatants that *could* protect other ships, like logistic ships, from air attack. The Pacific Command's warnings were ignored as resources became scarcer and key decisions about strategy remained unresolved. The consequences were within view now. But they were obscured, at least for the moment, by the success of manned and unmanned planes from the *Washington* in destroying a half-dozen enemy subs and interrupting the flow of additional troops and supplies from the mainland to Chinese troops that had landed on Taiwan.

President Algodón opened the National Security Council meeting the evening of December 8.

"General Zrebiec," the president called on the Joint Chiefs chairman.

"Sir, the good news is that the *Enterprise* will reach her position off the northwest Sumatran coast within seven days. I spoke with Admiral Krishnapur a few moments ago (President Algodón and the Indian prime minister's talks had gone well). The Indian government is worried about the skirmishing that began two days ago at Aksai Chin. The admiral said that INS *Vikrant* (a 40,000-ton aircraft carrier) and her escorts would join *Enterprise* east of Sri Lanka and assist in interdicting Chinese merchant traffic as well as engaging PLAN combatants. With the Australians covering the Lombok Straits and the Indians and us patrolling the Malacca and Sunda Straits, Chinese ships will not be able to transit between home waters and the Middle East."

"And the bad news?" asked Algodón.

The chairman turned to the Defense Intelligence Agency director.

"Sir, despite our successes against enemy subs around Taiwan, the Chinese maintain a large and potentially

decisive advantage in anti-ship cruise and ballistic missiles as well as fighter-bombers that carry several such
weapons. For the moment, our anti-missile and anti-
aircraft defenses can protect U.S. combatants in the area,
but when we run out, China will still have lots more to
throw at us."

"What," asked the president, "about the laser weapons
and rail guns that Navy Secretary Gideon and Admiral
Moreland briefed me on?"

Secretary Gideon uttered a low wheeze. "This isn't
the time for a history lesson. But none of your predecessors made basic decisions about what we would do if we
found ourselves in exactly this situation."

"What is that supposed to mean?"

Here, Admiral Moreland broke in. "It means that the
Navy failed to make strategic choices about operating
effectively in the South and East China Seas. It means
that we split our defenses against China's missile and aircraft superiority between upgrading traditional missiles
and newer technology. As a result, we are better equipped
today than in the past to shoot down both enemy missiles and the aircraft that follow them with even more
missiles. And it means that we are better equipped to use
lasers and rail guns as defenses against the same. But,"
he hesitated.

"But what?" said Algodón.

"We are ill-equipped to carry the fight to the enemy
fleet *and* to defend our own ships. Lasers and rail guns
require a huge amount of electricity. So do the radars that
integrate information about both incoming missiles and
aircraft. Generating electricity uses up space. More space
means bigger, more expensive ships. We asked for the
money to build them. Congress and the last two admin-

istrations said no. When we run out of missile defenses, only five destroyers and a single cruiser are equipped to defend themselves with lasers and rail guns. Our defenses are spotty."

The admiral was not asked, nor did he volunteer, that even if the twenty-three U.S. Navy surface ships and submarines in the fight were able to defend themselves, they were unprepared to operate as an integrated force to destroy the PLAN. Naval strategic planners had also failed to make the shift from the sea services' post–Cold War power projection mission to fighting and sinking another naval force. Tactics, weapons, and training were in the midst of a transition from projecting power to the mission they needed to conduct here, destroying another naval force at sea.

"The *Washington* must be protected," said Algodón, raising his voice.

The chairman replied. "I have ordered our rail-gun and laser-equipped surface ships to take up position in defense of the *Washington*. She will continue her anti-ship and anti-submarine warfare missions as safely as possible. Still, it is a risk."

"And when the ships that defend themselves with legacy weapons run out, then what?"

"Sir, they cannot be reloaded at sea. They will steam back to Japan for more missiles."

"Are you recommending that we leave one aircraft carrier and its escorts to defend Taiwan, sink the PLAN, and maintain a blockade of Chinese merchant ships?" asked the president.

General Zrebiec replied that the carrier's missions could be reduced while the guided-missile destroyers hurried back for more weapons. He picked up the laser pointer that was lying on the big table and pointed it at the middle screen in the Situation Room. The screen displayed a map of China's coast. He pointed to several positions in the Ningbo vicinity.

"These are the PLAN's intelligence, surveillance, and reconnaissance (ISR) nodules for their current operations in the South China Sea. Halberds (the land attack cruise missiles that replaced the old Tomahawks) launched from our attack subs can take them out. The PLAN will have to scramble to continue attacks on our ships.

"Sir," he added, "I have to tell you that the chiefs are divided about this. General Kash (the U.S. Air Force Chief of Staff) and General Carrey (the Army Chief of Staff) believe that, between satellites and airborne surveillance aircraft, the PLAN can cobble together a system that operates effectively in place of their land-based ISR nodules. All of us agree that it is difficult to predict how China will react to an attack on its mainland."

Secretary of State Halley frowned. "I don't like where this is going. The Chinese have been relatively restrained in their cyber attacks against us so far. A few financial institutions, military logistics centers, and civilian air transportation hubs. Our defenses have been spotty. What happens if they launch a massive attack? Our grid for moving food from growers in the West to Eastern and Midwestern consumers depends on computers. Could they close down the stock market? What do we do then? They rely on computers less than we do."

The secretary paused to drink some water. "Even if we retaliate," she continued, "a full-bore cyber war will hurt us more than it hurts them. And if they combine cyber attacks with kinetic ones after we strike their homeland, are we prepared? What prevents further escalation? We avoided an attack on Hawaii and our original plan was to prevent escalation by targeting their navy and merchant shipping. Aren't we changing that if we attack the mainland? And if we are, it's not in response to their escalation but because of our limitations."

President Algodón was faced with exceptionally difficult choices. He could conduct a naval campaign against a regional foe with superior offensive capability. He could escalate with unknowable and potentially dire consequences. Or, he could retreat. The first option risked large-scale losses at sea, including the possibility that a U.S. aircraft carrier might be sunk for the first time since World War II. Either retreat or defeat would ensure the end of the alliance structure that the United States had maintained in Asia since the end of World War II, along with certain damage to every other American alliance as well as the final chapter of the United States's position as the world's preeminent power. Escalation could also expose the United States to cyber attack, leaving the nation's financial services, electricity grids, transportation, and food supply crippled. It could bring in Russia and Iran on China's side, all of which were armed with nuclear weapons and ballistic missiles that could target any point in the United States.

There are strategic fulcrums in the world where the ability of the United States to deliver overwhelming seapower is indispensable to America's longtime goal of preventing hegemony on major land masses, preserving allies, ensuring our continued close economic and security interests, and demonstrating to friends and partners around the world that we remain reliable. East Asia is first among these fulcrums. Half the world lives in Asia, under the threat of Chinese domination. Our economic future and security is inseparable from an Asia made up of peaceful, prosperous, and self-governing states that regard the current international order as a benefit.

Seapower is key to our interests because it protects—or could threaten—commerce between Asia and the rest of the world, including especially us. Effective seapower requires a disciplined strategy, the means to implement such strategy, and the will to pay for its implementation. Today, the United States lacks all three. Far from having a strategy that addresses China's effort to deny us access to the Western Pacific and its global ambitions, U.S. policy makers remain hesitant to acknowledge what China's rulers have maintained for decades, that a strategic competition exists between us and them.

Moreover, American seapower has yet to make the transformation from projecting power to controlling the seas. China's strategy of denying us access to the region's oceanic spaces demands that the United States be able to control the seas to avoid escalation, defend our allies, and bring a conflict to an end as swiftly as possible by choking the adversary's economy. We are still thinking about projecting power when we need to be thinking about integrating our fleets so that they can fight and win battles at sea. Finally, as will be demonstrated, we are not designing the right kind of ships or enough ships to prevail at sea.

A U.S. president who is confronted by a grave crisis with China today would feel pressures that are similar to those of this scenario. Unless strategy, tactics, ships, and weapons stay ahead of the threat that China poses, the challenges described here will be those that face a U.S. president about a decade from now. The root of the crisis that the above scenario describes is the political failure to guarantee the superiority of American seapower. The roots of the failure grew in the nation's preoccupation with Middle Eastern land wars and fighting terror.

CHAPTER VIII

BUDGET APOCALYPSE

How Defense Cuts and the "Sequester" Came to Be

The final year of the George W. Bush presidency saw U.S. defense spending reach a historically unprecedented level, as the result of prolonged combat operations in Iraq and the seven-year military presence in Afghanistan.[1] Both the "base" defense budget—spending on personnel, equipment, and facilities—and "contingency" budget—spending on wartime operations—reached their highest levels since World War II, measured in 2016 dollars.

However, with Iraq withdrawal plans endorsed not only by President Bush but also by both the Republican and Democratic candidates in the 2008 election—John McCain and Barack Obama—the Department of Defense anticipated an end to the budgetary growth that had characterized the post-9/11 era. This became a certainty in September 2008, when the Wall Street financial crisis jolted the economy, foreshadowing reduced federal revenues in the coming years.[2]

When President Obama took office in January 2009, he

expected to reduce defense spending. Obama's first secretary of Defense, Robert Gates, launched an ambitious
effort to reform defense spending. At the same time, he
understood the need to prepare for an increase in security
challenges around the world. Gates wanted to cut what
he regarded as fat in defense spending and reinvest savings in defense programs that would enable the United
States to meet current and future security challenges.[3]
Gates expected that defense spending would stay relatively constant throughout the next several years. He proposed budget-neutral, strategy-driven reforms, and drew
up plans for the United States to maintain a high pace of
combat operations while shifting resources from the war
in Iraq to the one in Afghanistan.[4]

By the fall of 2010, the consequences for the defense
budget began to appear. The Obama administration's
intent to reduce America's military footprint abroad,
combined with a continued rise in deficit spending, led
to continued defense spending cuts beyond what Gates
had already achieved. Although Secretary Gates had cut
defense spending by $400 billion, the president wanted
more. He proposed an additional $400 billion decrease in
defense budgets, to be distributed over the next ten years.[5]

Under its first two budgets, the Obama administration
cut $478 billion from Defense. This was accomplished
by decreasing or canceling a host of future defense programs. It cut short the production of F-22 fifth-generation
fighters, eliminated the U.S. Army's next-generation tactical vehicle, and delayed indefinitely plans to build the
Navy's next-generation cruiser, which would replace aging
cruisers first commissioned thirty-four years ago. Gates's

cost-cutting also added an additional year's delay to the production of the Navy's new *Ford*-class aircraft carrier, among other programs.[6]

No explicit strategic justification was offered for curtailing or halting these programs. Implicit in the reductions was the assumption that the need for deterrence as well as the warfighting capability and capacity that these weapons would offer in a major conflict had diminished. Implicit also was the notion that the affected combat systems would become still less relevant as time passed. Terrorists, the administration believed—not deterring or fighting wars with peer or near-peer competitors—was the single most important future threat.

The expanding arms production and growing technological sophistication of weapons in such potential adversaries as China and Russia since Obama took office are discussed elsewhere in this book, particularly in chapters III and VI. The progress of these potential enemies in designing, manufacturing, and testing weapons for use in major conflicts suggests that the assumptions behind the Obama budget cuts were unwarranted. China, Russia, Iran, and North Korea's conventional and strategic weapons programs illustrate their rulers' belief that major conflicts are possible in the future. The actions of these potential adversaries underscore the national security risks that the United States accepts if it hesitates to deter major war against states that are hostile to the United States as well as others that regard us as strategic competitors.

Secretary Gates believed additional cuts to be imprudent and unfair. Other cabinet-level departments of the government had not been asked to accept equally deep budget cuts, and Defense had only recently undertaken its own spending cuts. At the same time, the Department of Defense was experiencing a disproportionately high increase in costs, for example, in personnel. Secretary Gates warned that the additional hundreds of billions in cuts would necessitate "reducing force structure and military capability."[7] After Gates left office, he expressed his views straightforwardly about the administration's defense budget cuts. He said that his discussions with President Obama revealed:

> A fundamental difference between us. I wanted to restructure defense spending to make it more efficient and disciplined, reducing bureaucratic overhead and waste and cancelling weak programs in order to preserve and enhance military capability. . . . The president felt that defense could and should be cut on its merits, but also to give him political space with his own party and constituents to cut domestic spending and entitlements. (At least that's what he told me).[8]

POLITICS AND THE DEFENSE BUDGET

While U.S. foreign policy in the early years of the Obama administration was marked by efforts to disengage from the Middle East, U.S. domestic politics were changing. In response to the Obama administration's progressive agenda, as well as federal financial support for several large U.S. corporations that sought relief from their respective financial crises, support for limited government and fiscal responsibility emerged as large objects on the political horizon. The "Tea Party" movement, as it came to be called, was a driving force behind a major Republican victory in the 2010 mid-term congressional elections. Republicans won sixty-three formerly Democratic seats in the House of Representatives and reclaimed majority control of that body.[9] Additionally, six Republicans won seats in the Senate, leaving the Democrats with a narrow majority in the upper house of Congress.[10]

With the decisive Tea Party victory, many freshman GOP representatives who came to Washington in early 2011 interpreted their election as a mandate for fiscal discipline.[11] While Congress has the responsibility to determine federal spending through the annual budget appropriations process, the Republican House sought a more ambitious means for reform, one that would impose fiscal discipline for longer than a single budget cycle. Tension emerged between the Democratic and Republican negotiating parties, especially over the extent and methods by which the deficit should be reduced. Republicans sought more extensive deficit reductions, achieved entirely through decreased spending. Democrats advocated a more modest deficit reduction, achieved through the combination of tax increases and lower levels of spending cuts.[12] The issue became unavoidable when the government's need for additional money to avoid default clashed with a congressionally established limit on the federal government's ability to borrow money.

After partisan feuding, a deal was reached. Republicans agreed to raise the debt ceiling by $2.1 trillion. In exchange, Democrats agreed to a deficit reduction of at least the same amount. The deal resulted in the Budget Control

Act (BCA) of 2011. The Act established a mechanism by which spending would be reduced. Over the course of ten years, from 2012 to 2021, cuts in discretionary spending would amount to $900 billion in savings.

The Act also established the Joint Select Committee on Deficit Reduction (also known as the "supercommittee"), a bipartisan committee of twelve members of Congress. Its task was to identify the additional $1.2 trillion in savings that were needed to reach the $2.1 trillion sum by which the national debt ceiling would be raised. The committee's deadline for agreement on the spending cuts was November 2011.

According to the BCA's provisions, the supercommittee's failure to agree on the source of additional savings would impose mandatory limits on discretionary spending. These limits would provide the required cuts in a process referred to as "sequestration."[13] The threat of sequestering funds across the board was conceived with the expectation that compromise would be reached to avoid cuts that must affect virtually every member of Congress. Sequestration was to apply equally to defense spending and domestic programs. The stakes were high for the advocates of each.[14] Everyone expected that with so great a threat compromise must be reached. Everyone was wrong.

The supercommittee offered no comprehensive legislative package to meet the $1.2 trillion deficit reduction needed to avoid budget cuts. This failure forced mandatory across-the-board cuts, beginning in Fiscal Year 2013.[15] The result was felt throughout the federal government, in particular by the Department of Defense. It became an increasingly vulnerable target, because newly elected

Republican members—whose party had once been the strongest supporter of a vigorous national defense—now included so-called budget hawks and Tea Party members whose concern about the nation's debt surpassed their support for defense spending.

The budget year of 2013 was the most painful for the Department of Defense in the years that followed 9/11. The FY 2013 budget resulted in drastic, indiscriminate, across-the-board cuts to military spending. This limited the entire department's ability to manage how the budget would be reduced. Heretofore, Defense had used the annual budget planning process, a rolling five-year budget forecast, as an opportunity to set priorities in lean as well as fat budget years. The legislature's action eliminated this process as sequestration was applied.

Defense sought to cut costs by trimming the nation's ability to execute long-term stability operations, such as those that were being conducted in Iraq and Afghanistan. As the certain effects of draconian cuts became clear, Congress relented. It softened the effects of the 2011 BCA budget cuts through the American Taxpayer Relief Act in 2013 and again in 2015. According to the Budget Control Act, sequestration would kick in if the Defense budget exceeded caps that the legislation had set.

Congress avoided this by raising the BCA caps and reducing defense cuts from the initially planned $63 billion to $37 billion.[16] While $37 billion seems like a small amount compared to a total budget of nearly $600 billion, the amount subtracted is all at the margin. If a family's annual budget is cut by 6 percent, the loss must be absorbed in utility payments, repairs, clothing, entertainment, food, and so on. At the Department of Defense, the money would have to come from weapons that were being constructed, research needed for modernization, operations and maintenance, or other integral parts of defense. Despite legislation that reduced the sequester's bite, the Department of Defense had to make difficult decisions, which came with significant costs to the military services' capability, morale, readiness, and industrial base, and thus to the ability of the United States to project and exercise hard power.

The election of Donald Trump as president in November 2016 appeared at the time as a sea change. But the picture remains unclear. The first Trump defense budget asked for an increase for fiscal year 2018 that was a hair's breadth from what his Democratic opponent would have requested if she had adopted the recommendations of the Obama five-year defense budget plan. The proposed 10 percent increase will start to address the state of disrepair that all the military services have experienced in recent years. It will not increase the size of America's combat fleet. Future Trump budgets may accomplish this, but there is no way to know that now.

Trump had promised significant changes to the defense budgets that the Obama administration requested. Mr. Trump pledged to increase the Navy from the current fleet size of 276 ships to at least 350, a significantly larger number than the previous administration's plan, which charted a course to reach a fleet size of 306 vessels by 2046. As Mr. Trump puts it, the new administration's plan will be "the largest effort at rebuilding our military since Ronald Reagan." It would give the Navy a fleet whose size has not been seen since the Cold War.[17] During the campaign,

Trump vowed that the military, including the Navy, would also seek to expand infrastructure, including shipbuilding in such places as the Philadelphia Navy Yard, New Hampshire, Maine, and Virginia.

Shipyards that had been shut down in recent years would be reopened, and the supporting infrastructure to shipbuilding and the shipyards would also be expanded. The president-elect did not offer specifics on what kinds of ships will be added to create the 350-ship Navy. Those who knew weren't saying. Those who didn't know were. The latter suggested the addition of two carriers, more *Virginia*-class attack submarines, littoral combat ships and their follow-on fast frigates, and large surface combatants.[18] As plans took shape, the incoming administration was said to favor modernization of all USS *Ticonderoga*-class cruisers, which the Obama administration had "sidelined," in order to extend their service lives.[19] The number of sailors in the Navy, too, would see a growth by nearly 50,000, from the current level of 330,000 to 380,000.[20]

In the waning months of 2016, the Navy made public a plan that went slightly beyond Trump's 350-ship Navy. It laid out a plan for a 355-ship fleet, through sharp increases in the number of large surface combatants, such as destroyers and attack submarines.[21] The estimate was the result of a year-long study that looked at how many ships the Navy would need to adequately address future global threats, including the rise of near-peer adversaries such as China and Russia.[22] But this mattered not, since the new administration would propose its own budget plan to Congress for the fiscal year that begins in September 2017.

The costs for Donald Trump's defense additions and

expansions have been estimated at nearly double the existing budget plans, with some estimates indicating almost a $1 trillion budget.[23] The expansive growth of the Navy that the Trump team advocated would reverse the Obama-era defense budget cuts. It would also end the legislative agreement to cap the defense budget and impose across-the-board reductions in defense spending—known as the sequester—if the mandated agreements were broken. In September 2016, two months before the election, candidate Trump called for an end to the sequester, urging Congress to "reinvest in our military."[24] Eliminating the elaborate structure that allowed federal borrowing to increase while imposing limits on defense spending will put the Trump administration at odds not only with Democrats who oppose defense spending but also with Republican budget hawks who oppose increases in the defense budget and government spending writ large. The Trump administration has promised the resources to put American seapower—and the U.S. military in general—back on its feet. Success is imperative for the nation's security and that of its allies and friends.

SEAPOWER SUFFERS FROM CUTS, SEQUESTER

President Trump's election was years away when the original sequester went into effect. This agreement between Congress and the president had large consequences. Reduced funding for the Navy and the Marine Corps forced leaders to choose between maintaining current capabilities and future ones. The Department of the Navy's budget is the largest of the three branches of the U.S. military, representing in recent years a consistent 30 percent of the total Department of Defense budget. The Navy not only maintains the United States's most pervasive and visible presence abroad but also, through the U.S. Marine Corps and special operations, serves as an immediate responder to crises as well as a deterrent to prevent crises from escalating into major conflicts.

The Department of Defense did its best to plan for the budget cuts that the Obama administration directed. However, the cuts from the sequester could not be anticipated; nor did the legislation allow the department discretion in executing the cuts. The result was a 6.8 percent reduction—$10.7 billion—from the sea services' budget in 2013.[25] It was clear that the cuts were on their way, but the extent of their effect was unknown.

Since FY 2012, the Navy's budget has shrunk, a result of the sequester and subsequent years of cuts.[26] Funding for Overseas Contingency Operations, the additional amount added to the defense budget to pay for operations abroad, has declined.[27] The budget for the Navy and Marine Corps is divided into several segments, including, but not limited to, Procurement, Operations and Maintenance, and RDT&E (Research, Development, Test, and Evaluation).

Defense budget cuts—both those planned prior to the sequester and those enacted by the sequester—have led to downward trends in all these categories. Weapon purchases; shipbuilding and conversion (the costs of both constructing naval vessels and refurbishing older vessels to meet demands); and aircraft acquisition (including the purchase of the new F-35 fifth-generation fighters) have dropped since 2012. The decline is a result both of the president's budget proposals to reduce costs of programs, as seen in Obama's FY 2011[28] and FY 2012[29] budget plans, and of simultaneous across-the-board caps from the 2013 sequester.[30]

Since the implementation of the Budget Control Act of 2011, both Navy and top Department of Defense officials have admitted that these cuts forced the Navy and Marine Corps to reduce readiness as well as the Department of the Navy's strategic reach. The Department of Defense Comptroller's FY 2016 report emphasized that the Navy's global presence was down 10 percent, with fewer U.S. ships patrolling the seas.[31] From reduced maintenance on aircraft and ships, extended deployments and gaps in the deployment of aircraft carriers, and shortfalls in acquisitions, cuts to the Department of the Navy have attenuated the ability of the United States to deploy forces rapidly to conflicts and crises around the globe.

For example, the United States was able to respond as the civil war in Libya began in 2011. But the military did not have the equipment in place to move 167 U.S. citizens to safety and protect them as they were departing. The U.S. forces that are trained for such missions—the Marines—were no longer assigned to the Mediterranean. The Pentagon had to rent a Malta-based ferry, while China had a modern frigate, the *Xuzhou*, that was diverted from anti-piracy operations in the Gulf of Aden to aid in the evacuation of Chinese nationals.

When events turned more violent in Benghazi the following year, U.S. seapower was still missing from the Mediterranean and was not able to provide the immediate response that could have avoided the deaths of four

Americans, including the U.S. ambassador to Libya. Responding to crises is important for the United States: our commercial, diplomatic, and security interests are spread around the world, where unanswered challenges encourage more serious provocations.

In contrast, when China launched a large volume of missile "tests" in the Taiwan Strait in 1995/1996, President Bill Clinton could order two aircraft carrier battle groups into the area. The administration's action reassured Taiwan, which was on the eve of a presidential election. Failure to provide American military support would have invited China to intimidate Taiwan and interfere with its democratic process, while at the same time it would have broadcast America's unreliability to friends as well as adversaries around the world. China may or may not have been testing its missiles. It was certainly testing the commitment of the United States to our friends and allies.

CONTRACTION

The lack of resources does not end with the sequester or the legislatively mandated possibility of its future resumption. For example, Congress, for the three fiscal years from 2014 through 2016, decreased funding for the Navy by a total of $22.7 billion. This not insignificant sum equals about 1.5 times the money that the Navy spends annually on shipbuilding.

Cuts to the budget left the Navy short of resources to pay for ships needed to replace aging vessels and modernize the fleet. The Department of the Navy still projects the optimistic targets of operating a 300-ship fleet by 2019 and reaching an optimal goal of 308 ships by 2021, according to then-Secretary of the Navy Raymond Mabus's 2016 testimony before the Senate Armed Services Committee.[32] In fact, fleet size is headed in the opposite direction, down. According to then-Chief of Naval Operations Admiral Jonathan Greenert, in his 2015 Senate Armed Services Committee testimony, the size of the Navy shrank by 23 ships and 63,000 personnel between 2002 and 2012.[33]

Since the time of that testimony—when there were 289 ships[34]—the Navy has decreased significantly, including 14 ships between FY 2015 and FY 2016, with the current level at about 275 ships. The decline in the number of ships in the Navy between 2015 and 2016 also coincided with 9 fewer ships on deployment across different combatant commands, the largest cut of which came with a significant drawdown in ships assigned to the 5th Fleet, in the Persian Gulf under Central Command.

For the Marine Corps, the Navy is currently operating a deficit of amphibious ships as well. While the sum of American global combatant commanders' requirement for amphibious ships is 50, the Navy believes that 38 amphibious ships constitute the minimum needed to meet national needs. Notwithstanding, the current amphibious fleet amounts to just 30 ships. Commenting on this shortfall, Chief of Naval Operations Admiral John Richardson told Congress that, in the current fiscal climate, the Navy's goal is to be able to operate 34 amphibious ships; he admitted explicitly that there is a "gap between the requirement and what [Navy] can resource."[35]

FAILING TO MAKE ENDS MEET

The number of ships is not the only significant way to measure the effect of budget cuts. The Navy also delayed or canceled ship deployments. Retaining commitments while postponing or restricting scheduled ship deployments increases the time away from home for ships that are deployed. Consequences follow. Longer deployments mean more wear and tear on equipment and pressure on sailors and their families. Delayed or shortened repairs and maintenance reduce the service life of a ship. The result is a decline in the readiness of American seapower. This is exactly what happened.

Delays in maintenance and modernization because of the sequester extended far beyond the period that the sequester lasted. For example, a mere six-day furlough of civilian naval employees and a subsequent hiring freeze on civilians, the result of overall Department of Defense budget cuts, interrupted normal maintenance. When ships return to port, civilian employees are vital to such tasks as maintaining engines, fire-control systems, navigational equipment, communications, and readying weapons for operations, including combat.

Morale among civilian employees suffered when the furloughs were applied selectively. Contracted staff continued to work, in several cases even working overtime to make up for the work not being done by others. Support staff formerly classified as critical were told to stay home. Among those who stayed on the job, many saw their salaries cut by 20 percent over the period of six weeks. Notwithstanding, employees continued to work the same number of hours, if not more. Military members expressed frustration as their own work proceeded unabated, and they were forced to work longer periods to complete their missions in the absence of support staff. The furlough lasted only six days (and it had been reduced from a previously planned eleven days), but its impact left the Navy six days further behind on work.[36] This was just a taste of the sequester's effect.

Natural attrition drains the pool of skilled civilians who perform critical tasks in constructing and maintaining ships.[37] Because of the maintenance backlog that the sequester generated and a freeze on hiring civilian employees that encouraged workers to seek greater job security in other professions, the industrial base that supports American seapower suffered.

Putting ships to sea for months is costly. Fuel is burned. Crews must be fed. Ammunition used in training raises the bill. So does maintenance and repair during port visits. When money budgeted to pay for these expenses was suddenly removed, costs had to be cut. In 2013 alone, five ship deployments were canceled because of the sequester, including the guided-missile frigates USS *Rentz*, USS *Kauffman*, the attack submarine USS *Jefferson City*, Military Sealift Command rescue and salvage ship USNS *Grasp*, and the hospital ship USNS *Comfort*.[38]

The deployment of the USS *Harry S. Truman*'s carrier strike group was delayed six months. The nuclear-powered attack submarine USS *Miami*, damaged in a 2012 fire, was decommissioned rather than repaired.[39] In 2014, routine work on eight submarines was backlogged, with wait times that lasted from two to nine months.[40] To meet the demands of the sequester, the Navy canceled $603 million in shipyard maintenance[41] on twenty-three warships, including two carriers, two minesweepers, two "big-deck" amphibious ships, two mid-sized amphibious ships, and fifteen destroyers, all vessels in high demand by combatant commanders seeking to counter rising maritime competition from China and Iran.[42] As with your home, deferred maintenance leads to greater future costs. American seapower is no different.

Because of the sequester, the Navy decided to lay up (i.e., remove from service) eleven older cruisers. In this case, the Navy planned to modernize the eleven ships so that they could be returned to active duty in the future. Congress balked at the prospect that eleven powerful ships would be absent from the fleet for an extended period. Members worried that the burden would fall on ships that remained operational and, a darker possibility, that the Navy might choose to save more of the money of which it was being shorn by decommissioning some of the cruisers. This concern was not a chimera: the administration had already indicated interest in decommissioning nine cruisers and amphibious ships.

The compromise was the so-called 2-4-6 Plan. According to the agreement reached with Congress, work would begin on modernizing two ships each year. By legislation, no ship would spend more than four years in the program. And no more than six ships could be in modernization at the same time. The Navy's original plan would have put all eleven cruisers in for modernization at once. With no crews aboard them and tied up at pier side, this would have saved money and also would have extended the last of the ships' service to 2043.[43] Congress's 2-4-6 Plan extends the ships' lives to 2037.[44] The Navy's plan allows the Navy to save money while keeping a cruiser together with a battle group for a longer period. Congress's plan allows more cruisers to remain in operational status, albeit for six fewer years. Neither strategy nor the operations of hostile navies force these dilemmas. Notwithstanding, they are consequential and occur because of entirely domestic political calculations about the budget.

Besides having enough large surface ships available in the event of the unforeseen, money is an issue here. Modernizing all the cruisers at once meant that the Navy would not have to pay for operating the ships and would have allowed for economies of scale in purchasing new equipment to extend a ship's life and improve its fighting capability. CNO Admiral John Greenert stated in written testimony to Congress at the time that "the Navy's original cruiser phased modernization plan would have saved approximately $4.5 billion over the entire program [fiscal year 2015–2026]. Under the current 2-4-6 plan mandated by Congress, those savings are $300–$400 million, primarily due to reduced manpower and operations savings."[45] The case for preserving a more robust fleet was found to be more compelling.

However, the difference between the Navy's plan to modernize its cruiser fleet and Congress's plan should not be allowed to obscure the fact that the Obama administration's initial cuts to the defense budget eliminated altogether the design and construction of nineteen next-generation cruisers. Modernizing the current and aging cruiser fleet will keep these ships operating for another two decades or so. But what then? The Obama administration offered no plans to build a next-generation cruiser after the ones afloat today are decommissioned.

A cruiser combines the advantage of being able to perform several different tasks—air defense, anti-submarine warfare, anti–surface ship warfare, and projecting power ashore—with large quantities of weapons and the potential for generating an abundant supply of electricity. The latter is particularly important, as weapons like high-power lasers and electromagnetic rail guns become operational and enter the Navy's arsenal. A long delay in replacing today's cruisers or having no replacement at all will diminish the fleet's combat power as China and Russia modernize their equivalent naval systems.

In the end, the most important question was a difference between the administration and Congress over the size and character of the U.S. combat fleet. The possibility of a $4.5-billion savings would please many in Congress; some who wanted to cut spending and others who saw no problem in reducing the fleet by what they regarded as a handful of ships. Mindful of this, an administration that sought to spend less on defense saw the cruisers as a useful instrument to trim the defense bill as it shrank the U.S. military's overall size.

The sequester also set back facilities and bases. It forced a 30 percent cut in funding for facilities restoration and modernization for FY 2013. Congress had already cut funding for facilities to 87 percent of what the Navy required to modernize both ports and airfields. The important point is that cutting money for shore facilities is a standard recourse for the Navy in anticipation of a falling budget axe. When budget cuts cannot be avoided and no other category exists to trim, those who are responsible for keeping up ports and airfields wait for bad news.

And it is bad news. If docks, storage tanks, fuel pumps, tarmacs, and the machinery to repair them go wanting, the consequences are not as immediate as if a battle group is absent in a crisis. But it's only a matter of time. Surgeons cannot operate without instruments, anesthesiologists, and adequate facilities. The Navy cannot execute its missions without logistical support, including functioning ports and airfields. Both the Marine Corps and naval aviation have experienced significant shortfalls due to the reduced budgets.

According to Lieutenant General Jon M. "Dog" Davis, then-USMC deputy commandant for aviation, 20 percent of the Marine Corps's F-18 fighters are "stuck" and unable to be moved to maintenance depots, owing to delayed repair and maintenance. In similar straits are several other key pieces of Marine Corps aviation, in particular the CH-53 Sea Stallion/Super Stallion helicopters, AV-8B Harriers, and MV-22 Ospreys. While he was Assistant Commandant of Marines, General John Paxton, now retired, said publicly as early as 2015 that "The F-18s are a very specific example of the badness [*sic*] of sequestration and furlough, because when we let the artisans [*sic*] and engineers go, we couldn't get the aircraft into maintenance that they need."[46] Naval aviation, similarly, finds itself with a 140-aircraft shortage between its planned inventory and its actual aircraft inventory. Budget cuts have cut significantly into the Navy's ability to buy new aircraft.[47]

The effects of these maintenance backlogs, cuts, and extended deployments have been to degrade a force that is already stretched thin by personnel reductions and the administration's orders to respond to global crises. A good example of the latter is the detachment of the USS *Harry S. Truman* from the Persian Gulf after six months to the Eastern Mediterranean, where its planes attacked ISIS targets. The usual length of deployment during the Cold War was six months. *Truman* was scheduled for a seven-month deployment. She returned to home port eight months after sailing.

The length of deployments of carrier strike groups, amphibious readiness groups, and guided-missile destroyers has increased from the long-standing norm of six months to eight or nine months, or more. Longer deployments not only are hard on sailors and their families but also increase the maintenance needed to return combat ships to sea following a deployment. Naval vessels, like family cars, need more work the longer that routine maintenance and repairs are postponed.

A 2016 Government Accountability Office (GAO) report found that the pace at which the Navy has been using its ships—due ultimately to a shrinking fleet—has "reduced the predictability of ship deployments for sailors and for the ship repair industrial base." The same report noted that decisions to honor commitments despite a shrinking number of ships "have also resulted in declining ship conditions across the fleet and have increased the amount of time that ships require to complete maintenance in the shipyards."[48] As then-CNO Admiral Jon Greenert noted during a 2014 speech aboard the USS *Kearsarge* in Norfolk, Virginia:

> The carriers and the other large ships that need a lot of shipyard time—the time to get the maintenance done so that you're not spilling over into the training phases, which spills over into the preparation for deployment, and then into deployment. Then you're not ready to go, you're not manned, all the maintenance didn't get done, too much was deferred—and you start down a vicious cycle.[49]

An example of what Admiral Greenert meant occurred in 2014. The aircraft carrier USS *Dwight D. Eisenhower* was scheduled to deploy from Norfolk, Virginia, to the Middle East. But repairs and maintenance to the ship had not been completed when she was scheduled to sail. The Navy substituted USS *Harry S. Truman*. An important reason for the swap was that the 2013 budget problems had resulted in the extraordinary measure of sending *Eisenhower*—which had been launched twenty-one years before *Truman*—back to the Persian Gulf two months after returning from it. This was a significant change. On her first deployment, in 1979, nine months separated her return from the Mediterranean and her departure to the Indian Ocean. Eight years later, seven months separated the *Ike*'s return to port from her departure for the Med.

The result of the *Ike*'s almost-immediate turnaround was that more of her systems required more repair. This meant a several-months' extension of the older carrier's time in the yards to prepare for the next deployment. Aside from the effect on the thousands of families of crew members who saw their husbands, wives, and parents leave for another deployment just weeks after returning from the previous one, the disruption also had operational consequences. *Truman* arrived in the Persian Gulf several months after the ship it was relieving, the USS *Theodore Roosevelt*, had departed.

A shortage of available carriers plus the Navy's effort to save on operational costs resulted in the gap in U.S. aircraft presence in the Persian Gulf. Iran's rulers could not possibly have failed to note the gap that began in early October 2015 and lasted until near the end of the year. In January 2016, the navy of Iran's Islamic Revolutionary Guard Corps (IRGC) captured and briefly held U.S. Navy sailors aboard riverine boats that were operating in the Persian Gulf. A Navy report subsequently found that lax standards, insufficient operational discipline, and an unclear understanding of the rules of engagement contributed to the incident. Beyond the purview of the Navy's investigation into the incident was the effect on the IRGC of the signals delivered by a recent gap in U.S. naval presence.

Several lessons can be learned from the Navy's having to scramble to maintain a presence in the Persian Gulf. The two most important are, first, that a short-lived cut in funds had effects that snowballed in the Navy's daily operations and could have had far more serious consequences in the Middle East. Had Iran chosen to take advantage of the actual gap in the U.S. carrier presence, an ordinarily tense Persian Gulf could have become a violent one. The second is that, even with ten operational carriers, maintaining a round-the-clock presence is a very difficult and complex task that must account for transit times from home port to duty stations and back, time to refresh training for crews of ships that replace those whose deployments are ending, routine maintenance, and also the extended maintenance needed to refuel a carrier's nuclear reactor.

Even with ten carriers, schedules are so tight and the demands of keeping a trained crew at the ready are so large that the United States is able to maintain a steady carrier presence in just two places, the West Pacific and the Persian Gulf. If conflict broke out in, for example, the Black or Baltic or Mediterranean Seas, the United States would be forced to choose between addressing the needs of the moment and removing carriers from the presence and deterrence missions that are sufficiently important to maintain powerful naval forces on station around the clock.

The "snowball effect" is not a matter of speculation. Shipbuilding procurement and maintenance were cut significantly enough to affect the Navy into the foreseeable future. The GAO reported in 2016 on the Navy's readiness, in particular the Optimized Fleet Response Plan (OFRP). In November 2014, the Navy implemented this plan, which was intended to improve the maintenance process. The GAO found that it had failed, and that maintenance delays have significantly harmed the Navy's ability to maintain readiness:

> The declining condition of ships has increased the duration of time that ships spend undergoing maintenance in the shipyards, which in turn compresses the time available in the schedule for training and operations.[50]

The Navy instituted the OFRP after 8 of 9 carriers and 74 of 103 surface combat ships saw overruns in maintenance times between 2011 and 2014. However, since the plan's implementation, none of the 3 carriers and only 15 of 83 surface cruisers and destroyers that have entered maintenance have completed maintenance on schedule. The GAO ascribes this to the Navy's failure to properly assess maintenance requirements, workforce inexperience, and workload fluctuations.[51]

Keeping ships too long at sea requires them to spend more time in the repair shop when they return. Runners who complete a marathon are advised to rest for a week. Weightlifters who stress large groups of muscles know that it is important to take at least a day off to allow the body to repair and regenerate after a strenuous workout. The same applies to ships and their crews. They require time to recover and repair. If this time is shortened, consequences follow—as excerpts from the U.S. Government Accountability Office May 2016 report noted below illustrate.

USS *George H. W. Bush*: "2015 planned maintenance availability for the USS *George H. W. Bush* (CVN 77) exceeded its 6-month availability by more than 2 months. To accommodate the increase, the Navy reduced the ship's employability to operational commanders by 3 weeks and compressed its scheduled training by 5 weeks."[52]

USS *Dwight D Eisenhower*: "USS *Dwight D. Eisenhower's* (CVN 69) maintenance availability, begun in 2013, was extended from a planned 14 months to more than 23 months to accommodate 2½ times more growth and new work than the Navy had planned for, as well as shipyard performance issues. . . . The *Eisenhower* maintenance delay had ripple effects that impacted the entire optimized carrier schedule."[53]

USS *Harry S. Truman*: "Extension required USS *Harry S. Truman* (CVN 75), which the Navy had intended to be the first aircraft carrier to transition to the OFRP, to complete back-to-back deployments to meet operational demands. This prevented the *Truman* from entering her OFRP maintenance phase at Norfolk Naval Shipyard as scheduled in fiscal year 2015."[54]

The GAO does not merely identify the OFRP's initial failure to maintain schedule with ship maintenance. The report goes on to lay a large part of the blame, based on interviews with both Navy and shipyard officials, on budget reductions and procurement delays, with sequestration identified as a contributing factor. Without necessary funding provided in a timely manner, the shipyards have struggled to "maintain the fleet and warfighting readiness."[55]

MARINE CORPS

The Marine Corps currently deploys more than 31,000 Marines, who engage in combat operations, training, and other activities, such as safeguarding U.S. embassies around the globe. To manage the significant reduction in funding that the Obama administration requested and Congress approved, the Marine Corps has been forced to cut capacity. The Marine Corps procurement money in the president's budget requests alone decreased 50 percent, from $3.1 billion[56] down to $1.5 billion[57] between FY 2011 and FY 2017.

President Obama's Defense budgets reduced money for the Marines, and the sequester's effects lingered. In

2013, the Marine Corps was left with a $1.4 billion shortfall for the fiscal year.[58] The USMC's priority is its funding for near-term readiness. The nation has interests that the Marines are best suited to protect—for example, in helping to drive ISIS from the territory that is a source of the terrorist organization's wealth and its claim to lead the Islamic world. The Marine Corps will meet its obligations. But an insufficient budget, and more, a declining one, is exhibit A of a zero-sum game. What is spent here cannot be spent there. The future readiness of the Corps is threatened by underinvestment in long-term modernization and infrastructure.[59]

The size of the USMC decreased from 202,100 active personnel in 2012 to 184,100 in 2015, with the intended goal of shrinking to 182,000 by 2017. In the period between fiscal years 2014 and 2015 alone, the Marine Corps shed two whole infantry battalions, down to twenty-three from twenty-five. Marine ground units are likely to face a "battlefield mobility gap," because replacements for the High Mobility Multipurpose Wheeled Vehicles (HMMWVs, or Humvees) have been delayed and face reduced procurement as well.

As of late 2016, a shortfall in senior enlisted leadership existed, a gap in the USMC's steel backbone of non-commissioned officers.[60] This opens a potential deficit in enlisted leadership, a key element to the USMC's effectiveness. Chairman of the Joint Chiefs and former Marine Commandant General Joseph Dunford has expressed fears that the current arrangement "will hollow the force and create unacceptable risk for our national defense."[61]

The current state of the force threatens combat capabilities and troop readiness of the Marines. Already under strain from the Obama administration's initial budget cuts, a return to sequester would devastate the Marines' ability to give its forces the rest they require following deployment. If funding cuts are implemented at full Budget Control Act levels, the deployment-to-dwell ratio—the ratio of those currently deployed to those either training, building up, or recently returned from deployments—for the Marine Corps has the potential to fall to 1:1.[62] This means that Marines would have only one month for rest, training, and workup for every month deployed, far from the ideal ratio of three months per every month deployed. These levels would exhaust Marines, forcing them and their families to bear the additional burden of a cycle in which Marines would spend half their time deployed.

The Marine Corps is not only facing daunting challenges to its current readiness; future readiness is threatened by today's constraints. General Dunford explains the possible effect on the Corps:

> Approximately half of [USMC] non-deployed units—and those are the ones that provide the bench to respond to unforeseen contingencies—are suffering personnel, equipment and training shortfalls. In a major conflict, those shortfalls will result in delayed response and/or the unnecessary loss of young American lives.[63]

Marine aviation, too, has suffered from the increased pace of operations that results when the force is asked to do more with less. Multiple Marine MV-22 Osprey and F/A-18 Hornet squadrons currently run at deployment ratios under 1:2. This means two months at home for every month deployed. Moreover, nearly one in five USMC aircraft is currently unavailable for use, awaiting repairs and spare parts, an aircraft inventory challenge that is exacerbated by reductions in the number of replacement F-35Cs procured. According to the 2016 USMC Aviation Report, USMC squadrons that deploy "achieve readiness 'just in time,'" but the next-to-deploy and non-deployed squadrons have not been afforded the adequate resources for training to fight immediately.[64] If an emergency substantially increased the number of Marines needed for combat, squadrons would have to go to war without sufficient training.

Lieutenant General Davis sums up the dangers of lack of training capabilities. He believes there is a connection between the "decrease in flight hours per month per aircrew and an uptick in our mishap rates."[65] "Global security commitments" now require a deployment-to-dwell ratio for the USMC's active aviation component of 1:2. This falls well below the ideal ratio of 1:3 and is likely to take a toll not only on the aircraft and equipment but also on pilots and maintenance crews.[66]

Marine pilots and maintenance have been shorted the number of flight hours for training. This means less experience for individual crews and for the entire aviation community. For example, in a snapshot taken in the spring of 2016, Marine Corps F/A-18 pilots saw flight hours reduced to 8.8 flight hours per month, less than half the 15.7 flight hours recommended.[67] A generation ago, the standard was closer to 25 hours per month, and Marine pilots were flying fewer combat missions then than today. Flying an advanced fourth-generation F/A-18 Hornet/Super Hornet is not like riding a bike. For the pilots and the aircrafts' ground crew to know their jobs, the aircraft needs to fly.

To address mounting deficits in parts and aircraft, the Marine Corps has been forced to scavenge. Without enough fighter attack jets, the Marine Corps announced in June 2016 that it planned to refurbish twenty-three mothballed F/A-18s from the 309th Aerospace Maintenance and Regeneration Center at Davis-Monthan Air Force Base in Arizona, also known as "the Boneyard."[68] For older airframes, such as the CH-53 Sea Stallion helicopter, many of the parts to maintain the older aircraft are no longer in production. Thus, ground crews strip other aircraft or scavenge. In some instances, Marines have reportedly cannibalized parts from sources as diverse and unreliable as aircraft in museums.[69] It's hardly a good solution. But what's the choice? Vital pieces of older airframes are no longer manufactured. Supply chains have shifted toward servicing replacement aircraft that, owing to budgetary delays under the Obama administration, have yet to enter service.[70] The older aircraft and antiquated parts that are being pressed into service put the lives of Marines at risk.[71]

Naval aviation, too, is facing a future shortfall similar to the Marine Corps, as the aging F/A-18 Hornets are replaced by new F-35s. Cuts to F-35 purchases by the Navy may leave the Navy short of thirty-eight aircraft, which would require extending the service lives of the currently used F/A-18s.[72]

Costs for maintaining aviation facilities are being cut. The base budget for FY 2015 funded only 80 percent of the requirement for aviation depots. This has led to fewer aircraft on the flight line and has forced the Navy and Marine

Corps to deploy partial squadrons. Moreover, the degradation of shore infrastructure, where sailors train and prepare, will harm readiness and lead predictably to increased risk.

Budget-linked readiness deficits in Navy and Marine Corps aviation have already cost lives. In January 2016, two CH-53 Sea Stallion helicopters collided off the North Shore of Oahu, killing twelve Marines.[73] Just three days prior to the incident, the Marine Corps had relieved the commander of the same unit for being unable "to maintain material readiness standards."[74] The first nine months of 2015 saw deaths in Marine Corps aviation reach a five-year high, with eighteen Marines killed; this was three more deaths than in 2014 and higher than any time since fifteen Marines died in 2012.[75]

For its part, the Navy has struggled to explain the loss of three aircraft in an eight-day period in May to June 2016. During this time, two F/A-18F Super Hornets collided off the coast of North Carolina, an EA-18G Growler suffered an "in-flight arresting gear engagement leading to nose landing gear and engine damage," and a Blue Angels F/A-18C Hornet crashed in Tennessee, killing the pilot. Naval Air Forces commander Vice Admiral Mike Shoemaker emphasized in a 2016 speech that, while these incidents could not be directly tied into readiness, the rising trend of aircraft incidents among the sea services poses uncomfortable questions.[76]

A Marine Corps aviation supply and maintenance officer, speaking on condition of anonymity, emphasized how "stretched to the limit" the Marine Corps is. The officer directly linked the lack of appropriate training for both pilots and maintenance crews in order to "troubleshoot" problems to fatal incidents. He referred to the 2014 fatal crash of a Navy MH-53E Sea Dragon, call sign Vulcan 543, as a result of improper handling of wiring, a symptom of the lack of adequate training and the loss of experienced senior enlisted personnel due to budget constraints.[77]

LOW MORALE

The current high rate of operations is taking a toll on the morale and enthusiasm of sailors and Marines alike. A 2014 survey of both enlisted sailors and officers found that 49.8 percent of enlisted sailors and 65.5 percent of officers felt that the current operational tempo was too high.[78] The dissatisfaction with the added stress of the budget-forced situation will eventually influence sailors' and Marines' decisions about whether to stay in the service. According to one study, the longer and more frequent deployments that have become the norm reduced reenlistment and retention rates between 1.3 percent and 1.9 percent.[79] While this is minor, the loss of talent and trained individuals degrades capability, especially as systems on naval platforms continue to become more advanced and demand greater technical skills, training, and expertise. Sailors and Marines sacrifice a lot, as do their families. It is unreasonable to imagine that their patience will last indefinitely.

CARRIER GAPS

For now, the nuclear-powered aircraft carrier is the backbone of the United States Navy and the preeminent tool for projecting U.S. military power abroad. However, as the

U.S. carrier fleet stands now at ten ships, budget cuts have strained their use. Shortfalls in deployments of carrier strike groups to different combatant commands in strategic regions have already occurred. More are likely. These "carrier gaps" leave different regions without an American aircraft carrier for a period of time, reflecting diminished U.S. influence. The Persian Gulf saw a carrier gap during the critical Iran deal period in the fall of 2015, as the USS *Theodore Roosevelt* departed the region on October 9, 2015, and the USS *Harry S. Truman* joined with the 5th Fleet beginning combat operations against ISIS for Operation Inherent Resolve on December 29, 2015.[80]

To avoid a carrier gap during the summer of 2016, *Truman* departed the Persian Gulf in June 2016, one month later than had been scheduled, and the USS *Dwight D. Eisenhower* deployed.[81] This avoided the possibility that USS *John C. Stennis*, stationed with the 7th Fleet in East Asia at the time, would become the only U.S. carrier to be on call to both the 5th Fleet in the Middle East and the 7th Fleet in East Asia. Had *Truman* not stayed the extra month, *Stennis* would have been the only carrier able to deploy rapidly to counter any significant escalation in the Persian Gulf, but would also have had to do so from a great distance.

However, the increased length of the deployment likely took a greater toll on *Truman* and its crew.[82] The temporary solution to this potential carrier gap situation, while it was immediately effective, pressured an already over-stretched carrier fleet. This is not a sole episode. As congressional budget caps restrict funds needed for operations, maintenance, and the construction of more ships, personnel costs rise. These costs cannot be avoided. The result is an increase in demand on sailors, Marines, and their ships and aircraft that affects all of U.S. seapower.

With the 2012 retirement of the USS *Enterprise*—which went into service the same year as the Cuban Missile Crisis—the U.S. fleet dropped to ten carriers, one fewer than the congressionally mandated number of eleven. The reduced number has put the remaining ships under stress, as it means longer—beyond the seven-month deployment goal—and more frequent deployments, or a reduced presence globally. The first of the next generation of carriers, the USS *Gerald R. Ford*, has been postponed, owing to the insistence of the Pentagon under the Obama administration that the *Ford* undergo extensive shock trials. With the delay, the period during which the fleet has ten carriers, which was initially intended to be fourteen months, will have lasted over four years.[83]

STRATEGIC IMPACT

The effects of the cuts to the naval budget have strategic implications beyond the current state of American seapower. The decreased presence caused by carrier gaps and the falling number of ships lessens the strategic influence of the United States around the globe, particularly in such regional hot spots as the Persian Gulf and East Asia. Combatant command operational requirements dictate that the Navy be able to "surge" three carrier strike groups and three amphibious readiness groups forward within thirty days in the event of a global crisis. However, current capabilities allow for only one carrier strike group and one amphibious readiness group to be forward deployed. Even if the additional two carriers were ready for deployment and entirely capable of conducting integrated operations with another one or two carriers, weeks would pass before they could arrive and begin combat operations.[84]

The long-term effects of maintenance backlogs and the increased workload on aging ships and aircraft *will* catch up with the fleet in the future. Canceling shipbuilding, too, will harm the future U.S. Navy. As then–Secretary of the Navy Raymond Mabus stated at a House Armed Services Appropriations Subcommittee hearing in 2015, "if you miss a ship . . . you never make that ship up."[85] CNO Admiral Greenert drew a more detailed picture:

> Disruptions in naval ship design and construction plans are significant because of the long-lead time, specialized skills, and extent of integration needed to build military ships. Because ship construction can span up to nine years, program procurement cancelled in FY 2016 will not be felt by the Combatant Commanders until several years later when the size of the battle force begins to shrink as those ships are not delivered to the fleet at the planned time.[86]

Had the election of 2016 gone differently, the resulting decline of the U.S. combat fleet would have coincided with the rise of other international actors, including the reinvigoration of the Russian Federation and the rapid naval expansion of China. The budget cuts of the Obama administration, due to their long-lasting effects, will take years from which to recover. As Admiral Greenert put it, "we've been forced to slow our Navy modernization. We have lost our momentum in fielding emerging critical capabilities for future fights. We are losing our technical edge."[87] The future that the new U.S. administration must address contains shortfall gaps in the fleet due both to the sequester and to congressionally imposed spending levels that are insufficient to meet executive branch–directed global commitments.

Until positive changes are enacted, the Obama shipbuilding plan means shortfalls in large surface combatants from 2034 to 2037, and thereafter from 2041 to at least 2046. The same plan would have small surface combatants suffer a shortfall for the entire planned thirty-year period, in part due to the most recent cut of ten littoral combat ships from the plan. Rounding out the combatant craft shortfalls are deficits in attack submarines from 2025 to 2036 and amphibious assault ships from 2017 to 2021, in 2040, and from 2042 to at least 2046.[88] President Trump has promised to change this and rebuild the fleet. His goal is reasonable.

The old thirty-year naval shipbuilding plan was like a suit of armor that had been fashioned with large and mobile gaping holes that shift from exposing one vital organ to another. The bet that the Pentagon made under prior leadership was that no sharp weapon would land a blow at this Swiss-cheese armor at the wrong moment. The large anticipated gaps in the future fleet were sacrifices that were made to preserve readiness. This was an unwise exchange, since without strong support for and understanding of seapower's strategic importance to the United States's global power, even the money for readiness is at risk.

Nor was this the end of the story as things stood after years of neglect. The nonpartisan Congressional Budget Office (CBO) includes in its estimate of future shipbuilding the considerable expense of refueling nuclear-powered aircraft carriers and purchases of new equipment after a ship has been delivered. The Navy's old thirty-year plan, however, included only the cost of building new ships. In addition, the CBO and the Navy generated different estimates for predictable increases in labor costs and the cost of future vessels. The Navy's view of future costs is more optimistic—that is, lower—than that of the CBO.

The CBO estimated that to complete even the envisioned Swiss-cheese construction program over the next three decades, the Navy would have to receive one-third more funding for shipbuilding than its historical average over the previous thirty years. This does not consider today's readiness, maintenance, spare parts, ammunition, and installation shortfalls. Resources needed to return these and other key elements of logistical support for U.S. seapower would likely cost many billions of dollars, perhaps even approaching a third of the entire Navy Department's 2016 budget.

In restoring American seapower, President Trump has a daunting task. The yoke is not easy nor is the burden light. Leaving aside non-shipbuilding deficiencies and assuming that the CBO's estimates are correct, the U.S. Navy will shrink as the fleets of its largest potential rivals, China and Russia, grow. The point of picturing the state of affairs in the Obama administration is not so much to cast blame as it is to illustrate the challenges that now face the new administration as it rebuilds the Navy and plans for its future. These challenges are not limited to ships and weapons.

CHAPTER IX

THEY ALSO SERVE
WHO ONLY STAND AND WAIT

*The accounts noted in this chapter are taken from face-to-face
interviews between the author and the wives of sailors and Marines
who currently serve in America's armed forces. The names used
to identify the interviewees are fictitious. The stories are true. I am
grateful for the naval and Marine spouses' forthrightness and
I hope that readers will share my admiration for their sacrifice.*

The greatest asset of America's military is not high-quality weapons, advanced technology, or global reach. What makes the American military great is its people, the men and women who sacrifice predictable nine-to-five jobs and sometimes their very lives in the service of the United States. These sailors, Marines, soldiers, and airmen work long hours under difficult and dangerous conditions. Their families support their service and sacrifice. In the last few years, military families have borne the brunt of the budget cuts, increased pace of operations, and wear and tear that has afflicted the military.

Wives are separated from husbands. Children grow up in households where one parent is often deployed. Spouses become virtual single parents, and the adaptation when the sailor or Marine returns home is not always as joyful as the long-anticipated moment of homecoming. Life milestones are missed. Lost time together cannot be regained. This chapter attempts faithfully to detail the effects on, as the military puts it, "those who also serve."

IMPACT OF BUDGET CUTS

FINANCIAL STRAIN

The post-9/11 U.S. national security objectives increased the deployment of American military personnel around the world. From Iraq to Afghanistan to counter-terrorism operations, the U.S. military were deployed with increasing frequency. The Department of Defense budget rose to support deployments and objectives. Eventually though, the Defense budget's growth became a political target for budget hawks who made common cause with an administration that saw virtue in reducing the U.S. military.

Navy and Marine wives speak from years of experience. "Becky," the wife of a senior chief petty officer in the submarine service, understands how important submarines are to the Navy. She correctly notes that the silent services "do not bear a lot of the brunt" of budgeting cuts in comparison to other commands. However, she saw her family's benefits decrease while she was working to finish her college degree. Having finished over half of her higher education, she found that "[the budget] took a huge cut to spouse education benefits." Owing to the constant moves that are part of being a Navy family, she could not find a full-time job to pay for her education in place of the lost benefits.

The cuts did not affect the spouses of service members at the E-5 level (Petty Officer Second Class) or below. But Becky's husband was an E-6, a Petty Officer First Class. She lost the assistance while she was in school as an active student, notwithstanding the fact that she had already signed up for the next semester of classes. Forced to "weigh out," she never returned. "Of all the things my husband sacrifices, and my family sacrifices, I had three semesters left . . . they just cut all the funding. . . . I feel as though I should just stay at home . . . have no career. . . . There's not even training for spouses . . . for careers that could help my husband and our family."

Defense budgets of the past few years have again raised the long-standing threat to close the commissaries that military families rely on for low-cost, name-brand groceries. The commissaries are a convenient target for budget cuts. They appear to be an extraneous benefit that would not directly affect base or military operations. However, most families use these stores. As a chief petty officer's wife said, "losing the commissary would be a huge blow to our monthly budget." One ombudsman—a volunteer who acts as a liaison between the command and the families of service members—said that she had received many similar calls from service families. Military families, she observed, plan their finances to take full advantage of these stores' reduced cost. The closures were prevented, but they are a good example of the uncertainty that pervades military lives.

Budget cuts have eaten away at reenlistment bonuses for enlisted sailors. The amounts offered during the 2000s benefited service members, particularly those in positions that demanded a high level of skill. The extra income helped offset the low rise in salaries during additional years under contract. Budget cuts eliminated the reenlistment bonuses of highly trained and experienced senior enlisted members of the Navy, those ranked E-7–Chief Petty Officer–and above: their eligibility ended. The ranks of E-6 and below can still get these bonuses, but the amounts "have been significantly lowered." "What does that say to your senior enlisted?" asks the wife of one senior enlisted serviceman. "You need those trained, senior personnel who have been here. If you've got everybody who wants to get out at eight years, or ten years, at some point somebody has got to have been there long enough to have been there, done that, and knows how to help run the ship."

"Melissa," the wife of a chief petty officer in the Navy's Explosive Ordinance Disposal (EOD) units, pointed out that her husband had pursued service under more dangerous circumstances in part because the role provided selective reenlistment bonuses. He did this for his family. However, the size of the bonuses has "been dwindling quickly." When this interview took place, her husband was up for reenlistment. He expected to receive a bonus less than half of what he would have been offered if he'd been up for reenlistment a year earlier. Melissa commented on the Navy's use of bonuses as reenlistment tools: "they dangle the carrot, then they dangle it a little further . . . so it's a gamble every year" about whether the reenlistment bonus would be worth more years in the service.

The reduction in the bonuses has increased the number of families in financial straits. This falls particularly hard on the submarine community. Becky notes, "As a submariner, if you're in financial hardship . . . you will lose your security clearance. You cannot work aboard a submarine without at least a secret security clearance." The "unplanned losses" caused by financial difficulties affect other families: filling vacancies caused by someone else's loss of security clearance pulls solvent service members from shore duty and away from the time they had expected to spend with their families.

Despite financial difficulties, many sailors are reluctant to seek help with the Navy–Marine Corps Relief Society or other places that might provide emergency loans. They worry that their commands might learn of their finances, even though the Society generally does not release private financial information except in cases of "repeat offenders." "Sometimes it becomes a security issue," says "Amy," whose husband is a fire controlman aboard a destroyer. "If they find that a family is in financial trouble, are they a risk to sell secrets?"

The benefits that came with deployments have not escaped the budgetary cheeseparing. Additional money for deploying once included family separation pay and tax-free income for extra pay received in areas that were designated as dangerous. Now, says Amy, those benefits have been reduced and, in some cases, ended. "I did not realize how much it affected, but my husband just did the last [deployment], and I am looking for tax-free and he never got it," she explains. "He never hit anywhere where he got it. During the previous deployment, we were tax-free the whole time, and on this deployment his ship went to the same places." Her husband's deployment pay is now being taxed. "We still get the family separation, but . . . now it's all taxed . . . as annual income." Even though her husband gets sea pay while on deployment, it is "nowhere near enough to live on."

The Basic Allowance for Housing (BAH) helps service members pay for housing based on the cost of living. Reductions in BAH have led to a decline in the standards of housing that Navy families can afford. Sometimes low-cost housing and safe places do not come in pairs. "They find the cheapest place they can . . . in the middle of the ghetto, and there's cars getting broken into." "One of our spouses . . . they had nine break-ins," said one ombudsman, "and that happens when sailors happen to be deployed, so the spouse has to deal with filing the police report and replacing the stuff, or just saying goodbye to it, and filing the claim with the insurance company. It puts a lot of stress on the families and the couples." "We don't get a lot of housing allowance if we live off base," said "Rachel," the wife of a Marine officer assigned to a landing dock ship, "and they're looking at reducing the BAH rates for military, which is scary."

DECLINE IN SERVICES AND ASSISTANCE

Budget cuts not only have directly affected families' pocketbooks but also have impaired services to families and hindered the people who provide the services. "Sarah," the wife of a Navy pilot, is also a clinical worker who supports Navy and Marine Corps families. She said that reduced budgets had resulted in a contract that was awarded to a lowest bidder who had no experience with military families. The new contractor cut costs by hiring under-qualified and underpaid staff. Experienced workers left. The new contractor cut Sarah's salary by $9,000 and complained that the employee was not at her desk. This was true. She was out of the office helping families that were experiencing medical, financial, and emotional problems. "You're never in the office!" her supervisors told her. "If I'm sitting in this chair," she says, pointing to the chair behind her desk, "I'm probably not doing my job."

Sarah also had to pay nearly $4,000 out-of-pocket expenses to travel to meet a ship in Europe to provide services to sailors and their families abroad. "We're paying to support the military. Literally." Why? "The services that are in Europe . . . don't have someone qualified to do what I do . . . they try to get the help in the region but they don't have it."

This climate has led to a high turnover rate of psychologists and specialists who provide family and counseling services. "There's a constant turnover . . . especially with the clinical psychologists. . . . I can refer them to somebody, and then go to refer somebody else in three months, and the psychologist's left, they're gone. There's definitely not consistency," one ombudsman lamented. Consistency is necessary in a psychologist's work, because it takes time to build trust—the foundation of successful treatment—between patient and care provider.

For spouses who managed to find employment within the Navy support community, budget cuts diminished their ability not only to assist service members but also to support their own families. Melissa, the wife of the EOD chief, worked at the Navy–Marine Corps Relief Society while the family lived at an overseas duty station. During the 2010 government shutdown, she had two months of her pay withheld. At the same time, the timing of her husband's paychecks became an unknown. "That was a very anxious time," she said. "You sign up for this job, you think you have security in your job, you think you have security in your housing, and all these things . . . to think everything you hold dearly to be secure, suddenly it's gone." While the couple had planned ahead and had savings to carry them over, she saw other couples that had not been prepared and struggled with their finances because of the pay suspensions.

The budget cuts in recent years have also further restricted health care for Navy families. "We've been at a civilian doctor for the past ten years," says "Jennifer," the wife of an enlisted man and mother of five. "Tricare [the current and unloved military health care system] just wasn't there when my kids needed it. I've spent five months trying to get them to give us some flexibility, but they won't unless we switch from prime to standard." Even urgent but non-emergency appointments for herself or her children require a two-day wait. Before the budget cuts, same-day appointments with pediatricians were possible. Parents with children who unexpectedly need immediate medical attention will understand the meaning of this change.

"Lauren," a Marine wife, found that budget cuts directly affected the military's health care system. Scheduling routine medical procedures became a problem. "Medical is the big thing. Going to the medical facilities that are run by the military, you can see the decline of helpfulness and getting an appointment. There are fewer doctors, fewer nurses. So it's much harder to get in when we need something." She spoke with a physician about a procedure and was placed on the waiting list. Two months later she called to see how things stood, and learned that her place on the list had not moved. She had no choice but to have the operation performed at another base, an hour's drive away.

FEWER SHIPS, MORE WORK

Defense budget cuts have less direct but still profound results on family life. As noted earlier, budget constraints and overall cuts have meant longer and more frequent deployments, often with very little warning. Long deployments that begin on short notice strain not only sailors and Marines, but also their families at home. "I have two little ones," one woman, whose husband is a Navy junior officer, explains. "We plan our schedules based on which one of us *isn't* on deployment."

Time away from home, even on ships with regular deployment schedules, is rarely limited to the length of a particular deployment. "They just got back from a seven-month deployment," says Rachel, "and they're actually gone this month as well. Then they'll be back for about three weeks, and then they'll be gone for another three weeks." Time is required to prepare crews before they sail, and more time is needed when they return as the process begins anew. As another wife notes, "With the budget cuts, we don't have as many ships that are ready to go out. . . . We've been in a constant cycle where we're constantly getting ready to go in the shipyard, or getting ready to go out of the shipyard. Getting ready to go on deployment, or getting ready to come back."

Melissa, mentioned above, relates that her husband was currently on his third deployment of the last five years. The deployments of EOD personnel have become longer and more frequent. Her husband's first deployment lasted five months; the second was six months; and the most recent is scheduled for eight months. As deployments lengthen, the time between them shortens. "It used to be on average that we'd have about a year and a half to two years," Melissa said. "Now the turnaround time is fifteen months. As soon as he got home he was put on a new team, and they immediately started to work up [that is, prepare for the next deployment]. And even when he is home, stateside, he's not home because he's gone for training. Even when he's home he's not home." The chief accrued over one hundred days of leave, but because of the increased demands placed on him, he hasn't been able to take the time off that he is owed.

Becky, too, indicated that the submarine community has experienced increased operational tempo since the budget cuts went into effect. "We've seen longer deployments. We've seen extended deployments. We've seen more of the 'back-to-back,' a lot less downtime between the deployments, which for a family is very difficult." She explained that, in the past, her husband and shipmates would deploy for a half year once every three years. Now, she said, the submarine community sees one deployment a year.

Being away regularly for half the year stresses families to the point where the retention rate has dropped. An ombudsman said, "We have seen many of our friends who would have stayed in just leave; they can't do it anymore." The enlisted community—where twenty years of service offers full retirement benefits—now sees senior enlisted personnel leave after thirteen, fourteen, or fifteen years because they "just cannot see the light at the end of the tunnel and can't do it anymore. They get out, even without the retirement benefits, because the frequency of deployments is too tough."

Amy tells the same story. Her family has seen increased deployments over the past five years at an average of one deployment per year, with the exception of 2011, when budget cuts forced the ship to remain in port. This means in the last half decade her husband was home less than six months per year.

RUN HARD, PUT AWAY WET

Budget cuts and increased operational tempo affect crews not just at sea but on return to home ports. Keeping ships at sea longer means more maintenance. More work is needed to put ships back to sea, and the sailors who do the work must spend extra hours to complete their assignments. "Ships failing inspections FOUR TIMES," exclaimed one wife. One ship "failed inspection to the point where the commodore moved on board so they could run inspections 24/7. They weren't sure it would receive a 'go' even after two years in the shipyard."

Sailors and their families are confused about official estimates for time in the yards. "We've been told several different things," says Lauren, the Marine's wife, whose husband's ship was to enter extended maintenance several weeks after the interview. "We've been told six months, we've been told eight months, we've been told eighteen months—they have no clue. They don't know the extent of the repairs and the renovations that they're doing, yet."

Assignment to the shipyards does not equal more time with families. Stress on family life does not lift. "They have to be at work earlier, they'll be there later, and they're doing a job that's not their job." Such assignments build a false expectation that the service members will be home more often, will have more time to spend with their kids, and will be able to help out more around the house. "It's causing financial issues, it's causing stress. Clinical counselors see people more when they're in the yards than when they're on deployment," said Lauren.

The submarine community faces a similar problem. Because of budget and contract cuts to the shipyards, submarines spend "much shorter times" in the shipyard. The result is that crews are required to work much longer hours. As Becky notes, "When they're in the shipyards, they will work fourteen, fifteen hours a day, every single day," and often also through weekends. "Project managers look at the Navy guys and think 'they're getting a paycheck whether they're on the job forty hours or eighty hours,'" while shipyard civilian workers get paid overtime and have limited hours. "So our guys end up picking up a lot of that extra work." Often, the needed parts are either not available or late to arrive. This forces the ship to delay its deployment—which affects others who are deployed at sea waiting to be relieved.

Sailors in the shipyards come home exhausted from their long days, and this does not lead to familial comity.

"You'd think that the service member husband is just a louse and a deadbeat because he comes home and just sits on the sofa," one social worker explains, "but he's exhausted. . . . The civilian spouses have to understand, this man's been awake for twenty-six hours: how would you function?"

Perceived inequality heightens dissatisfaction. "There's a big difference between the shipyards that are building the new boats, the new submarines, the new aircraft carriers, etc. Those seem to have plenty of funds because that's where all the attention is. The shipyards that do routine maintenance or upkeep just to put the Band-Aid on it . . . those don't seem to be funded very well. Those are where sailors really struggle." This, according to one enlisted man's wife, is a direct effect of the budget cuts on shipbuilding and maintenance, and therefore on the physical and mental health of the fleet.

The increasing workload, especially ashore, limits service members' access to psychological and mental health support. "They [the command] don't allow service members to get help because they can't spare them. . . . They can't even give a service member an hour to seek family or marriage counseling. I've seen it. A sailor says 'my family is falling apart. My wife is going to leave me, she's going to take the kids,' and the answer [from the command] is 'we're really sorry, but we don't have time for this right now,'" said a clinical consultant, who understands that the Navy is pulled between completing necessary work and caring for its sailors and their families.

SEPARATE LIVES OF SPOUSES

The tasks of men and women in the service, constant work, the long—and getting longer—deployments, and time away from their spouses and children, all strain family lives and the routines developed during time together as well as apart. "You go weeks and sometimes months without solid communication. Email can be down sometimes. If you get a phone call it can be a delayed phone call. . . . It's complete separation from the person that you love."

"Our struggles are when he is home," says "Kim," the wife of a lieutenant commander, about their together-and-apart lives. "We wives are so used to somebody being somewhere else, so it's natural to speak of 'my house, my kids, my cars.'" She jokes that her husband makes fun of her, but notes that, in his absence, she single-handedly runs the family, including its finances. "He knows that the electricity is on, but I'm not sure he knows who the power company is. Who," she asks, "is dependent on whom?" She is matter-of-fact about the idea that Navy wives are dependent on their husbands.

The reuniting of a family is wonderful and a cause for celebration. But it's not always the way it's pictured in the media. "Having to give up the reins for a little bit and letting someone else take over is hard. [When he's away,] what I want to have for dinner, that's what we're having. What I want to watch, or where I want to go, the decision is mine and it's final. I don't need anyone else's agreement," another woman says, reiterating the changes needed to resume the sharing of family responsibility when a spouse returns from months away on an extended deployment.

The ombudsmen play central roles in helping families in need and ensuring that they know what to expect during deployments. However, even though the ombudsmen have the experience to help spouses, it is not always enough. "The families are just overextended," says an ombudsman and wife of a senior enlisted man on a large surface ship, "especially the younger ones, they call us for everything. They don't understand that the sailors' hands are tied. Their duty does come first. When they're at their job, and they're on the ship, that job has to come first."

One counselor for Navy families also sees how obstacles emerge from the other side of a marriage—for example, if the husband or wife doesn't understand the demands that are placed on their military spouse. "When I have couples who are dual military, it's easier because each one understands the stresses that the other one is undergoing. The civilian spouse . . . doesn't really appreciate the demands that a service member is under, and there's oftentimes conflict with that. Increased workloads often turn a difficult situation into a mess." This can lead to misunderstanding, suspicion, and sometimes infidelity, which leaves the couples to pick up the pieces or sees the family fall apart. "You have to have a strong marriage, to have a Navy marriage," says the wife of a master chief.

CHILDREN OF THE MILITARY

Often, the children of service members grow up with one parent absent for extended periods. As budgetary pressures mount, the extended periods lengthen. "The kids think it's normal that half the parents are home." The absence of a parent and the stress of deployments show in military children's behavior and often weigh on young children.

"She acts out a little bit," one parent said of her daughter, speaking about when her husband was on deployment. "She might be particularly irritated or emotional. . . . When she gets in trouble at home, cries that she 'wants her daddy.'" Just taking an equipment bag to the car, she adds, is enough to have a child demanding to know "where are you going?" Young children's feelings are often directed against the absent parent as well. "When he calls, she doesn't want to talk to him," one mother says. "There seems to be a bit of animosity there, like she's upset at him for leaving and doesn't understand that he has no choice and can't tell her when he'll return."

Young children can experience psychological effects from having their father or mother away for extended periods. The wife of an operations officer saw the effect on her son—in kindergarten at the time—when his father was on an extended ten-month deployment. "It got to the point where he'd sleep in the doorway of his room. He'd bring his pillow and his blanket and he'd lie there," she said. "It took months, MONTHS, for him to go back even when his dad came home. It took months for him to go back to his own bed. He still struggles with anxiety." Now, she says, "he's stopped having bad dreams and sleeping in the hall," but the stress remains.

As deployment cycles lengthened, older military children develop a tolerance for their parent's absence that one woman finds uncanny, almost unnatural. "In what normal world do you look at a kid, and the military parent says he'll be gone for anything under six months and they say 'okay!' and think nothing of it." And what effect does she see on the children overall? "They are the most resilient, independent, flexible little things that I have ever seen," she beams. "They are going to be amazing adults."

Children of Navy and Marine families develop various responses to the culture of lengthening absence. "Erin," whose eldest daughter—a twenty-two-year-old—has lived through her father's career in the Navy, describes the girl as "very bitter." She "bore the brunt" of her father's deployments and his absence from home for extended periods. When the daughter was in high school, budget cuts forced the cancellation of a shipyard contract for the submarine aboard which her father was serving. Compensating for the change required the family to move three times in one year. The girl changed schools each time. "She's very supportive of her dad, and our country, and she loves what he's done, but it bothers her about what we had to sacrifice."

Notwithstanding, Erin's younger twins are in high school; they attended elementary school while their father was on shore duty, and both want to go into the Navy. One of the twins, the boy, wants to be a pilot in the Navy, while the other, a girl, wants to go into the Navy nurse program. Military children grow up with a more complex and nuanced understanding of the world and politics. They see and listen to their parents' description of their jobs and what they mean. "They don't think the world is a good place . . . they just know that there are people out there trying to make it better."

The relationship between children and their absent parent can be hurt, even more so after an active-duty parent returns to civilian life. "When you're not in that uniform anymore, and your kids are more attached to one parent or another . . . they have that bond to one parent. The dad is the absentee dad," even when he returns. While kids may see their father or mother in the military as the "fun parent," as one spouse described, when they need real help—to bandage a scraped knee, for example—they go to the one they know and rely on, the parent who has been there.

Another spouse points out that her children go to her, even when her Navy husband is home, to get permission to go somewhere or do something. "That gets under his skin a little bit." "When my husband leaves," yet another mom indicates, "I become mom and dad, and when [my husband] comes home I go back to being just mom, but my son's used to me being everything, so he leaves my husband out of it. It's rough with the transitions." A parent's decreased time at home with children adds to this tension within families.

Families adjust and adapt for their children, creating ways to keep the absent parent a little less absent. One woman put up a map of the world for her children to track their father's ship, and made a place to put letters to send to him while he was on deployment. "You have to have some sort of system so that they would feel connected." "My husband would take an old-fashioned tape recorder and he would tape common phrases, 'Son, I heard you misbehaved at school today,' or 'I heard you got a really good report card today, I'm so proud of you!'" She illustrated an innovative way to keep her children connected to their father. "Because of how often we're forced to deploy now, we're coming up with these ways to connect our families." But ingenuity cannot substitute for proximity. Inadequate budgets greatly complicate the already difficult separation of families.

MISSING LIFE MOMENTS:
THE GOOD AND THE BAD

Having a family and being in the military means missing out on many important occasions, such as births of children, birthdays, anniversaries, and even the stressful moments of being a parent. As Jennifer, the wife of a sailor serving aboard a destroyer, says, the biggest issue with her husband's absence is missing "the milestones, big life events. . . . Luckily he's been here for all of the five children's births except for the first one."

One wife, who has an eleven-year-old and a thirteen-year-old, says of her husband's absence for training, work, or deployment: "He's been gone more than half of their lives, by far."

The birth of the EOD chief's daughter occurred during one of the rare instances he could get away from work. "I had my daughter on a weeknight," Melissa says. "She was born at 1:51 in the morning, and he was back at work at 5 a.m., so I stayed at the hospital by myself for two days." Melissa has a job because she believes she has no choice. Without her husband, it's harder to take care of their daughter. She pays for afterschool and evening care, even weekends, for the four-year-old. How does the girl feel about it? "She's young, so she doesn't have a good concept of time. He left, and we explained he was going to be gone a long time and everything." About a week later, her daughter asked, "Will Daddy be home today?"

Deployed sailors and Marines miss important moments of celebration. They are also away during family crises. One officer was nearing the end of a lengthy deployment in Afghanistan when his daughter was diagnosed with a serious disease. As his wife explained: "The doctor told me at the time that she was going to die . . . and that she would need dialysis and a kidney transplant for the barest hope of living. . . . A friend of mine, her husband was an admiral. He put a call in and sent someone looking for my husband in Kabul to get him on the phone so I could tell him myself." The initial diagnosis turned out to be wrong. The young girl lives with the disease but is otherwise healthy. But the husband "was not the same, for sure not the same when he came back. . . . When he got back from his deployment, the pace of his drinking . . . really ramped up." Eventually, he managed to get help, and at the time of the interview had been sober ten months. Family emergencies that are missed on deployment can also have a harmful effect on both service member and family.

Technology may offer some relief from the separation between service members and their families back in the United States. One Navy wife hopes that reliable Internet services and social media could be a bridge that would allow family events to be shared. "My husband missed my daughter's graduation from high school, but he's going to be able to watch my son's graduation by web-link," she says. "It is no substitute for the real thing, but it does allow a kind of sharing that distance otherwise prevents."

PATRIOTISM

Two major themes characterize the comments of spouses of active-duty officers and enlisted on whom the burden of decreasing budget resources has fallen: a deep loyalty to the United States and to those who serve it; and an abiding concern that those who have no connection to the military do not understand the personal lives of the men and women of America's armed forces.

As Becky, a submariner's wife, puts it, "I think sometimes, the civilian world, outside the military, we hear this a lot, and we even hear it from our family members, 'oh, well, you've just got such great benefits as a military family.' That's right. But we also give up our husbands and our spouses and our dads and our fathers. I think sometimes the civilian world just thinks it's like Hollywood . . . smart uniforms and duty stations on tropical islands. The fact is, it's not always easy and it's not always fun. It's a sacrifice for all of us."

Another woman echoes the concern that the division between civilian and military society prevents the former from understanding the latter: "There's this perception that we're a bunch of wives who are just freeloading; that we don't work, because we don't want to. The fact is, it's hard to have a job if you are married to a member of the military." Wives are sometimes derogatorily referred to as "dependapotamus" because they are "just there to reap the benefits of military lives."

This is not a social science study. The experiences related here are anecdotal. But the author has heard the concerns expressed in this chapter since before he received his commission as a naval officer. Over recent years, the difference between then and now is that the U.S. military has been asked to work harder with fewer resources. This hasn't produced new problems. It has sharpened old ones. Changing where you live every couple of years or so; uprooting kids when they've made new friends; raising children with a partner whose presence is increasingly uncertain; trying to make ends meet inside a support system that is in a state of constant and unpredictable flux; and the anxiety of a spouse or child about a distant loved one—any one of these circumstances by itself is stressful. Together, they demand intelligent, resilient, determined men and women to keep families together, preserve relationships, and raise happy, confident children up to and through their teenage years.

Neither spouses nor children expect medals. When the family member who serves receives one for excellence, they stand by proudly. Commanding officers know the families' sacrifices from personal experience and publicly recognize family members by name on important occasions. This does not allay wives' anxiety that American society fails to understand the increased demands on military families that accompany pared-down defense budgets. The nonrecognition of demands placed on the families whose anecdotes are related here are as much an element of seablindness as a decreasing fleet that struggles to meet its national commitments. Society's recognition of the stresses described here would offer comfort. Spouses and families sense the absence of this recognition.

Notwithstanding, there is no self-pity. "My whole adult

life, all I've known is to be a military spouse, and I am so darn proud to be one. I've lived my life accordingly, and I've sunk my whole identity into it." One sentiment expressed by the wife of a senior enlisted man united the experience of all the women who were interviewed: "We're doing this for our country."

CHAPTER X

REBUILDING AMERICAN SEAPOWER

The U.S. Marine Corps

Marines and their families face similar problems as the result of fewer resources and more to do. When the *Wasp*-class amphibious assault ship USS *Bataan* arrived in Norfolk in the late winter of 2012, she had been gone for ten and a half months, the longest deployment of any U.S. combatant since the Vietnam War. Because of increased demand and fewer ships, other amphibious ships and aircraft carriers also experienced deployments that far exceeded the traditional six-month standard. Former Chief of Naval Operations Admiral Jonathan Greenert was justifiably pleased to decrease ship deployment lengths to seven months. Notwithstanding, the nation's security needs cannot be gauged by the details of supplying them. The geographic distance of the United States from the key choke points of the world's oceans, and from allies and adversaries, gives Marines the special place they occupy in defending the United States.

Amphibious operations allow ground troops transported over the sea to disembark, assault an enemy, and establish a secure position into which more troops and equipment can flow and from which further military gains can be made. The U.S. Marine Corps exists to conduct amphibious operations as well as the more general mission of projecting power from ship to shore: this was one task USS *Bataan* accomplished on its lengthy deployment, during which it enforced the no-fly zone over Libya. Amphibious operations are more complex than is apparent from movies. Opposed landings, for example, require exceptional attention to detail. Marines need everything from weapons, ammunition, and fuel to medical supplies, food, and toilet paper. This matériel must arrive when needed. Disorganization in the loading and transportation of men and supplies is deadly.

Geography underscores the value of amphibious operations. Oceans account for more than 70 percent of the Earth's surface and provide access to the Earth's land masses, which explains their military use. Indeed, the history of combat begins with an amphibious landing as the Achaean forces led by Agamemnon landed at Troy. Later, in the seventeenth year of the Peloponnesian War, an Athenian fleet landed on Sicily in an amphibious operation and surreptitiously forced an entry to the coastal city known today as Catania.

In 55 BC, the Britons contested Julius Caesar's landing several miles northeast of Dover. Caesar used catapults aboard his ships to subdue the defenders on land. Nearly two millennia later, on the opposite side of the English Channel, Allied forces landed at Normandy. The thousands of ships that were essential to the operation offered the only way that a beachhead could be established to allow the flow of troops and war matériel that would liberate the continent from its Nazi occupiers. Unless the oceans are drained, their immensity in relation to the Earth's land mass will demand most great and many small powers to field amphibious forces.

America's amphibious arm, the U.S. Marine Corps, has played a vital role in ensuring American security since 1775. Since 1945, it has provided the United States with a rapidly deployable ground and air combat force that can assault and hold opposed landing zones, respond to international crises, evacuate American noncombatants in a foreign crisis, and serve as extra frontline troops when surge capacity is needed. However, the modern USMC has declined significantly, particularly in personnel, aircraft, and ship-to-shore delivery systems.

Without a revitalization of the USMC, the United States will lose the capability of its most effective power projection tool. At an absolute minimum, this will damage the ability of the United States to secure the dry land that forms the world's strategic choke points; cripple the nation's ability to apply highly effective ground forces quickly throughout most of the globe's vast littorals; and relegate to an inferior position the single military institution that best embodies the United States's fighting spirit.

FOUNDING AND EARLY HISTORY

The Marine Corps story begins with the Barbary Wars of the early 1800s. From the assault on Derna, when eight Marines and a small force of mercenaries marched 600 miles through the desert and defeated a force ten times their number, to the bloody assault on Chapultepec during the Mexican-American War, the Marines were an essential element of major campaigns.[1] A Marine detachment held the center of Andrew Jackson's line during the Battle of New Orleans.[2] Marines were deployed throughout the Caribbean and Asia between the Civil War and World War I on twenty-eight separate occasions.[3]

Persistent combat operations created a highly experienced and battle-hardened noncommissioned and junior officer corps that proved invaluable in World War I. Marines served as the frontline assault troops for the American Expeditionary Forces in Europe, taking a key role at the Battle of Belleau Wood, where they engaged much larger German forces, and where Gunnery Sergeant Dan Daly, the recipient of two Medals of Honor, inspired his men saying, "Come on, you sons of bitches, do you want to live forever?" Contrary to popular lore, the Germans probably never called the Marines "Devil Dogs." But the Imperial Army held a deep respect for the USMC. Official German dispatches described the Marines as "vigorous, self-confident, and remarkable marksmen."[4]

The USMC played an even more critical role during World War II, providing a significant share of infantry and ground-based air forces in the Pacific until the end of the war. Their record of courage and sacrifice in the

Pacific island-hopping campaign is unsurpassed in American combat history. Secretary of the Navy James Forrestal was present when the 2nd Battalion, 28th Marines raised the American flag over Mount Suribachi on the island of Iwo Jima in February 1945. His remark, that "the raising of that flag means a Marine Corps for the next five hundred years," was testimony to the Marine Corps's valor and effectiveness. Marine pilots and infantrymen held off waves of Japanese attackers on Wake Island, giving Americans a sorely needed lift during the dark month of December 1941. Marine aviators fought alongside their naval counterparts during the Battle of Midway. Names like Tarawa, Guadalcanal, Iwo Jima, and Okinawa will ring down the years because of the sheer willpower of thousands of young "Devil Dogs" on scraps of dirt and rock that dot the vast Pacific.

World War II marked the emergence of the modern Marine Corps. Unlike the other military services, it dominates a mission set rather than a domain. While the Army fights on land, the Air Force in the sky, and the Navy at sea, the Marines specialize in amphibious assault. This is a direct outgrowth of America's experience in World War II. While the British employed their Marines in commando units, and the Soviets used naval infantry as special operations forces, the USMC fought bloody pitched siege battles in the Pacific, often as the primary ground force, or, at a minimum, as the first wave of shock troops.

Much thought went into the Pacific campaign in advance. Marine strategists between the two World Wars looked at Japan's aggression in Asia and identified Tokyo as the most likely enemy in a Pacific war. They calculated that choking resource-poor Japan's sea lines of communication would be key to victory. They grasped that the forward bases from which the U.S. Navy could sever Japan's sea lines of communication were the islands of the Western Pacific. Out of this planning grew the idea that "the wartime mission of the Corps was to accompany the Fleet for operations ashore in support of the Fleet."[5]

From this grew the concepts of surprise, the use of mobile platforms to achieve it, reinforcement, and close air support that describe today's Marine Corps. This set of operational ideas is no less applicable to a possible war with China, where the objective of holding or retaking islands in the Western Pacific would provide secure positions from which the U.S. Navy could sink China's fleet or threaten its strategic imports—oil, for example—or the exports on which its economy importantly depends. Amphibious warfare is to seapower as caissons are to a bridge.

TODAY'S STRUCTURE

The Marine Corps is divided into multiple Marine expeditionary forces (MEFs). The MEF is structured for operations ranging from counterinsurgency to large-scale amphibious assaults. The core of each MEF is a Marine division, along with a Marine aircraft wing and Marine logistics group. These form a self-contained combat unit that can conduct high-end warfighting operations. Supplementing the MEF's Marine division, aircraft wing, and logistics group are one Marine expeditionary brigade (MEB) and one or more battalion-sized Marine expeditionary units (MEUs). Every Marine deployment, regardless of its size, is known as a Marine air-ground task force, or MAGTF.

MAGTFs consist of four elements. The ground combat element includes infantry with artillery support, and light and heavy armored units. The aviation combat element changes, depending on the size and configuration of the MAGTF, and can include a mix of transport and combat fixed-wing and helicopter aircraft. The logistics and command elements tie the MAGTF together and provide supplies and infrastructure for independent operations.

The MAGTF is designed for independent operations. Even a 2,500-strong MEU can operate independently for fifteen days. The USMC achieves this independence by retaining a diverse range of capabilities, especially in the Marine aircraft wing. Ground forces are subject to attack from different quarters. None is more deadly than from the air. Possession of their own combat aircraft gives Marines the support that their specific missions require. The USMC operates multiple types of transport and combat aircraft from both amphibious assault ships and shore bases. On the ground, the USMC also retains a significant armored component, which includes the heavy M1 Abrams battle tank.

The Marines partner with the Navy, their parent service, to create the modern expeditionary strike group (ESG). Originally conceived during the early 2000s to increase combat coverage globally, the ESG mimics the carrier strike group (CSG) in design, replacing the supercarrier with a large-deck amphibious assault ship and other transports, but retaining the protective screen of guided-missile destroyers and submarines. The ESG is designed to be a robust power projection force that can deploy and support Marines globally. In recent years, the ESG has taken on roles typically reserved for the CSG, such as conducting sustained airstrikes against ground targets. From mid-2015 until early 2016, no American aircraft carrier operated in the Mediterranean. Several different ESGs filled this coverage gap on occasion, independently conducting strikes against ISIS.

CONTEMPORARY OPERATIONS

The Marine Corps's reputation is well established as a result of its combat record in U.S. history, as well as by its discipline, high standards, and appearance. No less important is what the Corps contributes today to protecting American and allied interests. Marines will be needed in the future to evacuate Americans from crises abroad. Future amphibious missions could include retaking islands in the West Pacific that China might seize in a conflict where they seek, among other objectives, to extend their strategic reach.

The Marines might also be required to conduct opposed landings if Russia attacks the Baltic States. Middle East tensions are sharpening, and this trend is not likely to change soon. Because most of the region's important states have coastlines, amphibious operations could be required there. The USMC's experience throughout its history, and especially over the past three decades, prepares it for these as well as other possible conflicts.

The USMC has fulfilled each of its core missions of projecting power, responding to crises, participating in small wars, and forward engagement with partners and allies since 1945. But focusing on the Corps's actions since 1980 is most relevant for understanding the USMC today. The modern Marine Corps's major actions in Operation Desert Shield/Desert Storm (First Gulf War), the United Nations Unified Task Force and Operation II in Somalia, and Operation Iraqi Freedom (Second Gulf War) all demonstrate the utility of a powerful, agile Marine Corps with a diverse set of capabilities.

The First Gulf War was the most recent conventional conflict in American military history where the Marine Corps projected significant power. Combat in the Second Gulf War included conventional operations, but these lasted from the invasion's beginning on March 20, 2003, until Baghdad fell on April 9. Thereafter, military activity took on the character of the low-intensity conflict guerrilla operations that continue today.

In the First Gulf War, from August 1990 to February 1991, the USMC engaged in operations against Saddam Hussein's forces from the beginning of Operation Desert Shield, and later played a key role in the Desert Storm offensive. Marines were immediately deployed to Saudi Arabia as part of Operation Desert Shield, adding strength to the U.S. Army and Air Force contingents that had already arrived in the kingdom. Elements from multiple Marine detachments were deployed throughout the conflict, with USMC forces swelling to around 60,000 men by Desert Storm. These forces included infantry, armored units, and aircraft. Marine aviators who flew out of Saudi Arabian airfields were the spine of the air campaign that destroyed Iraq's air-defense system. Marine electronic warfare aircraft supplemented the USAF's and USN's electronic warfare fleet. Their extra numbers helped make the Coalition Air Campaign one of the most successful in history.[6]

Marine ground forces were some of the first to encounter Saddam's army on a large scale, participating in the Battle of Khafji, which halted the dictator's offensive into Saudi Arabia.[7] During the actual invasion of Iraq and Kuwait, USMC units fixed on Saddam's army, allowing for its decimation and subsequent retreat. Elements of the 1st and 2nd Marine Divisions made frontal attacks on entrenched Iraqi positions. This convinced Saddam that the major coalition assault would come from the Persian Gulf.[8] The embarked 4th and 5th MEBs forced Saddam to commit a large portion of the Iraqi army to the Kuwaiti shoreline, to prevent a potential amphibious assault.[9] As the threat of a U.S. Marine assault held the enemy in place, coalition forces swept through the desert in a massive flanking movement, encircling Saddam's prized army and routing it in a matter of days. In the air, on land, and at sea, the Marine Corps played a vital role in the Coalition victory.

Since 1990, the USMC's largest crisis response action has been its operations in Somalia in 1992. USMC ground troops were the first of the U.N.-approved and U.S.-led multinational task force (UNITAF) that entered Somalia's war-torn capital of Mogadishu in December 1992.[10] This operation helped restore order almost immediately. The USMC's discipline intimidated the warring Somali factions to reach a tense but workable peace in early 1993.

The film *Black Hawk Down* gave the unsuccessful effort to end the Somali civil war a major place in American popular culture. Multiple issues contributed to the mission's breakdown. The one that is most often overlooked is the removal of a major USMC presence in Somalia. Without tough, respected Leathernecks patrolling the streets of Mogadishu, Somali militias became bolder and eventually broke the uneasy U.N.-brokered peace. While special operations forces were effective in small strike operations, they are neither designed nor trained to provide the constant visible presence of USMC ground troops.

The USMC returned to Iraq in large numbers in 2003 and provided valuable surge capacity to the U.S. military during the first years of the Second Gulf War. Fighting two major ground wars in Afghanistan and Iraq put substantial strain on the post–Cold War U.S. Army. Marine infantry filled the gap. The Iraq and Afghan wars spurred a major expansion in the USMC, which had shrunk significantly due to post–Cold War budget cuts. By the height of the Iraq War in 2006, the Corps was fielding 200,000 active-duty soldiers.

Despite aging equipment, all elements of the USMC performed their missions effectively. The service reprised the counterinsurgency role it had first conducted over a century earlier in the Caribbean and the Philippines. Marine forces conducted major operations from the earliest days of the conflict. After the Second Battle in the urban combat zone of Fallujah, four Marines received the Navy Cross for their conduct during the bloodiest engagement of the Iraq War. Marine aviation also provided a large amount of logistical and combat air support to Army and Marine ground units. The USMC's ability to conduct independent, extended operations enabled these contributions.

RELEVANCE

The Marine Corps provides American policy makers with high value at relatively low cost. In 2016, this amounted to about $26 billion, or about 20 percent of the Department of the Navy's total annual budget. Agile, mobile, highly disciplined forces that can operate nearly autonomously are particularly valuable in an increasingly volatile environment where the possibilities of noncombatant evacuations, failing states, and continued operations against terrorists are good. The Marine Corps provides insurance against these and other contingencies, while also boosting the nation's entire combat capability.

The ability to conduct amphibious operations against hardened targets is a critical element of American conventional deterrence. Having a strong USMC tells Chinese leadership that the United States possesses the capability to contest China's effort at increasing its influence in the West Pacific islands within which Beijing would like to operate with impunity. Few measures enforce international usage and ensure allied or friendly state sovereignty better than a Marine air-ground task force, supported by an embarked Marine expeditionary brigade.

The USMC's ability to respond to contingencies and crises increases the global power and flexibility of American policy. An embarked Marine expeditionary unit can transition from conducting stabilization missions in Africa, striking insurgent targets in the Middle East, delivering relief supplies in Asia, and supplementing NATO forces in Latvia in a matter of weeks, given proper logistics. In an increasingly turbulent global environment, such flexibility is invaluable. Finally, a robust USMC provides substantial surge capacity to American ground and air forces. Without this surge capacity, the United States is less able to fight a major ground conflict.

The USMC provides this utility at a comparatively low cost. Only 4 to 6 percent of the United States's annual military budget goes to the Marine Corps, despite its usefulness as America's most flexible military tool.

CONTEMPORARY ISSUES

The Corps faces three issues today: personnel, aircraft, and amphibious ship-to-shore delivery systems. These three categories depend on one another for successful combat operations and are linked by the consequences to their effectiveness of years of budget reductions.

PERSONNEL

Marine personnel issues are connected to force size. A smaller force not only decreases the USMC's ability to fulfill its core missions but also puts stress on Marines, including aviators, who are frequently deployed. American policy makers must choose between a smaller, cheaper USMC that can carry out fewer missions, or a larger and adequately funded force that can execute and adapt its historical mission as the world grows more turbulent.

During the 1990s, the Marines fielded 190,000 active-duty soldiers. A force of this size was able to dedicate nearly half its number to a major ground campaign in Iraq while retaining the ability to respond to international crises. At the end of the Obama administration, following the post-Iraq drawdown, sequestration, and other Defense Department budget cuts, the USMC had shrunk to 182,000 soldiers. This is the smallest the force has been since before 9/11, when it could field only 172,000 soldiers. Multiple sources within the Corps, including its 35th commandant, General James Amos, have stated that the smallest force the USMC can field while still meeting its global commitments is 174,000, close to its size in 2000.

A smaller force places greater stress on the Corps, because fewer officers and men are required to perform the same, or a larger, number of missions. Since the 1990s, the U.S. military has attempted to ensure a 1:3 "deployment-to-dwell time ratio" for its warfighters. The ratio means that, for each month deployed, Marines spend three months at home. If current operational requirements do not increase, the USMC will not be able to maintain this 1:3 ratio without at least 182,000 active-duty Marines—the level of the Corps as of this writing.

The minimum acceptable force would allow service personnel to spend only two months at home for each month deployed. Not only does this ratio undermine morale but it also decreases training time between deployments and leads to more operational accidents, especially among the Marines' aviation community. In 2015, Marine Corps aviation accidents reached a five-year high—of eighteen deaths—three months before the end of the year.[11] The Obama administration proposed in its 2016 budget request that the Marine Corps be cut to 179,000.

Evidence of increased stress on a smaller pool of soldiers already exists. The fraction of forces deployed overseas has remained the same since January 2014, despite a

10,000-man cut in the size of the Corps. That higher operational tempo has taken its toll, especially on KC-130 and V-22 squadrons. V-22 squadron members currently receive fewer than two months at home per month deployed.

Marine retention rates have declined since 2010. In response, Marine leadership has aggressively recruited first-term Marines for new contracts. In November 2015, the Corps reported that twenty-three military occupational specialties (MOSs)—a defense-wide term for particular jobs in the uniformed services—required significant reenlistment to ensure that those tasks are properly executed. Among the specialties of particular concern are infantrymen, motor transport, data communications, artillery, and aviation. The USMC reckoned that it would need 7 percent to 20 percent of first-term Marines in each MOS to reenlist for another contract to preserve combat readiness. Although the Marines met their retention goals for 2015, the fact that major concerns exist in retaining under one-fifth of first-term personnel indicates long-term retention problems.

Extra funding would help the USMC increase its recruiting and expand by several thousand Marines. Even a minimal expansion would decrease the strain on currently deployed personnel, aiding retention rates by improving morale throughout the force. The total budget of the Department of the Navy should be sufficiently increased to add $8 billion annually to the USMC budget. This would raise the current USMC budget of $24 billion to around $32 billion, similar to the level of funding that a 200,000-strong Corps received at the height of the Iraq War between 2007 and 2009.

As things stand today, the USMC is divided into three Marine expeditionary forces. Each MEF contains a full division, an aircraft wing, a logistics group, a Marine expeditionary brigade, and three Marine expeditionary units (aside from the 3rd MEF, which has only one MEU). Additionally, the USMC must maintain a reserve MEF for training purposes, containing 40,000 personnel. Plans require each MEF to be able to respond to any sort of global crisis; the MEU is dispatched for such contained operations as responding to the 2010 Haiti earthquake and limited operations in Afghanistan; the MEB is employed for such wider-spread operations as the Battle of Marjah, the large 2010 coalition combat operation in the Afghanistan War; and the full MEF with its aircraft wing and division is used for high-end warfighting.

Counting the United States's current commitments, the USMC must provide:

- Seven MEUs (ideally nine) for deployment on expeditionary strike groups globally. Historically, four MEUs are Pacific based, and three are Atlantic based.

- Full crisis coverage in the Asia-Pacific. A full MEF is based in Japan, along with the forward-deployed elements of the United States Navy.

- Enough additional forces to respond to other global contingencies in four other theaters of operations (Africa, the Middle East, Europe, and South America).

Thus, the United States is planning to leave approximately 100,000 men, divided into two divisions, two brigades, two aircraft wings, six MEUs, and two logistics groups to respond to every global contingency outside of the Asia-Pacific. One hundred thousand soldiers and aviators must be prepared to conduct amphibious landings in the Black Sea, reinforce ground troops in a counterinsurgency campaign in the Middle East, conduct peacekeeping missions in the Caribbean, and deliver disaster relief supplies to Africa simultaneously.

In the Pacific, slightly fewer than 50,000 men must be prepared to conduct missions ranging from opposed landings against entrenched enemy forces in the South China Sea, delivering tsunami relief supplies to Asian island states, and intercepting enemy strike aircraft. The United States is placing the lion's share of its crisis response tasks in the hands of 180,000 overworked Marines. Unless the budget trends of the Obama years are reversed, this force is likely to continue shrinking. An increase of $10 billion in funding would enable an expansion equivalent to another division and brigade. This would greatly ease the stress on active-duty Marines and open up new possibilities for forward deployment globally.

If the USMC were to engage in a Gulf War–style operation in the near future, it would have to commit two divisions, two brigades, and a MEU, along with 406 combat aircraft. In 1991, the USMC had nearly 200,000 active-duty personnel. The world was more stable then than now. The USSR had disappeared as a major threat. China seemed more a partner than a potential rival. Iran was still recovering from its war with Iraq, and terrorism had not risen to the level of a persistent international threat.

It takes little imagination to identify areas where an extra MEB or MEU would be pivotal. A forward-deployed MEB in Australia or the Philippines would bolster American operations in the Pacific. A forward-deployed MEU in Greece or Haifa would remind Russia and Iran that the United States retains major commitments in the Middle East. An additional Marine air group and MEB in Estonia would increase America's ability to counter regional Russian expansionism.

Conversely, if the current trend continues, a future U.S. president may be forced to choose which crisis to respond to. Does the possibility of an embassy siege in Cuba carry more or less weight than providing air support to local forces engaged in fighting North African terrorists? Should the 3rd MEB be deployed to a revamped Subic Bay to deter China, or to Romania as part of the Black Sea Area Support Team? Regardless, a smaller USMC means that the United States will be less able to respond to crises and less able to deter situations that otherwise could develop into a major conflict.

AIRCRAFT

Before the airplane became an effective combat instrument, the artillery fire that preceded an infantry assault was the bane of ground forces. Once combat planes were sufficiently deadly and could be coordinated with armor as well as ground operations generally, air support of ground forces in action became a necessity. In anticipation of the event and during the five months before D-Day, Allied air forces virtually destroyed the Luftwaffe's fighters, killing one-fourth of the Nazis' fighter pilots during May 1944, the month before the invasion.[12]

General Eisenhower's son, John S. D. Eisenhower, who graduated from West Point on June 6, 1944, was driving with his father later the same month in northern France and found the logjam of Allied combat and logistic vehicles chaotic and inconsistent with the orderly doctrines he'd learned at the U.S. Military Academy. He said to his father, "You'd never get away with this if you didn't have air supremacy." Ike was not amused. He replied, "If I didn't have air supremacy, I wouldn't be here."[13]

Marine experience in the Korean War supported Eisenhower's retort. In March 1950, Marines were ordered to destroy units of the North Korean 4th Division, which had crossed the Nakdong River and established a position on a commanding ridge within the Allies' western defensive perimeter. Marine F4U Corsairs provided ground forces with reconnaissance and close air support during the battle for the ridge, in which the 2nd Battalion, 5th Marines experienced 60 percent casualties.[14] The North Koreans were pushed back to where they could no longer threaten the port city of Pusan. During the engagement, USMC close air support attacked the enemy so close to Leatherneck ground positions that John S. Thach, the Navy officer commanding the carrier escort from which the Corsairs flew, became concerned at how close the air support actually was. Two decades later, then-Admiral Thach (USN, ret.) told an interviewer:

They [the USMC F4Us] had to fly right down over the ridge, then start shooting right away, or start shooting really before they got to the ridge, with rockets. After the first one came down, the Marines on the ridge were standing up and looking. They wanted to watch the shells! The last pilot that came down after they'd put these rockets in there called the controller again and he said: "Would you please have the people in the front row be seated? I can see the back of their heads in my gunsight and it makes me nervous!" That's how close these Corsairs were.[15]

Marine aviation remains a critical part of the Corps as a whole. The organic Marine aircraft wing allows the USMC to operate without extensive support from the Air Force or the Army. This greatly increases the Marines' ability to conduct expeditionary operations in high-threat environments. Notwithstanding the Defense Department's arthritic prostration before the statues of joint equipment, joint tours for officers, joint doctrine, joint total asset visibility—to name a very few joints—the ability to act decisively, swiftly, and effectively cannot be separated from the ability to act without having to coordinate everything.

A lethal, experienced aircraft wing that can conduct every land-based combat mission is indispensable to the USMC's warfighting success. Increased finances are needed to replace old airframes, repair degraded equipment, ensure sufficient spare parts, train mechanics, and provide quality hours for pilots who fly combat missions.

Known as "America's Third Air Force," the Marine aircraft wing is arguably the most diverse aerial service in the United States military. The USMC operates a wide variety of fixed- and rotary-wing aircraft from ships and shore installations to support Marines during opposed landings. The F/A-18 A++, C, and D Hornets form the backbone of Marine strike and air superiority capabilities, typically operated from shore installations. The AV-8B Harrier II ground attack aircraft can be operated from both landing helicopter dock vessels (LHDs) and landing helicopter assault ships (LHAs). Because of the Harrier's vertical takeoff and landing/short takeoff and vertical landing (VTOL/STOVL) capabilities, it can also operate from small remote fields. In the near future, both aircraft will be replaced by the VTOL/STOVL-capable F-35B Lightning II strike fighter.

Marine EA-6B Prowlers have been the only land-based tactical electronic warfare aircraft operated by U.S. forces since the First Gulf War. The KC-130 tanker's ability to refuel other planes in flight extends the range of Marine fixed-wing aircraft. Rotary-wing aircraft include the AH-1W and AH-1Z attack helicopters and the CH-53E heavy-lift helicopter.

The most modern Marine aircraft is the tilt-rotor MV-22 Osprey, used for transport and force insertion. The Osprey has two jet-driven propellers mounted on its wings. The wings can be tilted up to allow takeoff from a helicopter-sized landing pad. Then they are tilted forward so that the aircraft can fly in a straight line at speeds much higher than any helicopter. The platform carries twenty-four combat troops. It gives an amphibious force at sea greater flexibility in choosing from where to launch an assault than would slower helicopters or even slower surface landing craft.

The Marines' diverse aircraft wing, especially when working with U.S. Navy fighters, can effectively dominate enemy airspace against a majority of enemy targets. However, Marine aviators first must be able to get their planes and helicopters aloft.

A decade of warfare has severely degraded Marine aviation. From 2001 onward, Marine aviators were deployed in the harsh desert and high-plateau operating environments of Iraq and Afghanistan, constantly supporting American and allied ground troops. A high operational tempo delayed or prevented necessary maintenance and encouraged mechanics to pursue quick fixes. Doing so meant cannibalizing old or damaged aircraft. After Marine withdrawal from Iraq in 2010, budget cuts forced USMC and Navy department leadership to choose between funding combat units and maintenance.

To sustain readiness, the Marines chose the former, resulting in a further decline in the condition of the aircraft wing. In addition to reducing the Marines by 10,000, sequestration cuts also forced the USMC to cut maintenance personnel to preserve immediate operational capability. To compound the dilemma, the tempo of combat operations in the Middle East caused the USMC to cut back on long-term maintenance and repair training for its mechanics; instead, quick fixes were prioritized to sustain combat missions.

As the Obama administration ended, the Marine aircraft wing was in a state of crisis. Damaged airframes were cannibalized for their spare parts. Limited funds that did not cover proper maintenance, combined with a fleet whose age required more than the usual maintenance, all but eliminated the purchase of new parts. The CH-53E troop transport helicopter was no longer in production. An important result is that spare parts are increasingly difficult to find, aside from those aboard grounded aircraft.

Additionally, the USMC declined to buy the F/A-18E/F Super Hornet fighter aircraft in the late 1990s.

That decision assumed that the F-35B would be ready for frontline service as scheduled in 2006.[16] It wasn't. Instead of gliding smoothly from the middle-aged Hornets to the stealthy F-35s in the late 2000s, the F-35 program's decade-long developmental delay has forced the Corps to refurbish old F/A-18Cs from the Boeing boneyard and extend their lifespan from 6,000 to 8,000 flight hours. Personnel cuts have hampered service life extension program (SLEP) efforts. The consequences have been felt throughout the sea services: the Navy's reallocation of engineers to refurbish USMC Hornets caused a major readiness deficit in its own F/A-18 E/F fleet.[17]

The self-consuming cycle emaciated the Marine aircraft wing. In 2009, between 73 percent and 77 percent of the aviation wing's F/A-18 variants were mission capable. In the same year, only 63 percent of the heavy-lift CH-53 Super Stallion helicopters were mission capable, and 39 percent of the large helos were fully mission capable. As President Obama left office, 31 percent of USMC F/A-18s and 28 percent of USMC CH-53s were just flyable.[18]

"Readiness" sounds like a term that Defense Department civilians and military toss around often. It is. This does not detract from its seriousness. As then–Secretary of Defense Donald Rumsfeld noted in 2004, "You go to war with the army you have, not the army you want or wish to have at a later time."[19] This remark applies to other services, to ships, tanks, and planes . . . and to readiness. A reduced Marine Corps ability to transport men and equipment from ship to shore, or to protect Marines from air attack once they have arrived, would restrict the United States's ability in hostilities from the Baltic States to the Mediterranean to the South China Sea.

The lesson of the CH-53 heavy-lift helicopter is instructive. In early 2015, USMC aviation leadership identified growing safety concerns in the CH-53E fleet and its variants, which are used for heavy lifting and anti-submarine warfare in the USMC and Navy.[20] A January 2015 spot check of CH-53 airframes yielded disturbing results: 20 of the 28 examined helicopters were found to have potentially fatal fuel line and wiring mishaps. These events, along with other poor inspection results and several crashes, prompted the deputy commandant for aviation to initiate the Super Stallion Independent Readiness Review (SSIRR), which resulted in the fleet's grounding in 2015.[21] The SSIRR has given way to a decade-long reset project, aimed at returning all 149 remaining CH-53Es to full combat readiness.

But even with complete success, the USMC would, by its own estimate, be short 50 airframes. Unlike the F/A-18C, of which there is an abundance whose service lives can be extended to supplement the fleet, there are no additional CH-53Es in storage for refurbishment.[22] In any major conflict, the USMC would have to press every aircraft in its CH-53 fleet into service. The impressment would not approach fulfilling combat requirements.[23]

While the higher-profile F/A-18s receive most of the public attention on readiness issues, the CH-53 fleet's deficiency is both greater and arguably more consequential. The Air Force and Navy can perform the same missions as the USMC's tactical fighter force, even during expeditionary operations. However, without enough CH-53E heavy-lift helicopters carrying every piece of equipment in the USMC's inventory (from Humvees to artillery to armored personnel carriers), the Corps's ability to conduct expeditionary operations and secure bridgeheads at sea and inland would be at risk.

The issue is broader than combat readiness. The precipitous decline in airframe condition across the fleet has resulted in more accidents for Marine aviators, further compounding the USMC's personnel and training problems. From January to September 2015, eighteen Marine aviators were killed in aviation accidents, greater than the 2012 record of fifteen killed.[24] Marine fighter pilots currently train between eight and nine hours per month (less than one hour per day), rather than the fifteen to twenty-five quality hours per month needed to ensure proficiency. "Quality hours" means time spent training for actual combat as opposed to simply flying an aircraft from one place to another.

Insufficient training leads to more accidents, which kills aviators and damages or destroys airframes, decreasing fleet size even further. The state of rotary aviation is even worse. Major accidents like the September 2015 Camp Pendleton crash—which killed one and injured eighteen—result from poor maintenance, whereas incidents like the January 2016 CH-53 collision stem from insufficient flight time.[25] The Trump administration has a large task ahead to provide the budgets and supplies that Marine aviation needs to reverse further deterioration.

Finally, the current deployment structure overworks

particular elements of the air wing, while balking at deploying others. V-22 squadrons are modern and highly capable. They are deployed more frequently than almost any other unit. The V-22 serves as the aviation combat element (ACE) in the Marine air-ground task force (MAGTF). The ACE is the sole aerial component in smaller MAGTFs, particularly in Marine expeditionary unit (MEU)–sized deployments. All other airframes, particularly the heavy-lift CH-53 and the AH-1 attack helicopter squadrons, only deploy as supplemental forces alongside the V-22.

Dubious personnel management, training, and rigid funding procedures have brought the Marine aircraft wing to its current state, but these are motes compared to the lack of funds that would have bought needed replacements for aging equipment sooner. This situation is very different from the USMC's participation in the 1991 Gulf War. The Marine Corps's 3rd Aircraft Wing deployed forty squadrons to Saudi Arabia and kept operations running smoothly throughout the conflict. Immediately before the invasion of Kuwait, the USMC deployed seventy-eight F/A-18s and eighty-four AV-8Bs to Saudi Arabia. A similar buildup today would require the USMC to deploy all but nine of its airworthy F/A-18s, and all of its airworthy AV-8Bs to the combat theater in question.[26] The USMC's CH-53 fleet will not be able to meet combat needs in major contingency operations.

The regrettable state of the USMC's aircraft wing is harming its capacity to defend American interests globally. If called upon to form a major bridgehead by conducting an opposed landing, the USMC would not be able to field more than ten or twenty fighter aircraft to defend its ground troops. Its ground attack aircraft would not fare any better. Unable to find replacement parts for older airframes, the Marines would need to cannibalize to repair battle damage, further shrinking needed ground support. Even if Marines could secure an initial beachhead, expanding it to secure initial gains and allow the safe arrival of additional forces might prove beyond their reach. The Corps's transport helicopters run the real risk of falling out of the sky.

American society has not been so politically divided in over a century and a half. Both major political parties are split, and the influence of the more radical factions is waxing. The 2016 presidential primaries experienced a small but troubling measure of political violence. This accelerated following the 2016 election. Growing cultural divisions are concentrated on college campuses, where the suppression of free speech claims a position of respect that was once accorded to freedom of speech. We are in a cold civil war where even the need for security is open to question.

None of the military services can escape this climate, in which traditional supporters of a strong defense have divided into groups that fear deficits more than the possibility that the United States would lose the ability to defend its interests at great distances from our homeland. Parts of both major political parties feel the longtime pull of American isolationism. The Marine Corps is particularly vulnerable, because it embodies the warrior ethos, the highest expression of manliness and pugnacious fighting spirit in this society, characteristics that will be increasingly questioned as the cold civil war grows colder.

The forward-leaning officers and men of the Corps, ever willing to respond to crises and defeat enemies—with or without the help of other services—not only perform an important practical service in protecting Americans but also embody the spiritual center of gravity of a nation that has, thus far, excelled because of energy, drive, ingenuity, and resolute defiance in the face of some very determined enemies. If this core is excised—whether by incremental budget reductions, through forgetfulness that our freedom is best protected at a distance from our borders, or by a rejection of the manly virtue that the military services (the Marine Corps most conspicuously) represent, or some combination of these—the nation will lose the most spirited part of its soul.

One demonstration of this spiritedness is that the majority of Marines, regardless of their specialty, want to be deployed. They are attracted, not repelled, by the prospect of danger. Long hours become less relevant when they perform the missions they signed up to master in the service of deterring and defeating America's enemies. When these same Marines are posted to bases in North Carolina, where they are greeted with a host of problems that are the result of insufficient resources and sporadic organizational support, the opportunities for disillusionment grow along with the temptation to look for work elsewhere. The issues that plague the Marine aircraft wing morph into personnel problems, and make smooth the highway to more decline.

Increased funding is not the only short-term solution to improve Marine aviation. Reorganizing the aerial component of the MAGTF to allow different squadrons to deploy more frequently and increasing flexibility in the use of funds would help increase morale and improve readiness and maintenance. Still, there is no substitute for funding when it comes to obtaining new parts, tools, and airframes. In the current situation, every additional dollar goes a long way.

AMPHIBIOUS DELIVERY

Ironically, amphibious delivery is the least discussed set of Marine capabilities. The USMC's explicitly amphibious mission ought to direct attention to how best to deliver men and matériel from ship to shore. However, the Marines largely rely on the Navy for transport and deployment. This means that the actual deployment mechanisms get lost in debates about various types of amphibious assault ships that the Marines and Navy use. Although these two discussions are connected, the core issue for the Marines is amphibious delivery vehicles. They are in need of a major overhaul.

Amphibious delivery is cheaper than aerial delivery for transporting large quantities of men and matériel from ship to shore. Even the critical V-22 or the heavy-lift CH-53 cannot deliver heavy assets to shore as amphibious vehicles can. Thus, amphibious delivery vessels are integral to the Marine Corps mission.

The USMC uses two platforms as their combat-capable amphibious delivery systems: the landing craft air cushion (LCAC) and assault amphibious vehicle (AAV). The fan-powered LCAC can carry up to 75 tons of men and vehicles to shore on its flat bottom.[27] Using LCACs, the USMC can launch a pre-dawn attack from over the horizon of any exposed coastline in the world—from as far as

500 miles away and twenty-four hours before a landing. The LCAC's speed and payload allows the Marine Corps to conduct amphibious assaults without visibly building up assets until the last possible moment, helping to ensure the element of surprise.

The other major USMC delivery mechanism is the AAV. The result of a marriage between an armored personnel carrier and a DUKW, or "duck" boat, the AAV is designed to provide Marines with a survivable amphibious platform that is useful on land.[28] Despite its slow speed in the water, the AAV, when combined with the LCAC, provides the Marine Corps with an effective infantry delivery mechanism.

Both the LCAC and AAV fleets have experienced significant wear and tear throughout their decades in service. The AAV first operated in 1972 and, following the cancellation of the expeditionary fighting vehicle (EFV) program, is slated for retirement in 2030, after over half a century of service. While the USMC has replaced the EFV program with the amphibious combat vehicle (ACV) program, the Corps must still maintain its existing AAV fleet for the next decade. There is no way to avoid paying for the AAV life-extension program. Withholding funds to cut costs will only add to the Marine Air Wing's current predicament. Similarly, LCAC life extension programs must receive proper funding, as must the ship-to-shore connector (SSC) program. Like the LCAC, the SSC rides over water and beach on a cushion of air. To accommodate increasingly heavy combat equipment, the new vessel will be larger and more powerful than the LCAC.

Other smaller programs, like the life-extension program for the light armored vehicle (LAV), require steady funding for the near future. Steady funding for the U.S. military is like a "solution" to the Middle East's problems: highly desirable but eternally elusive. Marine Corps LAVs provide MAGTFs with amphibious-capable fast reconnaissance units. Increasing interchangeability with the U.S. Army's Stryker family of vehicles would help mitigate costs, but consistent funding, which the chance of reimposed sequestration threatens, remains critical.

The long-range missile capabilities in the Russo-Sino-Iranian anti-access and area denial (A2AD) network have forced the Corps to reevaluate its previous delivery system requirements. The LCAC remains unrivaled in delivering heavy vehicles like M1 Abrams main battle tanks from ship to shore, but amphibious assault ships can no longer assume that deploying from over the horizon will offer them protection. A prolonged amphibious assault akin to Iwo Jima will also be impossible in the age of precision weapons, unmanned systems, and thoroughly distributed anti-ship and anti-air missiles.

In a report published by the Center for Strategic and Budgetary Assessments entitled *Advancing beyond the Beach: Amphibious Operations in a Brave New World*, Bryan Clark and Jesse Sloman make it clear that unarmored landing craft operating close to shore for extended periods of time will be destroyed by cheap anti-ship weapons.[29] In addition, modern commanders are unlikely to position a capital ship directly offshore in a highly contested environment. The days of Marines storming contested beaches under the shadow of battleship guns, or with an aircraft carrier in sight, are past. The USMC must shift its traditional assault paradigm.

Clark and Sloman make several recommendations that will help the USMC create new operational concepts for amphibious assault. First, they suggest the Marines establish advanced bases that house up to a battalion of troops in contested littorals.[30] These bases can create gaps in an enemy A2AD network, using anti-ship and anti-air missiles along with unmanned systems and electronic warfare measures to disrupt enemy defense lines. This combination could be even more effective if it is paired with a larger attack submarine and small surface combatant fleet. While Marine forces harass land targets, submarines and small frigates and corvettes can establish limited sea control, constraining an adversary's ability to operate. Complex small island chains, like the Philippines and Ryukyu Islands, could become naval trenches, providing an initial bulwark against Chinese forces.[31] Such an operational concept would require changing the purpose of Marine and naval amphibious raids. Rather than using them as power projection tools, Marine and naval raids against coastal installations would support sea control missions by destroying shore-based anti-ship, anti-air, and command and control sites.

Second, Clark and Sloman argue that the Marines should focus on range for ship-to-shore connectors, rather than building hybrid vehicles like the AAV and its canceled replacement, the EFV.[32] A larger number of faster, modernized LCACs that can be deployed from further out to sea will spend less time in the risk zone close to shore, increasing their chances of safely delivering Marines and vehicles onto a beach.

Third, Clark and Sloman emphasize airborne delivery

for initial assault waves, because of the greater range on airframes like the MV-22 as compared to the LCAC.[33] Developing lighter vehicles, like the internally transportable vehicle (ITV), would allow the Marines to benefit from the Osprey's full combat radius of 400 nautical miles. Making the most of this concept, the USMC could equip an entire MEU or MEB for air and airborne assault (helicopter and parachute insertion), much as the Army equips the brigade combat teams of the 82nd and 101st Airborne Divisions.

Amphibious delivery systems enable all Marine Corps operations. Next to proper personnel levels and funding, effective, modern amphibious delivery systems in the water and the air are critical to ensure that the USMC remains combat effective.

UNCERTAIN FUTURE

Today's Marine Corps is at a tipping point. The corrosive effects of a decade of constant warfare, combined with executive and legislative branch budget cuts, have gutted the USMC's aircraft wing, undermined training throughout the Corps, and slashed it to its lowest levels in modern history.

During peacetime, ignoring military readiness has been commonplace. Accidents, rather than combat fatalities, account for the death toll. For the public, the chain of accidents, reports of unpreparedness, and training deficiencies do not reach the visibility of local crimes, national scandal, or international events. Marines deploy in expeditionary strike groups and conduct training and presence missions globally. The Corps produces a "Top Shot" montage each week, transmitting those missions to the American public. The handful of accidents and mechanical failures, the dwindling force, the aging AAV and LCAC fleet—all these issues are nearly invisible to general audiences during peacetime.

In wartime, the situation changes. It is easy to imagine a future conflict in which the Marines are called on to deploy, within forty-eight hours, to the Baltics, Cyprus, the Mediterranean coast, or a small Pacific island. Those same poorly maintained helicopters, irreplaceable fighter jets, and under-prepared Marines will know the pressures and stresses of combat.

A Scenario It is easy to envision a future conflict in which a Marine expeditionary unit (MEU) forms a bridgehead on a hostile beach and hunkers down to await follow-on support. They expect CH-53 heavy-lift choppers to deliver supplies, artillery, and vehicles to their forward operating positions, while F/A-18s and a handful of F-35s provide air cover from makeshift airfields or a large-deck ship offshore. Once fully constituted, this force is designed to sustain itself for weeks, protecting the lodgment it has created until additional forces can arrive.

On arrival, one of the CH-53s transporting an M777 howitzer—one of the USMC's mainstay fire support systems—experiences a mechanical failure and crashes. Over the next week, combat attrition and mechanical failures decimate the CH-53 force that has been deployed to the operation. This slows additional necessaries destined for forward positions to a trickle. The F/A-18 fleet fares little better: a combination of insufficient training and poor repair cripples half of the twenty-four Hornets based at the Marine airfields in under ten days. The twelve-strong squadron of high-tech F-35 strike fighters must take on more operational tasks than expected. Without heavy-lift helicopters, spare parts for damaged F-35s are few and far between.

Although follow-on forces from the regionally based Marine expeditionary brigade (MEB) slowly arrive, the USMC's personnel cuts have decreased the number of troops available for rapid reaction. The MEU, typically 2,200 strong, has shrunk to 1,800 due to force cuts. The reinforcing MEB, typically able to field a reinforced infantry regiment with additional support forces, can provide only another 2,000 ground forces, along with a handful of engineers and combat support personnel. Few mechanics arrive, and even fewer among those are sufficiently trained to repair damaged CH-53s and F/A-18s. This small force of Marines, isolated and lacking adequate support, is slowly driven back to the beachhead and into the sea.

This scenario is imaginable if the trend of declining forces established during the Obama years were to continue. Even more likely is the possibility that the United States will not be able to respond to contingencies at all. The Marines will not have enough troops to provide the United States with a rapid reaction force if the Obama force cuts persist. U.S. leaders will be placed in an impossible bind: they must choose between placing Marines in hopeless situations and refusing to send forces to a crisis in which an enemy challenges American interests.

If a Chinese invasion of Japan's Senkaku Islands in

the East China Sea required U.S. action to honor treaty obligations and ensure Japan's security, an opposed amphibious landing would likely be necessary. A decimated Marine force that could not accomplish its mission would result in the loss of American lives, those of our Japanese partners, and call into doubt the alliance that has served the interests of the United States and Japan for two-thirds of a century.

The Marine Corps is essential to American seapower. It is a means of projecting power from the sea to the land and underscores the truth that commanding the seas is not an end in itself but rather a means to affect events on land, by diplomacy, good works, crisis response, deterrence if possible, and war where necessary. If political leadership fails to address the problems that this chapter describes, the United States will find a withered arm where a strong one is needed to assist in protecting vital choke points, rescuing Americans in mortal danger abroad, and responding swiftly to crises on land that neither land- nor aircraft carrier–based air or missiles can.

This requires halting and then reversing the Marine Corps's declining size. It necessitates renewed attention to, and resources for, mechanical and technical training. It demands the purchase of more fixed-wing aircraft to ensure support for Marines who fight on the ground and additional CH-53K helicopters to transport men and equipment from ship to shore. Eventually unmanned aerial vehicles that can reconnoiter, gather intelligence, and launch supporting strikes will be needed to increase combat power. Finally, an increase in funding for the Department of the Navy of about $8 billion is needed so that the USMC can carry out these initiatives and expand the force to 200,000 men.

This will allow the USMC to remain a forward-deployed fighting force that safeguards America's global interests and responds to international crises. Without such action, the United States faces the prospect that the corrosive effects of recent years will spread in the military service that is best suited to deter or, if need be, restrain a potential enemy on very short notice. America's leaders would then be faced with the choice between defeat and disengagement. Either way, American power would wane further.

CHAPTER XI

NAVAL REARMAMENT

The proud 594-ship active-duty U.S. Fleet that helped win the Cold War is a memory. It has been replaced by an aging and overworked 276-ship force. With the decades-long contraction of America's effective Cold War–era Fleet, industrializing countries have been busy filling the security vacuum, developing or recapitalizing their own naval forces, fielding advanced capabilities, conducting independent operations, and projecting regional power.

As America's maritime dominance has declined, so has order at sea. The simple black-and-white bilateral organizing template of the Cold War, is, with America's help, fragmenting into a crazy quilt of contentious multilateral rivalries. Since the late 1990s America's maritime leadership has sought increased influence through partnership efforts with emerging navies; by 2006, these efforts were working toward what was optimistically called the "1,000-Ship Navy." But that well-intentioned attempt to meld minor navies into a cohesive, U.S.-led instrument came a cropper, displacing U.S. leadership at sea by empowering smaller navies to pursue limited maritime aims outside the interests of the United States.

Chile, for example, was one of the first beneficiaries of the 1,000-ship Navy concept. The Chilean navy became the grateful recipient of a surplus American oiler, the USNS *Andrew J. Higgins*, which, under a trade agreement, was renamed the *Almirante Montt* and tasked to supply U.S. and allied vessels as they transited through the Southern oceans. Although the 2008–2009 transaction was a successful demonstration of how the 1,000-ship Navy might encourage regional collaboration, the acquisition facilitated a Chilean naval buildup that challenged a disputed maritime border with Chile's northern neighbor, Peru. A more cautionary tale is the Philippines. While the Philippine navy is busy absorbing four *Hamilton*-class Coast Guard cutters, destroyer-sized U.S. castoffs, Philippine President Rodrigo Duterte threatened in October 2016 to end a longstanding U.S. alliance in favor of China.

Rather than uniting around a single, easily defined strategic aim, Chile, the Philippines, and other emerging regional navies are motivated by their own local interests, driven, in large part, by the United Nations Convention on the Law of the Sea (UNCLOS). This treaty, which came into force in 1994, mandated the expansion of national exclusive economic zones; as competitors arm themselves either to seize or "control and patrol" these newly valuable regions, America's ability unilaterally to impose order within the global maritime is in doubt. Unless the U.S. Navy is recapitalized and funded to meet the challenge posed by nascent, independent-minded navies, increasingly contested and fractious oceans will pose a serious threat to American security.

Complicating matters, the nature of maritime aggression has changed. The prospect of fleet-on-fleet battles has been replaced by an irregular mix of fishing and sovereignty violations, near collisions, and other deliberate harassments by a changing array of state-supported militias, terrorists, commercial interests, and other subnational actors. For nearly two years, ISIS controlled the Libyan port city of Sirte and other coastal towns. Hezbollah operates from parts of the Lebanese coast. Iran now threatens to build naval bases in Yemen and Syria.[1] The relatively simple bilateral challenge from an established rival is being replaced by an array of shifting alliances, state-supported criminal enterprises, and a general collapse of maritime order that is as inconstant as it is potentially disruptive.

The end of this chaos is not in sight. Global naval inventories continue to increase. While the media focuses on China and Russia's naval expansion, other regional powers—such as India, Vietnam, and Indonesia—are also quietly developing their navies. Seas that have been largely calm since the Cold War are reverting to their historical form. In the Mediterranean, outside of U.S. or Russian contributions, local nations operate more than fifty modern submarines; although most serve under the NATO banner, a weakened NATO, or the loss of Turkey, Spain, or some other key NATO alliance member, would seriously threaten U.S. operations and trade routes through this strategic sea. On the other side of the world, off the South China Sea, Association of Southeast Asian Nations

(ASEAN) members have quadrupled their submarine fleets over the past thirty years, with many more set to enter service. At some point, the pressure to use these investments, possibly in a provocative way that defies quick attribution, is likely to prove irresistible.

The extent of the global maritime buildup is not just quantitative. It is hidden in qualitative measures that are often overlooked. Naval combatants are getting bigger and increasingly complex. In a trend commonly associated with naval arms races, smaller, less-capable warships are being swapped for larger, more capable vessels. This process echoes the naval buildup that preceded World War I, when maritime competition pressed the United Kingdom and Germany to increase the displacement of their dreadnaught battleships by approximately 55 percent.

Similar dynamics are at work today: pressure by both China and South Korea has spurred Japan to grow its fleet in both numbers and ship size. But while Japan's fleet growth over the last two decades has been slow and deliberate, the displacement of Japan's guided-missile destroyer fleet has grown by an impressive 65 percent, its conventional destroyer fleet has increased by 69 percent, and the displacement of its helicopter destroyers has grown by a whopping 275 percent. The helicopter destroyers have taken on a distinctly aircraft carrier–like flat-deck layout.

The maritime arms race is not limited to vessels. Weapons and sensors are becoming easier to obtain and operate. The rash of missile attacks against U.S. destroyers off Yemen in late 2016 underscores a proliferation of new technologies that makes the seas far more challenging. Modest forces now have opportunities to deploy hard-hitting long-range surface-to-surface missiles or other weaponry capable of challenging U.S. ships. The challenge isn't just near shore. An array of new commercial sensors gives states and other actors an understanding of ship movement through the oceans that is more comprehensive than ever. Constant, real-time monitoring and the ability to strike high-end military targets are within the reach of more and more states and can be obtained by many non-state actors.

The proliferation of highly capable weaponry threatens to change the world's littoral waters—where most naval contests are resolved—into increasingly perilous spaces. The comforting numerical and technological margins that traditionally favored the U.S. Navy are dwindling, and the resources once available to support a swift U.S. maritime response to impose order are either gone or diverted to other priorities.

The challenge facing the Trump administration and Congress is either to continue to demand the U.S. Navy do more with less, or provide the money needed to grow the fleet so it can adequately protect America's moat. As a candidate, Donald Trump supported the latter course, working toward a goal of a 350-ship fleet. Changing course to achieve a fleet of this size would reestablish America's global naval dominance.

PROTECTING THE GREAT MOAT?

Though it is easy for modern-day Americans to forget, the ocean is both a protective bulwark and a source of vulnerability. This dichotomy was well understood in the early days of the American republic. It informed the Founders' earliest decisions about defending the nation. Of the fifty-five delegates at the Constitutional convention, thirteen were merchants, dependent upon the sea for goods and market access. Three were in the maritime shipping business. One was a shipbuilder. Their product, the U.S. Constitution, reflected the experience of men who were intimately familiar with the sea.

The Founders took great pains to ensure the existence of a Navy. Article I, section 8 of the Constitution distinguishes between ground and naval forces. "The Congress," it states, "shall have Power . . . to raise and support Armies." But the founders also demanded that Congress "provide and maintain a Navy." Despite the high cost of building and maintaining a Navy, the fledgling nation recognized a basic strategic fact—the thirteen states' 25,536-mile coastline and the new nation's burgeoning sea trade had to be protected. The founding leaders also knew that powerful ships could not be built overnight—much less equipped, manned, and trained for combat—without long-term investment and planning.

Similar planning and foresight is not in evidence today. Future ship demand is guided by the U.S. Navy's Force Structure Assessment (FSA) process. But that process plows on largely unencumbered by strategy. Despite the vigorous decades-long modernization of an increasingly ambitious and adventurous Chinese navy and the ongoing reassertion of Russian naval activity, the latest shipbuilding plan from 2015 is not significantly different from the shipbuilding plan of 2001, except that the number of ships required shrank from 310-312 to 308.

The FSA looks backward. It determines long-term platform demand by evaluating current presence requirements and battle plans. This framework champions the status quo. It shapes the "future" fleet to mirror the existing one. Ultimately, it forces America's maritime security planners away from strategy and into an exercise that is conducted with scant strategic justification, one that perpetuates the shape and size of American seapower.

Lacking a strong strategic keel, the Navy has been set adrift as naval leaders vigorously defended a strategically unjustified fleet size target of 308 to 312. For more than a decade, the Navy has been essentially frozen in place while strategic circumstances, events, and technology changed around it. The failure to base naval vessel requirements on a well-articulated strategic vision, coupled with a single-minded focus on fleet numbers, has led to less-than-enthusiastic funding support from the executive and legislative branches of government. Today, the federal budget fails to meet the minimum demand for Navy ships generated by the Department of Defense. The Congressional Budget Office (CBO) notes that the resources needed to build a 308-ship fleet are 36 percent higher than the average amount of constant dollars that the Navy has received for shipbuilding over the past three decades. And it only gets worse. If the sea services are forced to tap the Navy's shipbuilding accounts to replace twelve aging *Ohio*-class ballistic-missile submarines, the nation's undersea leg of the nuclear triad, the CBO estimates that the fleet would dwindle to 237 ships by 2045.[2]

This strategic vacuum has done little to help the Navy

build support in Congress or with the electorate. Today, the Navy's contribution to American life is more removed than ever from the general public. The cities that America's founding fathers inhabited are no longer focused on the seas, and the land of Mark Twain, where rural life once depended on the unvexed flow of the Mississippi and her tributaries to the sea, is no longer visible to the average voter. News of maritime fishing disputes, which stakeholders in America's once-large commercial fishing industry followed in the newspapers, now lacks an audience and is consigned to specialist journals. Yet, while the fraction of American citizens who live and work on the water has declined, America's dependence upon maritime supply lines for food, fuel, and other goods has increased.

Today, political leadership sees the Navy and naval shipbuilding less as a matter of national security and more as a question of the jobs at the disposal of large defense contractors. Strong leaders such as former Navy assistant secretaries Theodore Roosevelt and Franklin Delano Roosevelt or former Secretary of the Navy John Lehman were vigorous and talented enough to make a national case for a larger, more active Navy. But with a naval leadership vacuum of many years, the national argument for shipbuilding has been lost, consigned to the occasional Fleet Week or recruiting advertisement. American seapower needs more than funding. It needs articulate, strategic-minded leadership that can connect national seapower goals with persuasive arguments to achieve them.

WHAT IS TO BE DONE?

The Trump administration should take a large step forward and conduct a comprehensive assessment of American seapower that includes the goals, size, and character of the nation's combat fleet. The mere act of assessment would acknowledge that the United States is a maritime state that possesses basic security requirements, and that its position as a great power rests on the fulfillment of these requirements.

The core of such an assessment is developing the strategy that ought to guide America's broad security goals and, in particular, the role that seapower should take in meeting these goals. The Navy conforms to each new president's strategic direction, as expressed in the National Security Strategy. While national strategies change from one administration to the next, the primary mission is to ensure the security of American citizens and the survival of the United States.

This means that the first priority of the U.S. military must be to turn back existential threats. America's primary external existential threat is nuclear war. The strategy to prevent nuclear war is largely based on maintaining the nuclear triad of land-based bombers, intercontinental ballistic missiles, and missiles launched from submarines, all equipped with nuclear weapons. For the Navy, the nuclear mission dates from 1960, when the nuclear ballistic missile-equipped submarine USS *George Washington* departed on her first deterrence patrol. This mission remains a central function of U.S. seapower.

The second priority for America's seapower is to conduct high-level, sustained maritime warfare at and from the sea. This requires all the large carrier battle groups, strike fighters, surface combatants, amphibious ships, and supporting fleet train—the resupply and maintenance vessels—that are needed to ensure victory in sustained large-scale warfare.

The third priority, of no less importance than defeating an enemy, is to deter or respond immediately to regional aggressions. While prevailing in conflict is a necessity for the security of the United States and its allies, preventing wars honorably is to be preferred. The ability of naval forces to deter and rebuff aggression has been amply demonstrated—as, for example, when the United States sent large naval forces to the Taiwan Strait in 1995 as a response to China's missile tests, which were meant to intimidate Taiwan. Seapower's largest weapons do not always demand the active use of force. A destroyer's passage through international waters wrongfully claimed as sovereign sends a low-level signal of American interest. In different circumstances—where aggression must be met immediately by compelling force—combat support, provided by powerfully lethal combatants, offers the United States an instrument to engage aggressors without endangering many of the large, valuable combatants that sustained high-end warfare demands.

A fourth priority comprises the important actions of surveillance and crisis management. Forces for these purposes are composed of a shifting set of Navy amphibious assault vessels, civilian-crewed ships, and other assets. They already sail about the globe, monitoring the South Pacific, the Antarctic, the African coast, and other areas of potential unrest, providing support for endangered U.S. citizens or other American interests that offer less potential as flashpoints for regional or global conflagration.

A fifth priority is to provide for coastal defense. Although American seapower keeps threats far from the United States, border security and exclusive economic zone (EEZ) enforcement remains important to ensure homeland security and the protection of large economic interests, such as fishing and extracting mineral resources from the seabed. America maintains a vast EEZ, second only to France. America's 3.4 million square miles of sovereign undersea territory must be secured from aggressive encroachment, smugglers, and terrorist attempts to infiltrate the United States. As more navies develop and resource constraints increase the relative value of seafloor resources, incursions into the American EEZ will increase. These predictable challenges demand constant monitoring, escorts, and the exhibition of credible combat power by the Department of Defense, the Navy, the U.S. Coast Guard, and Customs and Border Patrol assets.

These five strategic missions are at the core of a robust maritime strategy and should be reflected in the force structure that is built to confront multiplying challenges at sea.

THREATS REPRISED

A resurgent, revanchist Russia and the ruling mullahs of Iran (the latter being implacably hostile to the West and on the threshold of possessing nuclear weapons along with ballistic missiles) pose a serious challenge. Russia is diplomatically and militarily active but economically fragile, while a weaker Iran is set to invest billions in recapitalizing a navy long—and prudently—denied foreign funding and arms sources. These two nations pose near- and long-term threats. However, over the next decade, a modernizing, prospering China—with an integrated global military, economic, and diplomatic strategy—poses the primary challenge to America's position in the world and the seapower that is our nation's first line of defense.

STRATEGIC NUCLEAR THREATS

As major nuclear powers, Russia and China are long-standing threats. However, Russia's undersea nuclear deterrence forces are a known quantity and are gradually being replaced with modern boats as Cold War assets age. New *Borey*-class ballistic missile–carrying and nuclear-powered submarines (SSBNs, also known as "boomers"), which have been under construction for more than a decade, are slowly being integrated with a new and somewhat unreliable Bulava intercontinental ballistic missile. Eight to twelve of those boats will slowly replace twelve aging and obsolete Delta IV-, Typhoon-, and Delta III–class SSBNs. The new boomers will supplement seven existing Oscar II–class nuclear-powered cruise-missile submarines.

China is working diligently to advance submarine technology and to establish a bastion for strategic-missile submarines in the South China Sea. China's first deterrence patrols will be conducted by a fleet of up to five relatively noisy Jin-class SSBNs, joined, over the course of the next decade, by a more advanced class of advanced strategic-missile submarines.

Ballistic-missile submarines pose a significant security challenge to the United States as well as our allies throughout and beyond the West Pacific. Although the number of Chinese and Russian ballistic-missile submarines is limited, significant naval assets are required to track and monitor these boats around the clock. In addition, France, India, Britain, and other nuclear-armed countries—possibly including North Korea—are either developing or operating ballistic-missile submarines of their own, and some of those vessels may occasionally demand additional American surveillance or anti-submarine resources.

The seaborne nuclear threat could also present itself on the surface. Ships in China's large and poorly monitored state merchant fleet could easily house nuclear missiles or devices within their cargo spaces, offering China a cost-effective means to threaten international security.

SUSTAINED MARITIME WARFARE THREATS

Conducting a sustained global fight at sea remains an exclusively American capability. Although Russian provocations across Europe and the Middle East are on the rise, and Iran continues its preparations to roil the Persian Gulf's waters, no other nation outside of China is likely to use seapower for sustained combat operations to contest the United States.

Only China has sufficient maritime resources to develop a global navy that could sustain high-level combat far from home. Though it is currently a small-to-mid-sized-ship navy designed for littoral operations, the PLAN is expanding rapidly, adding blue-water combatants and integrating the country's global commercial interests with rudimentary command-and-control and logistical support structures needed for sustained transoceanic war. To support sustained naval warfare globally, China is developing carrier forces and the doctrine to support them. It possesses the industrial potential to follow America's lead of building and operating supercarriers.

Memories are short. It is easy to forget how America shocked Russia in 1961 by suddenly deploying three carriers (the USS *Kitty Hawk, Constellation*, and *Enterprise*) in a single year. China is introducing large surface escorts into its fleet at a rapid pace. They offer accelerating improvements in anti-surface and anti-air capabilities. The expansion is impressive: a fleet of thirty to sixty smaller, capable 1,500- to 1,600-ton escorts like the Type 056 patrol corvette are being built at a rate that mirrors that of the 1970s-era *Knox*-class frigate—the United States commissioned forty-six of these simple escorts in just five years. America as well as Asia will be required to respond when large Chinese naval combatants and their accompanying escort fleets begin to enter service.

Chinese submarine forces are modernizing as well. While these forces remain regional, China's fleet of five nuclear attack submarines will grow. China's current fleet of fifty-three diesel-powered attack submarines will extend its reach or be deployed to operate out of forward bases in critical regions. However, China's expected goal of seventy to eighty submarines looks increasingly achievable as it becomes clear that the fleet will still retain aging but useful Project 033, Project 035, and early Kilo-class submarines.

The Project 033 is an offshoot of the 1950s-era Russian Romeo-class, which itself was derived from German World

War II–era submarines. The PLAN modernized the boats, reduced their noise, and computerized functions that were previously executed manually. The improvements are a useful measure of the PLAN's determined effort to build a more capable fleet. American submarines will be increasingly stressed by very complex undersea operational challenges in Asia as newer, more capable Chinese submarines, aided by uncontested access to the South China Sea, encounter a range of Japanese, South Korean, and other modern submarines and sensor networks.

China, like the United States, is also capable of cultivating and recruiting regional naval powers to support Beijing's global combat ambitions. China has integrated its diplomatic and economic activities to establish economic and military opportunities around the globe. A growing network of bases between China and the Red Sea and commercial holdings in the Aegean, the Caribbean, and Central/South American states make smooth the highway for a rapid set of alliance-shifts to effectively contain American seapower.

The Pakistani navy, for example, is working closely with China. The cooperation is useful to both states. Over the next decade, Pakistan's navy is being prepared to operate a range of modern Chinese-sourced or -designed submarines, replenishment auxiliaries, fast attack craft, and frigates. This relationship, coupled with the Chinese-owned port infrastructure at Gwadar in Pakistan, offers China an opportunity to extend the cooperation into an alliance that would threaten the Indian Ocean's stability and the subcontinent itself.

For the United States, the likelihood of forward Chinese

naval bases in the Western Hemisphere is real. Germany tried to exploit anti-U.S. sentiment in Mexico in World War I. The Soviets were more successful in Cuba. Given the likely friction with South and Central America over a range of issues, the possibility that China may gain operational access to Mexico or other nearby states for forward operations must be considered. Each new alliance and every new forward base increases China's ability to support sustained, high-level combat at sea.

REGIONAL AGGRESSION

The likelihood of short, sharp regional conflict is increasing. China, Russia, Iran, and other regional militaries can conduct naval operations against the United States in the Western Pacific, the Persian Gulf, and the Baltic, Arctic, and Mediterranean Seas using a range of small surface, undersea, or clandestine commercial forces. This sort of aggression is opportunistic and is commonly undertaken in pursuit of limited aims. It would be preceded by irregular and paramilitary forces, political intimidation and agitation, and subversion as the aggressor tries to create a fait accompli. The umbrella name for these operations is "gray-zone tactics."

In the past, U.S. forces have massed to halt regional aggression, as they did in the Balkans and in driving Saddam Hussein's army from Kuwait. These operations were characterized by an intentionally disproportionate response that required much time and enormous cost to set in place. They are consistent with a particular style of warfare popularized by the Powell doctrine, and which advocates overwhelming force. Potential foes have noted that America's

mass mobilizations take time. Likely aggressors are working to exploit this vulnerability by coupling small, intri-
cately linked goals with deceptive tactics that calibrate
hostile acts to spur debate among an adversary's national
security advisors over the provocation's gravity and the
appropriate response.

China's building and arming of islands in the South
China Sea is a textbook example. The islands themselves
are less tactically important than the underwhelming U.S.
debate over how best to respond and the mild character
of the limited freedom of navigation operations that the
Obama administration favored. China and others in the
region saw the low-level U.S. response as a sign of weakness. *Lingchi*, or "death by a thousand cuts," is a Mandarin
term for a form of execution in which parts of the body are
cut off over an extended period. It is an apt metaphor to
describe an aggressive policy that moves slowly toward its
object in small steps. This is the gray zone.

The threat from regional aggression varies from theater to theater. In the North Atlantic and Baltic, the naval
threat is largely from Russian undersea assets, small surface combatants, and land-based aircraft and missiles. In
the Western Pacific, the threat ranges from the movement
of massed, quasi-militarized fishing fleets to a coordinated
response from China's large quantity of coastal defense
assets.

In the Arabian Sea, Iran's patrol boat navy will expand
and modernize as the Iranian economy experiences new
infusions of revenue. The Iranian navy has been demonstrably resourceful despite its scarcity of resources, so even
a modest recapitalization may encourage a far more ambi-

tious range of activity—and possibly confrontation—as the Iranian armed forces enjoy additional investments in contemporary technology.

However, the deck is not simply stacked against us. Would-be aggressors must consider consequences in their calculus. And the presence of the right number of nearby battle-ready and appropriately armed U.S. combatants remains a powerful deterrent.

The challenge is to prevent Russia, China, and Iran from forming operational alliances with either themselves or other strong, well-positioned allies. Material support from a new ally, or a sudden change in nearby alliance networks could offer the navies of hostile states a wider span of action or force the United States to cede the initiative at sea. As the Philippines' President Duterte's late 2016 shift toward China away from the United States demonstrates, alliances can be fragile. In critical regions, sudden reversals can dislodge the established maritime order, sending unnatural shocks to long-standing American national security interests.

SURVEILLANCE AND CRISIS MANAGEMENT

China is building a blue-water amphibious force that mimics U.S. force structure. Where Beijing lacked any serious amphibious capability two decades ago, the PLAN is now reaching for effective means to support what the PRC would claim as threatened nationals living on weak and sometimes lawless Pacific islands—an action that could pose a Grenada-like challenge to long-term U.S. strategic interests in the Pacific. Possession of these atolls would give China the ability to project power deeper into the Pacific and threaten U.S communications with its treaty allies in the region.

China's first-generation blue-water amphibious landing platform dock, the Type 071 LPD, has entered service, and an expected fleet of six will soon be joined by a Type 081 flat-deck amphibious assault ship, granting China the capability to carry out a range of complex amphibious assault missions far from home.

China and Russia are vigorously pursuing a range of surveillance activities that extend into all the oceans and to both poles. Some of these activities, like the routine transit of Russian tugs and trawlers through spacecraft launch zones, over undersea cables, and over other undersea infrastructures, are overt intelligence-gathering exercises. Others, like China's reinforcement of a range of Antarctic outposts, set the stage for future territorial claims or gray-zone aggression.

Outside of the conventional threat that China's surveillance assets raise by providing intelligence to their commanders, the sheer volume of commercial surveillance activities poses a hazard to naval units. The threat is complex, ranging from semi-nationalized fishing boats that report on ship movements to privately funded surveillance satellites or seafloor sensors. The challenge of engaging these sensors, shutting them down to allow undetected passage, or fooling them to show tracks that do not exist, has yet to be fully accepted as an instrument of American seapower.

COASTAL DEFENSE

In the home oceans and American EEZ, the Navy must focus on controlling the flow of migrants, drugs, and weapon of mass destruction (WMD) contraband into the United States. The U.S. Coast Guard forces are overwhelmed and able to respond to only 20 percent of the known maritime movements of illicit drugs.[3]

Maintaining the integrity of the border is a critical responsibility of a sovereign nation. If current anti-smuggling support from Central and South American states is withdrawn, or if China gains a forward lodgment in the Western hemisphere, the maintenance of border security—conducting standard national security missions while managing smuggler and migrant flows—will become a serious challenge.

GLOBAL WHOLE, REGIONAL PARTS

The chief issue facing American seapower for now and in the foreseeable future are the forces that, like a thick blanket of nettles, envelop the Eurasian landmass, including the Middle East and subcontinent. Any effective U.S. maritime strategy must measure these forces and consider how to deter or cripple them.

In the South China Sea, the U.S. Navy faces the Chinese South Sea Fleet, which has twenty-two attack submarines, seven destroyers, twenty-nine frigates and corvettes, and thirty-eight small missile patrol craft. In the East China and Yellow Seas, China has positioned some forty attack submarines, an aircraft carrier, sixteen destroyers, forty-six frigates and corvettes, and forty-eight missile patrol craft.

The Chinese Navy is supplemented by numerous lightly armed Coast Guard–like vessels, as well as an increasingly well-organized maritime militia. Each of these ships is positioned to operate within China's capable land-based missile umbrella, protected by an air force that is composed of about 2,100 combatants. The PLA air force is modernizing, growing a fleet of 600 fourth-generation fighters and supplementing these with fifth-generation aircraft over time. Each of these combatants is backed by a warfighting strategy that is focused on disrupting the electronic communications and logistical backbone on which the U.S. Navy depends in combat.

Russia also maintains a powerful Pacific Fleet of seventeen attack submarines, one cruiser, six destroyers, and twenty-four patrol boats.

To confront these fleets, the United States maintains twenty-eight attack submarines, two guided-missile submarines, five aircraft carriers (of varying levels of readiness), twelve cruisers, thirty-two destroyers, and eight littoral combat ships based in the Pacific. These numbers do not provide parity, though the odds get better if the formidable navies of Japan and South Korea assist in monitoring patrols and assuming responsibility if U.S. forces go into action elsewhere.

In the North Atlantic, Baltic Sea, and the Black and Mediterranean Seas, an active Russian Navy uses a small and aged force as recapitalization efforts get under way. The Northern Fleet is a formidable, submarine-heavy force of twenty-three attack submarines, an aircraft carrier, three large surface combatants, five destroyers, and twelve patrol craft of less than 1,000 tons. In the Baltic is a small force of two submarines, two destroyers, seven frigates, and eighteen patrol craft. Assigned to the Black Sea are four submarines, a cruiser, a destroyer, two frigates, and fifteen patrol boats whose patrols can extend into the Mediterranean.

American ships based on the Atlantic seaboard include twenty-four attack submarines, two guided-missile submarines, ten cruisers, twenty-eight destroyers, and five nuclear aircraft carriers—a substantial force that would be challenged by conflict in the three seas and ocean that abut the European peninsula and enclose the British Isles.

While Russia's smaller Baltic and Black Sea Fleets are supported by Russia's numerous land-based air-defense, surface-to-surface, and electronic warfare assets, both regions would, in a wider conflict, face powerful NATO neighbors that could hold their own against the current fleet. To the north, any attempt by a set of increasingly sophisticated Russian submarines to break out of areas covered by Russia's layered defenses would be challenged from above by America's P-8 anti-submarine patrol aircraft fleet together with an aggressive undersea attack by American attack submarines.

The particular challenge in these theaters is the likelihood that Russia's high command will coordinate combat at sea and on land using amphibious operations to set backfires in the West's rear and support their advances on land. The Western alliance is a strong bulwark, but NATO is a slow-moving instrument, and the strike packages from the five Atlantic-based carriers, if by unimaginable chance they were all in the area and combat-ready, offer the only "quick response" strike capability in the region.

In the Persian Gulf, a motley Iranian Navy, composed of marginally useful and aging showpiece vessels, is supplemented by a far more aggressive small-boat navy run by the Iranian Islamic Revolutionary Guard Corps. Today, this force is confronted by the capable small-boat navies of the Gulf, which are supplemented by a modest U.S. force of ten small Cyclone-class patrol boats and four mine countermeasure boats based in Manama, Bahrain.

U.S. seapower in the Gulf, supplemented by bigger combatants as needed, is sufficient to meet the threat, but Iran is enjoying an infusion of money as a result of the 2015 Joint Comprehensive Plan of Action. The likelihood that Iran's naval forces will receive more funds is excellent. So is the possibility of a permanent Iranian naval presence in the Red Sea and perhaps in the Mediterranean. Couple these prospects with the Iranian navy's willingness to apply Iranian power at a distance and the more combative nature of the Iranian Guard Corps' small boat fleet. Every indication points toward the emergence of Iranian seapower as a formidable regional force.

The geographic and technological range of land- and sea-based threats to America's forward defense—its seapower—is curving upward today. The arc of the curve is certain to increase in the next few years and over time. If the United States can depend on its allies to increase their own navies and meet their alliance obligations in a major crisis, the goal of a 350-ship fleet that President Trump has set will suffice. A 350-ship fleet will also relieve current pressure on every element of U.S. seapower. However, if allies reduce their navies and fail to meet commitments in extremis, the U.S. will require at least a 400-ship fleet to preserve its global superiority and keep threats at a distance from our hemisphere.

WHAT IS NEEDED?

To successfully carry out the five major missions of American seapower, the Trump administration must rely on a wise mix of strategy and brute economic force as it grows the Navy to the 350 ships that candidate Trump set as a goal during the 2016 presidential campaign. The ideas below about the character and size of American seapower anticipate changes that have occurred as our competitors' fleets multiply and continue their transformation into a more dispersed, globally capable threat.

Because of the complexity and relative growth in the size and strength of hostile and potentially hostile navies around the world, U.S. seapower must exploit every geographic and diplomatic advantage possible. To achieve such advantages, the Navy will benefit from developing and maintaining a vibrant in-house strategic wing of its own. This would help the State Department and other diplomatic stakeholders understand and advance such fundamental seapower strategic priorities as forward-basing, operational support, and alliance requirements. Also required is a clear identification of potentially dangerous maritime partnerships that would assist the State Department in advancing American interests.

Maritime security in a world of growing competitors, small and large, requires other new means. The seas, their environs, and littoral regions are complex. Platforms that can carry out hostile acts with little or no attribution are proliferating. The United States needs to be able to anticipate, identify, and gather solid evidence about acts of aggression that range from attacks with weapons of mass destruction to conventional arms. The work that was undertaken to link North Korea to the 2010 attack on the *Pohang*-class corvette ROKS *Cheonan* will need to be repeated—and repeated under far more tense circumstances—as more countries, criminal networks, and terrorists acquire the means to attack vessels while denying their involvement.

RESPONDING TO STRATEGIC NUCLEAR THREATS

To preserve America's undersea deterrent and continue its essential deterrence mission, the current force of aging *Ohio*-class strategic ballistic-missile submarines (SSBN) should, as currently planned, be replaced with twelve modern *Columbia*-class SSBNs. While these ships will face a far more contested sea than when the first SSBNs entered the water, America's 3.4 million square miles of EEZ provide ample protection, including the Papahanaumokuakea Marine National Monument in the northern Hawaiian Islands. The national monuments offer additional safe bastions where essential vessels can lurk, while the U.S. Coast Guard and federal agencies limit the deployment of sensors and other surveillance craft that are certain to proliferate over the forty-two-year operational life of the *Ohio*-class replacement submarines.

If a bastion strategy—where ballistic missile–carrying submarines operate in large, relatively safe tracts of ocean—

is still regarded as insufficiently secure, SSBN operations ought to be reviewed. One alternative is an SSBN task force that copies the current aircraft carrier strike group model. U.S. aircraft carriers rely on escorts for their safety and survival as they operate on the high seas and in places where action is most likely, in contested littoral areas or areas immediately adjacent to operations ashore.

Another option is to supplement the SSBN's highly successful Trident II/D5 submarine-launched ballistic missiles with nuclear-tipped medium-range ballistic missiles designed to fit in the *Virginia*-class attack submarines' payload tubes. This would allow the new *Virginia*-class submarines substantial flexibility in the missions they are assigned.

Nuclear-tipped warheads sitting atop submarine-launched missiles are useless without strong command-and-control elements. Current naval plans are correct to capitalize and protect critical links in the command chain, from the E-6B Mercury aircraft to other classified systems required to relay commands to a submerged SSBN.

To supplement deterrence, resources to detect and "find, fix, and finish" opposing strategic-missile submarines are needed. Sensors, unmanned systems coupled with P-8 Poseidon anti-submarine warfare aircraft, *Virginia*-class attack submarines, and surface anti-submarine warfare teams will all be required to keep track of a competitor's strategic submarines throughout their patrols. P-8 purchases should be increased well beyond current plans to buy 117 aircraft, and the 48-boat *Virginia*-class attack submarine fleet should be supplemented by large displacement unmanned undersea vehicles (LDUUVs) and surface vessels. A good start would be to double the current annual construction rate of two *Virginia*-class boats each year to four.

RESPONDING TO SUSTAINED MARITIME COMBAT THREATS

The history of warfare on land and at sea is also a history of dashed hopes that sharp, intensive operations would resolve violent disagreements quickly. The Achaean coalition did not expect to fight on the Trojan plain for ten years. Although the struggle against today's jihadists is understood to be a "Long War," no one at the time that the United States invaded Afghanistan in 2001 expected that combat operations would last for more than a decade and a half. The rise of near-peer competitors and nuclear proliferation in Iran and North Korea suggest not only that large-scale warfare remains possible but also that such conflict could last for years.

To conduct sustained, high-level warfare, large U.S.-based surface action groups, composed of aircraft carriers, large surface combatants, and amphibious assault elements, must be able to operate throughout the Pacific, Atlantic, and other seas, working with allies capable of supporting complex, sustained combat at sea. These ships would also be focused on fighting in contested seas, battling rival carrier battle groups, ensuring the safety of choke points, clearing sea-lanes, and supporting ground elements that have been ordered into an area where weapons of mass destruction could be, or have been, used.

The centerpiece of these fleets will for the foreseeable future remain the strike aircraft carrier. Ten large, nuclear-powered *Nimitz*-class carriers already exist. A single *Ford*-class aircraft carrier is nearly ready to enter the arsenal. As the *Nimitz*-class carriers reach the end of their useful service lives, they should be replaced with carriers that are no less capable. A good start would be the simultaneous construction of two carriers, which should begin as soon as possible. These new carriers are needed to place decisive combat force near likely flashpoints. A single carrier battle group attempting to challenge the combined threats of coastal China would be unlikely to survive, but a multi-carrier group, practiced in coordinated sea control and strike operations, would present a serious deterrent and warfighting threat to China's in-depth defensive measures.

Dedicating these lethal carrier battle groups to handle the "crisis of the day" risks a grave tactical mistake as the possibility of a major power conflict grows. The dangers that China, for example, is building in its littoral areas suggest that such powerful and high-value U.S. aircraft carrier strike groups should remain far out to sea while large numbers of smaller vessels establish sea control. Such control is a necessary predicate for the sustained combat that the coordinated abilities of large carriers and their escorts can provide. In much the same way, the Navy used large, multi-carrier "fast carrier task forces" to overcome Japanese defenses in World War II.

To complement the larger carriers and free them for their focus on the full range of tasks needed in conflict with a peer or near-peer competitor, the time is right to consider the design and construction of smaller, non-nuclear aircraft carriers. The smaller carriers could perform combat duties closer to an enemy's coast and allow the supercarriers to focus on the full range of combat missions, which include anti-submarine, anti-air, and anti-surface ship warfare, as well as defense of the carrier strike group and possibly strike missions. The missions of the smaller carriers would include the support of the U.S. Marine Corps and such necessities as surveillance and reconnaissance, which would otherwise reduce the punch of the larger assault fleet.

Smaller carriers would allow the current fleet of nine Marine Corps flat-deck/amphibious assault-ship hybrids (the *America*-class landing helicopter assault ships [LHAs] and *Wasp*-class landing helicopter dock ships [LHDs]) to become aviation-only platforms. The smaller carriers would be designed to conform to global canal requirements in order to speed their movement between oceans. The result would be increased combat power, as ships like the current aviation-only 45,000-ton USS *America* (LHA 6) were replaced by a more strike-oriented CATOBAR (catapult assisted takeoff but arrested recovery) carrier similar to the equivalently sized *Midway*-class carriers that were commissioned just after World War II. The strike focus would offer a qualitative improvement to the airborne strike and support capabilities the Marine Corps needs, while enabling broader missions and a more diffused challenge to an enemy than the LHA/LHDs possess today.

Air warfare, conducted almost exclusively by variants of the F/A-18 strike fighter, requires sufficient funding to support the rapid pace of aerospace developments. There is no serious dispute that unmanned craft, including air as well as surface and subsurface platforms, will assume increasing importance in American seapower. As these aircraft are introduced, naval aviation needs an opportunity to test various models. The loss rate for unmanned platforms should not be an issue. Naval aviation should be encouraged to extract as much knowledge as possible to ensure its superiority over other manned and unmanned systems.

The manned versions that follow the F/A-18—the F-35 Lightning strike fighter—will remain useful, since the campaigns in the Middle East and Central Asia are wearing down F/A-18 airframes at a rapid pace. Development of longer-range sensors and missiles is needed to supplement the legacy short-range F/A-18 and F-35 strike fighters. Naval leadership understands this and is right to address it.

The current fleet's aircraft carriers continue to need the support of at least seventy surface escorts, each capable of undertaking complex undersea warfare, air-defense, and strike/anti-ship tasks in the face of threats from electromagnetic, chemical, biological, radiological, and nuclear weapons. Today, these missions are conducted by sixty-three *Arleigh Burke*-class destroyers and twenty-two *Ticonderoga*-class cruisers, and may be supported, over time, by a modernized "Flight III" *Arleigh Burke*-class destroyer or a larger surface combatant based on either the LPD-17 or DDG-1000 hull-form. Under the Obama administration's final long-range plans and over the next decade, the number of large surface combatants will increase to about one hundred. This is insufficient to meet the naval buildups of potential adversaries. The United States should aim for a mix of frigates and destroyers at least 40 percent larger than it now plans.

These expensive surface combatants need better weapons, sensors, and electronic warfare systems to maintain their superiority over potential enemies' ongoing advances in technology. The legacy anti-ship Harpoon missile's range needs to be doubled to keep pace with Chinese and Russian advances in their anti-ship missiles' range. Similarly the next-generation anti-ship modifications of Standard Missiles—which had heretofore defended against hostile aircraft and missiles—must continue so that our ships have increased long-range protection against enemy ships. In greater range lies greater safety, as David understood when he chose a slingshot to oppose Goliath's heavy javelin.

The continued viability of the successful Aegis Combat System, which integrates the defenses of surface ships against both enemy aircraft and missiles, is a necessity. Communications systems that are needed to weld disparate systems into a cohesive instrument must be integrated into the larger combatants and electronic warfare systems. Existing and improved defenses must continue to provide the protection needed against the advanced missiles and electronic warfare measures that advanced adversaries will deploy against U.S. forces.

Amphibious assault units are well suited to rotate in and out of the large surface action groups as they respond to crises in areas such as those near Okinawa or Guam, where a Marine Corps presence is necessary to deter regional aggression from both North Korea and China. Marines would be supported by aviation-focused aircraft carriers while amphibious support would be assumed exclusively by greater numbers of small-deck amphibious vessels.

In support of the deployed fleet, a range of logistical

support craft are required to provide enough ammunition, food, and fuel to prevail in sustained conflict. Today's fleet of thirty-six combat logistics and fleet support ships will grow with the planned addition of seventeen next-generation T-AO(X) tankers. Chinese and Russian investments in naval modernization make for an increasingly dangerous environment. The defenses of new logistics ships should be improved to include strike weapons. In addition, the Navy plans to design and build tug and salvage ships to recover damaged combatants after action so that they can be returned to service.

To increase their combat usefulness, the thirty-seven supply and cargo vessels that make up the fleets of the Military Sealift Command, which are needed to sustain troops ashore, should be equipped with self-defenses, for example air-defense systems. Implementing these recommendations will improve America's ability to fight at sea in a major conflict. More effort is needed to ensure that logistics vessels can quickly offload and unite troops with their combat gear in any WMD scenario. Older vessels in the ready reserve fleets should be evaluated and, where necessary, replaced. Doing so offers work for a range of emerging American cargo ship manufacturers that are needed to sustain the industrial base of U.S. seapower.

RESPONDING TO REGIONAL AGGRESSION

Major naval battles are rarely fought far from land. The Battle of Salamis in 480 BC, in which Athens and its allies defeated the Persian navy, took place in the confined waters of the Saronic Gulf. Octavian, in the Battle of Actium, ended Rome's civil conflict by defeating the naval forces of Mark Antony and Cleopatra in the Ionian Sea at the entrance to the enclosed Ambracian Gulf. The 1571 Battle of Lepanto, in which Venice, the Papal States, and Spain turned back the Ottoman navy, occurred south of Actium, in the Gulf of Patras. The fulcrum of the 1942 Battle of Midway was the island of Midway, which the Japanese Empire sought to capture to advance their forward position in the Pacific. The Battle of the Atlantic is an exception, but not much of one, because the stakes were America's ability to sustain the allied effort against the Nazis. The essence of naval power is to affect events on land.

Today is no exception. China's attempt to control the international waters of the South and East China Seas and their bracketing island chains imperils the ability of the United States to communicate with its Asian allies and partners. In areas of tension or where hostilities are possible, such as in the South and East China Seas or in the Eastern Mediterranean or Persian Gulf, naval leadership is aware that a mix of submarines and smaller, battle-ready surface action groups could be substituted for today's carrier strike group to deter aggression. This sensible modification to traditional practice would allow large carriers to be held in reserve and be prepared for multi-carrier operations both to deter conflict and to increase the lethality of a U.S. response if deterrence fails.

These surface action groups should be tailored to regional threats. Their common denominator would be a mix of small carriers, large surface combatants, and logistical vessels—including command and control and tender/maintenance craft. But their essence would be submarines and smaller forward-deployed vessels—frigates and patrol boats—that can move swiftly to answer aggression and counter gray-zone tactics, serving as a deterrence force by demonstrating the ability to punish an ambitious foe.

Smaller craft—forward-deployed frigates and combat-ready patrol boats—would be the backbone of this force. The mission that 115 frigates and numerous minesweepers once supported during the Cold War has been handed off to a motley fleet of 8 commissioned littoral combat ships (LCSs) and thirteen small, 300-ton *Cyclone*-class patrol ships. Ultimately, between 40 and 52 LCSs are planned for commissioning.

Either more lethal and numerous LCS platforms or an updated, robust frigate should be added to the fleet; a large number of highly armed 600–700-ton patrol gun-boats would usefully augment the fleet's sea control ability. These small craft, armed with anti-ship missiles and carrying a mix of smaller anti-surface, anti-air, and other innovative capabilities, can deliver swift offensive power while offering junior officers a command. For reconnaissance, surveillance, picket duty, and immediate and lethal response in the close-to-land parts of the ocean where naval engagements have traditionally been fought, smaller vessels are critical for ensuring access for American seapower to a region's contested waters.

As these small ships work further forward, they will need the same types of combat systems with which larger combatants are equipped. Their weapons systems, sensors, and electronic warfare systems must be sufficiently scalable to conform to the limited space and weight of smaller combatants as well as even smaller unmanned combatants. However, a particularly important tactical advance for surface combatants will be the tactical unmanned aerial vehicle (UAV). These already exist, in part, in the RQ-21 Blackjack Small Tactical UAV and the MQ-8B/C Fire Scout UAV helicopters.

These platforms are likely to be forebears to a more sophisticated UAV called the Tactically Exploited Reconnaissance Node (TERN), which is currently under development by the Defense Advanced Research Projects Agency (DARPA) and the Office of Naval Research. The ability to field a small, high-endurance rotary-wing sensor platform will allow small platforms to range far away from a mother ship and gain the advantage of time to engage potential threats before they are able to inflict damage on our forces. The particulars of these systems need not trouble a general audience. Their combined effect is to gain competitive advantage by outranging an enemy with weapons of greater lethality.

PROVIDING SURVEILLANCE AND CRISIS MANAGEMENT CAPABILITIES

Technology in the form of sensors, advanced detection of enemy systems, satellites, and the integration of tactical data already exists or will shortly become available. This includes such defenses against these same measures as stealthily shaped and reflective surfaces. The net result has slewed the focus of contemporary warfare toward a greater and more precise knowledge of the battlefield. But the goal of knowing an enemy's intent and capability is as old as warfare. Today's technology represents a large step toward gaining this knowledge.

Surveillance, monitoring, and contingency response

provide critical support in combat. These functions are undertaken by a range of different platforms. At sea, oceanographic research ships, EP-3E Aries II aircraft, MQ-4C Triton UAVs, P-8 Poseidon patrol aircraft, submarines, and a growing constellation of unmanned ships, submersibles, and other fixed surveillance systems work together to provide intelligence to the sailor.

As intelligence-gathering efforts expand and more countries struggle with the challenges of unmanned platforms, more resources will be needed to track, monitor, and confuse or defeat hostile data-gathering efforts. Twelve fast, utilitarian *Spearhead*-class expeditionary fast transports (T-EPFs), supported by two *Montford Point*-class expeditionary transfer docks (T-ESD) and two to three *Louis B. Puller*-class expeditionary mobile bases (T-ESB), will be entering the fleet. They could also serve as interim support vehicles for a wide range of new unmanned platforms as they evolve from an exotic, unreliable prototype to a reliable weapon, ready for the front lines.

To meet a growing number of contingencies, an expanded U.S. Marine Corps will require additional resources if the flat-deck ships are transformed to increase naval air power. The stores and supplies that the large-deck LHAs and LHDs usually carry would be transferred to a growing amphibious fleet, one that is currently composed of a planned eleven LX(R) ships and twelve *San Antonio*-class landing platform dock LPD-17 ships. This would allow the landing and sustainment of assault elements of two Marine expeditionary brigades.

Over the past decade, as America fought wars far from the sea, amphibious warfare has been neglected. The current requirement for amphibious vessels was allowed to slump to thirty-four to thirty-eight ships. But future demand, the result of China's construction and arming of South China Sea islands, as well as their rapidly increasing fleet of blue-water amphibious assault ships which threaten the entire first island chain, are powerful arguments to build more than fifty of these useful vessels. Amphibious warfare will be important and a constant in warfare as long as oceans abut continents.

The large LPD-17–based hull form has potential to be particularly useful. Though the first LPD-17 ships were plagued by quality and engineering issues, these problems have been largely resolved. Now that the ships have become reliable, the advanced capabilities that were discarded as the ships were introduced into the fleet can now be reintroduced. Existing LPD-17s could be equipped with missiles and an accompanying vertical launching system as well as other combatant capabilities. At the same time, the LX(R), an LPD derivative, could leverage the existing LPD-17 production line, expanding the amphibious fleet to meet the challenge posed by the global proliferation of amphibious fleets. The Navy's critical "connectors" that move troops and gear from the ship to shore are being sensibly and efficiently recapitalized.

In aviation, the amphibious fleet maintains some of the most advanced platforms available today. The venerable Huey has been replaced with 160 UH-1Y Huey/Venoms and 189 AH-1Z Super Cobras. They offer the fleet modern reliable utility and attack helicopters. The aging troop-carrying CH-43 Sea King is being replaced by 360 MV-22 Osprey, an innovative tilt-wing helicopter-airplane hybrid, which, after a long teething period, has emerged as an integral troop transport for the USMC. Larger heavy-lift CH-53K King Stallion helicopters are working through their extended development process, but, once delivered, the Marine Corps will reap the benefits of maintaining very high performance requirements and an ambitious operational doctrine.

In some regions—particularly in the Pacific, anti-Chinese ethnic unrest could spur Beijing's intervention. Acquiring a toehold in the Central or Southern Pacific would require such faster, lighter-equipped response vessels as the joint high-speed vehicle, a fast, low-cost and low-draft naval transport that carries troops and equipment.

PROVIDING FOR COASTAL DEFENSE

At home, the transit of illegal drugs remains a significant problem for the U.S. Coast Guard and Customs and Border Patrol. The USCG estimates that it has actionable intelligence information on 90 percent of the maritime movements of drugs toward the United States, but only enough surface resources to intercept 20 percent of the illicit traffic. This is unacceptable. The Navy can expect that the USCG's two classes of large, ocean-going USCG cutters will be supplemented by naval vessels to shut down the known maritime movement of illegal immigrants, drugs, and other contraband into the United States.

By working to expand collaboration with the U.S. Coast Guard, Navy platforms can support stronger border protection and restrict the maritime flow of drugs and other illicit contraband. If collaboration and support for anti-drug efforts decline in Central and South America,

Louis B. Puller-class expeditionary mobile bases (T-ESB) can serve as interim locations for counter-smuggling law-enforcement platforms.

CAN IT BE DONE?

Can it be done? The answer depends on what the "it" is. U.S. seapower can certainly be greatly increased. The more difficult questions are: What strategy governs the ships and aircraft to be built? How, and to what specific purposes, will they be deployed? Will we continue to emphasize projecting strike power from the sea to the shore, as has been the practice since the Cold War ended? Will we shift toward being prepared for great power conflict by emphasizing control of the seas? How can alliances, both naval and continental, be marshaled to support our security aims and deny the enemy room to maneuver? American seapower has a sporadic record—sometimes excellent, sometimes deficient—of addressing strategic questions. The prospect of servicing a $20 trillion national debt should have little effect on our will to defend the nation. It should weigh importantly as we choose how best to accomplish this.

The thirty-year shipbuilding plan for fiscal year 2017 recommends a fleet of 308 ships. The changes recommended in this chapter would increase the American carrier fleet by two additional large-deck ships and ten smaller conventional ones. The recommendations would convert or replace ten of today's amphibious flat-deck ships to serve as a more aircraft-focused design. To compensate for the lost amphibious lift, about ten additional "small-deck" amphibious ships would be added to the existing amphibious fleet. To escort these ships, twelve large surface combatants would be added, along with more than twenty attack submarines.

This would result in a battle fleet of about 350 vessels, the absolute minimum if there is hope of prevailing in conflict with the threats described above. Small patrol gunboats, which are not included in the current battle fleet, could be used to supplement these numbers and provide presence as needed. Several recommendations, such as the one that would greatly increase the number of large surface combatants, would result in a fleet that is substantially larger than 350, one that could unilaterally preserve the decisive advantage of U.S. seapower in a global conflagration.

Recapitalizing a navy takes time. Additional ships may be ordered quickly, but they are built much more slowly. A significantly measurable increase in fleet size is unlikely until the end of the decade. The stockpile of reserve ships that contributed to rapid buildups in the past—that helped expand the fleet during the buildups of the Korean War, the Vietnam War, and the Cold War to 600 ships—no longer exists. The only useful ships are the two fast and battle-hardened *Supply*-class replenishment ships currently held in reserve. The resupply ships *Rainer* and *Bridge* are barely halfway through their operational lives. A refit, always expensive, would still cost less than the billions needed for replacement ships with equivalent capabilities.

Without classifying ships that were not built for combat as combat vessels, the underutilized national shipbuilding industrial base is still able to build more ships than it is today. Doing so would bring additional combatants into the fleet at a faster pace. The submarine industrial base is expanding to build large, new ballistic-missile submarines. This workforce can—and should—be augmented to build attack submarines at a rate higher than the current two boats per year. Large surface combatants are produced by shipyards owned by Huntington Ingalls Industries and General Dynamics. Both companies can support a rapid buildup of larger, more complex combatant craft. VT Halter Marine, Philly Shipyard, and Vigor Industrial are working on larger ships and could support large shipbuilding projects.

The American shipbuilding industrial base is particularly suited to increase the construction of smaller combatants. Two yards, Austal USA and Marinette Marine, are building littoral combat ships. Eastern Shipbuilding is preparing to construct the Coast Guard's offshore patrol cutter, and Bollinger Shipyards is turning out the small 350-ton fast response cutter for the Coast Guard. Yards owned by Edison Chouest Offshore, Vigor Industrial, and VT Halter Marine lack business because of the collapse of America's offshore petrochemical extraction sector and could easily and swiftly produce smaller, less complex combatants.

A part of the naval industrial base is well situated to increase production. A large range of hungry new shipyards are vying for position as smaller and often unmanned surface and undersea platforms start to enter the fleet. These new "research and development" yards would benefit from a steady stream of funding to support innovative prototypes and nurture the development of the next John

Ericsson or Donald Roebling, respectively the inventors of the USS *Monitor* and the "amtrac" tracked amphibious landing craft.

The ground vehicle and aviation/aerospace sectors are prepared to accommodate the anticipated buildup of the U.S. Marine Corps and expanded aviation requirements of a larger, more energized Navy.

The Navy is technically ready to advance a range of innovative communications and electronic warfare initiatives. But the Navy's internal research and development infrastructure demands additional investment. The Naval Research Laboratory and the Office of Naval Research have done a good job tailoring their work to address new fleet challenges, and their efforts have enabled public-private partnerships that hasten the delivery of such new technologies as lasers and rail guns. But new technology for the military is like a statue without a pedestal. The challenge is to drive these new innovations through the slower, bureaucratically hidebound government acquisition directorates.

Innovation is also stymied by the large, terminally sclerotic procurement bureaucracies, such as the Space and Naval Warfare Systems Command (SPAWAR) and Naval Sea Systems Command (NAVSEA). These bureaucratic organizations throttle innovation and limit the Navy's ability to quickly and efficiently exploit technological innovations across the fleet—often delivering nonfunctional, nearly obsolete equipment. As innovations accelerate the latest technology into the commercial world—and rival navies—the delivery of electronics that are generations behind those of peers is unhelpful. SPAWAR and NAVSEA would benefit from a clear delineation of their core function by cutting the enormous amount of support they receive from outside contractors and executing their management functions internally, without contracted note-takers, schedule-makers, and other dubious overhead expenses.

American seapower's bureaucratic problems are not isolated. According to news reports published in December 2016, the Pentagon chose not to release its own study on the Defense Department's wasteful management practices.[4] Among other findings, the report noted that the Defense Department's purchasing departments employed 207,000 full-time workers, placing it among the top thirty private employers in the United States.[5] Also mentioned were the Defense Department's 457,000 full-time logistics jobs, more than the United Parcel Service's entire workforce.[6] The same internal study found that the Department of Defense could save $125 billion over a five-year period if it used attrition and early retirement, eliminated high-priced contractors, and improved its use of information technology.[7]

To some extent, the shape of the future Navy depends upon when the nation might expect conflict. If conflict is expected over the short term, readiness and proven systems must suffice; but, if there is time for innovation, then the new U.S. administration would benefit from determining what old technology and practices make sense to be set aside in favor of a tougher, riskier road to innovation.

Ultimately, a 350-ship Navy is a realistic and achievable goal. If America's seapower has a powerful advocate, who can marshal public opinion and link intelligent strategy to its practical execution, Congress is likely to be persuaded—

as they have been in the past. If the Trump administration can make significant progress toward this goal and set in place the plans and funding to see the job through, it will have done America an exceptional service, setting the framework to preserve American naval dominance for another three decades or more. The price will not be low, and there are serious questions about how to pay it. But the economic and security cost of surrendering our strength at sea is far greater. A thorough reform of the management practices in the Department of Defense would go a long way toward paying for revitalizing America's forces, at sea, on land, and in the air.

Command of the seas is not an end in itself but rather a long-armed lever for influencing events on shore. It offers its possessor economic, military, diplomatic, and political leverage over an adversary in peace and war alike. If the Persian navy of antiquity could not supply its army and outflank the Greek city-states' land forces, they could not win. When Xerxes's forces were defeated at the sea battles of Salamis and Mycale, the Persians were forced to withdraw. If the United States could not enforce a blockade of Cuba, the Soviets might turn the island into a nuclear quiver adjacent to the mainland.

Conversely, maritime alliances or empires cannot survive without being able to communicate by sea. If an alliance of states that sits on or near the Atlantic is prevented from using it to communicate, the alliance is toothless. Powers whose geography connects control of the seas with their greatness must retreat when they forget their dependence on seapower.

This volume's final scenario is set in the Mediterranean, the ancient parent of maritime strategic competition, whose maritime states—including such external ones as England and the United States—have seen their influence wax and wane with the ability to command the seas and, in some cases, project their power ashore.

CHAPTER XII

THE MEDITERRANEAN TIDE SHIFTS

A Scenario Bt 2025, Iran was close to consolidating its
grip on what had been the Middle East's Muslim states.
Greater firepower in the form of intercontinental ballistic
missiles and nuclear weapons, as well as the diplomatic
heft that the United States had handed over ten years
earlier, had given Shiites the whip hand in their contest
with Sunni Islam, whose Wahhabi adherents' pact with
Saudi Arabian rulers cracked and then crumbled.

The borders that existed before the so-called Arab
Spring, which began in Tunisia in 2010, had long since
shattered. These were the borders that the Sykes-Picot
agreement of 1916 had established to divide the Middle
East between English and French spheres of influence
after the Ottoman Empire collapsed. In the new Middle
East, Syria and Iraq were administered as Iranian protec-
torates. Kurdistan had become a self-governed state composed of what had been northern Iraq and surprisingly
large chunks of southeastern Turkey. Jordan had fought

hard but lost its large eastern wing to an Iranian-led puppet army. This was a bitter defeat.

The Jordanian royals were compensated by the fall of the House of Saud. The old Saudi patriarchs died off. They succeeded in begetting many progeny but failed to encourage seriousness in them. Moreover, the sheer number of Saudi princes defied the aging King Salman's ability to concentrate power in a single individual to ensure the House of Saud's succession. The old ruler's sons' and grandsons' taste for expensive Italian cars, Monaco, and the pleasures of Paris and Amsterdam grew. Those sons who attended West Point neither attended to their studies nor participated in sports. They frequented East Side bars and Belmont.

Oil prices had dropped to less than $40 per barrel in 2016 and hovered in the same vicinity for long enough to unhinge the Saudis' economy. Slightly more than $100 per barrel was necessary to balance the Saudi budget. As Riyadh's cash reserves had long since been spent, the already disgruntled Wahhabis had withdrawn their support for the Saudi royals. Young military officers helped push aside the dissolute royal military retainers. The junior officers sought a figurehead and settled on the Hashemite family in Amman.

Centuries ago, the Hashemite dynasty had ruled the western belt of land on the Arabian Peninsula that contained Islam's two holiest sites, Mecca, where Muhammad was born, and Medina, where he is buried. The Hashemite family—small, self-restrained, and untroubled by problems of succession—was a bulwark of discipline compared to the multitude of libertine Saudi princes. According to the deal worked out with the Saudi military, the Hashemites would become the monarchs

of the combined kingdoms of Jordan and the old Saudi
Arabia. They were more likely to slow Iran's domination
of the Islamic Middle East. Iran's influence appeared
to be on the step of a capstone achievement as the U.S.
Navy's evanescing fleet reduced naval presence in the
Persian Gulf from a single carrier with accompanying
escorts to a rotating schedule where one cruiser and several destroyers alternated to provide a presence of fluctu-
ating strength.

With its control secure in Baghdad, Damascus, and
Lebanon, Iran turned its attention to Egypt. The Muslim
Brotherhood's hatred of Abdel Fattah el-Sisi trumped
their ideological differences with the Iranian Shiites.
Handsome bribes, smuggled weapons, and the promise
of military support—if needed—encouraged them to rise
up against the Egyptian president. Suicide bombers hurl-
ing themselves off buildings combined with drone strikes
vaporized el-Sisi's motorcade. He went, as had Morsi,
Mubarak, and Sadat before him.

Egypt was not the lapdog that Iran had established in
the old states of the Levant. But the Brotherhood had no
problem either in offering military access to Iran nor in
allowing Iranian troops and air and naval forces to use
its territory for launch points of military expeditions into
neighboring Libya and beyond. The mullahs became the
dominant political and religious influence not only in
Libya but also in Tunisia and Algeria. Iranian destroyers,
amphibious vessels, and frigates patrolled from eastern
Morocco to Egypt's coast, including in the Gulf of Suez
and the Red Sea. Iranian naval vessels regularly called at
Tripoli, Tunis, and Algiers. Nor did the mullahs ignore
the Mediterranean's northern shore. Iranian relief societ-
ies as well as more sinister organizations had been active

in Bosnia, Albania, and Kosovo in the 1990s. Thirty years later, they picked up where they had left off.

If Turkey could be Finlandized or pinched between its old enemy Russia and the growing Shiite empire to its south, the Iranians might consolidate their influence so that it extended from the Adriatic to the western Maghreb. In Iran's way Greece stood, though "wobbled" would be a more accurate description. The default on its loans, expulsion from the Eurozone, hyperinflation, and perforated defenses had turned Greece into NATO's biggest single liability. NATO's Article 5 (the provision that an attack on one alliance state would be considered as an attack on all) was very well and good. But which member would commit ground forces to the defense of a state whose combat pilots were down to a single hour of flight training time per month?

Athens had a reasonable answer. Natural gas had been discovered in large quantities off the Israeli coast in 2010. More reserves were found south of Cyprus the following year. Natural gas reserves that were approximately ten times the size of those in Cyprus's exclusive economic zone were discovered in Egypt in 2015. Exploration of the Aegean began in 2017 and resulted in the discovery of large additional natural gas deposits.

Below its seafloor, the Eastern Mediterranean turned out to be a giant, if segmented, cavern of natural gas. Drilling rigs, onshore liquefied natural gas processing plants, floating liquefied natural gas ships (FLNGs) that processed the gas at sea, vessels whose decks were occupied by huge domes that carried 10 million cubic feet of natural gas, and underwater pipelines dotted and crisscrossed the Eastern Mediterranean. Greece profited not only from the sale and liquefaction of natural gas but also from the use of its territory for pipelines that moved the gas to Western Europe. The possibility once again existed for the country to stand on its own economic feet. However, the gas business needed peace to turn a profit.

Iran's leaders had other ideas. They would be a force from the Mediterranean's north and eastern shores to most of its southern coast. Turkey's Finlandization would mean a stop to its nuclear weapons manufacturing and ballistic-missile development and an end of its efforts to support half-hearted Sunni insurgents in what had once been Iraq and Syria. Iran, along with its Russian patron, would be pleased to have Sultan Erdogan—he'd changed his title from president to sultan—concentrate on dismembering Kurdistan.

But Turkey would not be Finlandized. The sultan accepted the risk of continuing his nuclear weapons and ballistic-missile programs. Erdogan, still in power eleven years after having become chief of state, scaled back his support for Sunni insurgents and policed his southern border with greater attention. Since he had lost to the east and south, he turned his attention—like his fifteenth-century predecessors—west, toward the Balkans, in particular toward Greece. This did not please NATO. But Turkey, possessing Europe's largest naval and land forces and strengthened by the long-awaited incorporation of F-35 strike fighters into its air force, was the alliance's best bet against Iran's ambitions across the Aegean—and further.

Iran's rulers' forebears had invaded Greece in 492 BC and then twelve years later. They were thinking about Greece again. If they could bring enough pressure to wield influence in the Balkans, the Turks would lose an important outpost, Iranian influence would approach

313

Western Europe more closely, and Greece would be pinched between adversaries to its northwest and across the Aegean. Where Darius had failed, the jihadist clerics might succeed.

The commanding officer of the U.S. 6th Fleet, Vice Admiral George Huffman, was also thinking about Greece. During the Cold War, the 6th Fleet had prowled the Mediterranean armed with robust amphibious forces, two carrier strike groups, dozens of surface escorts, and submarines, and had been aided by large bases from Crete to Sicily to Spain.

Now, the 6th Fleet had a handful of littoral combat ships based in Spain and a command ship in central Italy. That was it—except for when a surface action group or the occasional carrier strike group passed from the Suez to Gibraltar or in the opposite direction, heading to or from the Persian Gulf. Then, operational control of the carrier became Vice Admiral Huffman's responsibility. This happened once every ten months when the naval flotillas relieved each other. But the ten-month cycle was erratic. Sometimes two or three months would pass before the arrival of the relieving carrier filled the gap left by the departed one. If a crisis blew up in the Mediterranean, the U.S. president had to trust to good fortune that sufficient firepower would be on the scene.

The advanced destroyer USS *Zumwalt* had exited the Mediterranean en route to the Persian Gulf a month earlier. It filled a gap left by the USS *Theodore Roosevelt*, which had sailed home three months before.

The admiral was sitting at the desk in his in-port cabin aboard the USS *Mount Whitney*, going over the stack of intelligence messages that had arrived during the mid-watch. One of his littoral combat ships was in port for regular maintenance at Toulon. A second was at a Spanish shipyard having its main drive shaft aligned. The third was visiting Augusta Bay, Sicily. A fourth patrolled in the international waters close to the Suez's mouth.

Message traffic was normal. A host of Panamanian-, Chinese-, and Palauan-flagged tankers trundled westbound from Suez for North and South American ports; ships laden with cargoes of ballast headed in the opposite direction to take on Iranian and Saudi oil; refrigerated ships with Israeli and Turkish fruit plodded for Western Europe; scores of Italian and Bulgarian fishing vessels hunted from Gibraltar to Sochi, on the Black Sea's eastern shore. Nothing interesting.

Or was there? The admiral's staff had highlighted a message from a couple of days earlier that showed the route of a Palauan-flagged dry goods ship on a course from Sukhumi in Georgia to Rabat on Morocco's Atlantic coast. Sukhumi was the capital of Abkhazia, the area that had broken away from Georgia to join Russia in 1993.

The MV *Voronezh* carried fertilizer and copper ore. It had crossed paths in the central Mediterranean with a Liberian-registered ship out of Valletta, the capital of Malta. The *Callixtus*, loaded with electrical generators and pharmaceuticals, was bound for New Orleans. Both ships carried containers on their decks in addition to bulk cargo below decks. There was nothing noteworthy about the two ships' courses except that they intersected at the same time (0300 local) and place.

The Maltese speak their own Semitic language as well as Arabic, Italian, and English. The island lies between Sicily and Libya. Italian diplomacy and patrol boats had prevented Malta from being swallowed by the Shiite wave that flooded the Maghreb littoral. But, like Casablanca during World War II, it had become a magnet for espionage that remained squarely in the sights of North Africa's Iranian puppets.

Admiral Huffman looked at the asterisk that appeared in the Office of Naval Intelligence (ONI) report on both ships and saw that an Iraqi national captained the ship that had come out of Sukhumi. He called his intelligence officer.

"What do you think of this, Bob?" the admiral asked, pointing to the course intersection of the two westbound merchant ships. "You think it's a coincidence that they crossed the same point at the same time?" The 6th Fleet's intel officer, Captain Robert Sloss, was approaching his twenty-two-year mark as a naval officer. He thought that coincidences happened when Manchester United defeated a rival at the same time that the National Zoo in Washington fed its pandas.

Sloss looked over the message date/time group so that he could call up the same message on his computer.

"Sir, I'll get with Defense Intelligence Agency (DIA) and see if there's any signals intelligence on comms between the two ships. If something was going on out there, they might have been talking."

"Good."

"Also," the captain continued, "they'll need to take a closer look at the ships' previous port calls, the crews, owners, the whole nine yards."

Sloss knocked on the admiral's door later in the afternoon. "Sir, I checked with DIA. There's no record of any communications between *Callixtus* and the *Voronezh*. The Liberian-registered ship's owner is a small Greek company. A Bulgarian consortium bought the *Voronezh* from

its previous owner and
eight years ago. The t
same port at the same
nections between the
Med and runs the Med
yearly. *Voronezh* mostly s
of the occasional call at

"Did *Voronezh* call any
the admiral.

"Sir, her last recorded
was Qatar. Neither *Voron*
'watch' list. Both vessels
they crossed paths. They still are."

"Watch them, Bob," said the admiral, shaking his
head. "This doesn't smell right."

Vice Admiral Huffman had a good nose. After taking on cargo at Sukhumi in Georgia, the *Voronezh* had
delivered several hundred tons of vegetables and fruit
from two Mediterranean ports to Qatar. With this cargo
offloaded, she took on several intermodal freight containers filled with gas turbine parts and sailed east toward the
Strait of Hormuz.

Approaching the narrow choke point where the Persian Gulf empties into the Indian Ocean, her second
mate complained of acute pain in his lower right abdo-
men. The ship's captain, Ahmed Hossein, an Iraqi who
had migrated to Bulgaria, expected this. Hossein was a
devout Shiite. Saddam Hussein's regime had imprisoned
his father on trumped-up charges just after the First
Gulf War.

Iranian intelligence subsequently recruited Ahmed.
At the time he was still a young man. He heard nothing
from the Iranians for years, until the *Voronezh* tied up in

Sukhumi. An Iranian agent contacted Hossein and said
that one of his crew members would become ill at sea and
that he must contact the company for instructions. At the
same meeting, Hossein learned that a freight container
would be placed aboard his ship while they were in port
offloading the sick crew member, and that a rendezvous
at sea with another vessel would be required to transfer
the freight container. The rendezvous would conclude
this unusual mission. The spymaster said that its successful execution would net him a $100,000 cash reward.

Voronezh put to sea and events unfolded as its master
had been told. The second mate complained of acute
abdominal discomfort twenty-three hours after leaving
Doha. When the pain worsened, Hossein dutifully called
the owners. The radio communication was brief. A few
minutes later, the owners' agent in Sofia responded. The
shipping company's doctor diagnosed the pain as acute
appendicitis and recommended immediate medical attention. The captain was instructed to put into the Iranian
port of Bandar Abbas, seventeen miles ahead. It would
be cheaper to dock there and offload the sick man than
to pay for land-based helicopter emergency services.

Voronezh hailed the Iranian port authorities, who had
an ambulance waiting when the ship arrived at a dimly lit
pier less than two hours later, about 0400. The Iranians
also had a single intermodal freight container to add to
the ones stacked on the ship's deck.

The moon had already set. Most of the ship's crew
slept. Those on watch were gathered on the port side to
help the groaning patient into the ambulance. Captain
Hossein remained on the bridge, alone. A large derrick's
arm reached across the slip and deposited the container—
which held a nuclear device and radio-activated detona-

tor hidden under piles of machine-manufactured rugs—on the *Voronezh*'s starboard side. A watch stander noticed but was unconcerned. Containers were on- and off-loaded at most ports. Nothing exceptional here. With her mooring lines cast from their bollards, the *Voronezh* gave three short blasts on her horn and backed away from the pier.

Hossein stood on the bridge as the pilot reversed direction and nosed the ship out into the quiet waters of the Persian Gulf. The *Voronezh* was an hour and a half behind schedule, just as the owners' agent had predicted.

Eleven days later, the *Voronezh* completed her transit of the Suez and rounded Port Said, heading for Malta. The rendezvous with the *Callixtus* represented the completion of Captain Hossein's special instructions. The instructions had gone into effect while the *Voronezh* was pierside in Qatar. There, she had had a new crane installed. The procedure took longer than usual. Mounting a crane on gimbals would allow cargo to be transferred between ships at sea. It was a delicate matter, even with recent advances that allowed computers to anticipate and compensate for the roll of both ships as a transfer was executed. Calibrate it wrong, and the movement of any piece of heavy cargo from one ship to another, even in a calm sea, could turn into a loss of property and life.

The final step depended on the Mediterranean's cooperation. Even a gimbal crane could not set a container down safely on another ship in a pitching sea. The operation took place in August, when the inland sea comes closest to a glass sheet, and at night, when the heated winds from close-by land masses would abate.

The *Voronezh* and *Callixtus* had each been equipped with a set of ultraviolet light-emitting diode (LED) signaling devices. They used them to communicate as the distance between them closed, and the container that had been taken aboard at Bandar Abbas was transferred to the *Callixtus*. The entire operation lasted 45 minutes. Crew members were informed that a change in shipping insurance regulations necessitated the transfer.

The master of the *Callixtus* had been told only that the transferred freight consisted of antique Persian rugs (which were still forbidden for importing to the United States), bootlegged cigarettes, and a large shipment of diamonds. He didn't believe a word of it and figured that the cargo was drugs. But, he reckoned, it was a slight risk compared to the promised reward, including the handsome down payment of 5,000 Euros that he had received. He looked forward to having done with the business and pocketing the promised balance of 45,000 Euros. Both ships resumed speed and separated as the slower *Voronezh* fell behind on her course toward Rabat.

Admiral Huffman sent a message to the European Command Commander with copies to Chairman of the Joint Chiefs General McKelan, USAF, and the other members of the Joint Chiefs as well as the Joint Staff. The message reported the fact of the two merchant ships' occupying the same geographic position at the same time along with other relevant information about ownership and prior ports of call. Huffman recommended that *Callixtus* be boarded and searched on the high seas long before her arrival at the port of New Orleans. He stored the merchant ship issue in a mental file, went over the fleet's monthly expense ledger, and made his way down to the wardroom for the daily intelligence briefing.

Huffman's message went through the usual channels. The usual channels ignored it. Where the Office of Naval Intelligence had once had a 15,000-square-foot room

filled with hundreds of analysts who watched the world-
wide movement of certain merchant ships, cutbacks had
been necessary as service on a $29 trillion federal debt ate
into both defense and non-defense spending. ONI guide-
lines did not call for monitoring friendly flagged foreign
vessels with a spotless history of ownership, cargoes, and
ports of call.

The same financial problems decimated the fleet. Even
if the ONI decided to put *Callixtus* on its "watch" list,
there was only one Navy frigate and two Coast Guard
cutters to patrol the Gulf of Mexico and the Caribbean.
Chinese and Russian "research" ships plied the area just
outside of U.S. coastal waters from Miami to Browns-
ville, Texas. Submarines from the same two countries
also came to snoop and reconnoiter. Worsening relations between Washington and Mexico had resulted in
the Mexican president's willingness to accept a Chinese
naval facility at the port of Lázaro Cárdenas on Mexico's
Pacific coast. A Chinese destroyer maintained a constant
presence off Nicaragua's east coast, where a new, wider
canal linking the Atlantic with the Pacific was about
to open.

A single Greek and another Bulgarian-owned merchant ship might conceivably attract ONI's attention, but
sending an armed U.S. ship to investigate meant aban-
doning surveillance on Chinese and Russian spy vessels,
surface combatants, and subs.

Admiral Huffman had done what he could. He seated
himself in the wardroom. Captain Sloss began the morning briefing.

"Sir, Russian naval dispositions are the same: one
carrier, one amphibious ship, two guided-missile cruisers, six destroyers, two subs, three logistics ships, and

a pair of mine-sweepers. No change. They remain on patrol between the mouth of the Adriatic and the eastern Aegean."

"Wonderful. Any new developments with the Turks and Iranians?"

Captain Sloss reviewed the events of the previous two weeks. A suicide bomber had blown himself up at a Turkish-sponsored kindergarten in Albania's capital, Tirana, killing three teachers and nineteen toddlers. Almost to the minute, another suicide bomber detonated his vest at a mosque, killing twelve men, including a local cleric, in the Turkish city of Gaziantep, about 30 miles north of the border that separated the old Syria from Turkey. A Hezbollah terrorist leader in Beirut claimed responsibility for both bombings. He said that they were in response to the ambush of an Iranian convoy the previous week as it traveled west from Iran toward Lebanon.

Sloss went on. "Erdogan answered back. The intelligence community has confirmed that the Turkish-supported terror group, Islamic Caliphate (IC) carried out drone attacks that had killed two dozen Houthi Shiite military officers and government officials in Yemen last Thursday." Backed by Iranian support, the Shiite tribesmen had toppled the military government that ruled Yemen in 2019.

Admiral Huffman leaned forward in his chair.

"So?" he asked.

"Well, here's where it gets interesting," Sloss responded. "A Turkish surface squadron is conducting interoperability maneuvers with four Egyptian frigates in the vicinity of the Zohr gas field."

"I know."

The Italian energy giant, ENI, had discovered the

Zohr natural gas field, with proven reserves of 30 trillion cubic feet, in 2015. Zohr lies off the Egyptian coast, within Egypt's exclusive economic zone. Since the discovery, Egypt, Israel, Cyprus, and Greece had signed a defense cooperation agreement to protect one another's natural gas drilling rigs, natural gas transport ships, and liquefied natural gas plants in their respective exclusive economic zones.

The immediate reason to establish a defense agreement was Sultan Erdogan's threat to use force if the Greek Cypriots exported the natural gas that had been discovered in 2011. Diplomatic, security, environmental, logistic, and commercial dilemmas had delayed the actual sale of Cyprus's natural gas until now. Turkey's threat had been discounted—for good reason. Almost a decade and a half earlier, Ankara had failed to carry out its threat to use force if Cyprus so much as drilled for gas. But, as the new agreement suggested, the region's natural gas-rich states were nervous.

Huffman shifted about in his chair. "Please continue."

"Well, Iran increased its naval presence in the Med last night. An amphibious ship, two destroyers, and five frigates are operating midway between Cyprus and Egypt. This morning at 0530 our P-8 squadron reported that a couple of Iranian *Varshavyanka*-class subs had arrived on scene to escort the amphibs."

"This isn't the first time that Iran has put two subs in the Med at the same time," remarked the admiral, "but the timing of their arrival has been staggered. Have they ever sent two in at once?"

"This is the first time," answered Sloss. "It is also the first time that Iran has deployed a nuclear-tipped anti-ship missile aboard one of its new Russian submarines."

The *Varshavyanka*-class, also called Type 636.3, is an advanced diesel-electric boat. It displaces 4,000 tons submerged and, besides its six torpedo tubes, is armed with anti-ship and surface-to-air missiles.

"Do the Turks know?" asked Huffman. "And if they don't, are we going to tell them?"

Relations between Washington and Ankara were frosty, but Turkey was still a NATO member. And Article 5, which required member states to regard an attack on one as an attack on all, remained in effect. Huffman didn't want to see that provision invoked and he wanted even less to see it invoked and ignored. That would be NATO's end.

"Sir, the Turkish navy knows. There's been an unusual volume of traffic between the Palace, the naval command headquarters in Ankara, and the navy base at Gölcük. But there's more."

The admiral leaned forward and reached for his coffee.

"Yes, sir. Do you recall the small Turkish carrier and amphibious ship that were conducting pre-deployment workups in the Sea of Marmara?"

Turkey had commissioned a 30,000-ton flattop in 2022. The *Anadolu* carried a small number of F-35 fighter-bombers, helicopters, landing craft, tanks, and troops.

"Sure."

"They sailed through the Dardanelles yesterday and are headed south into the Aegean, accompanied by a couple of destroyers."

"Destination?"

"Message traffic is unclear, sir. But there's been more than a few mentions of Cyprus and also the Red Sea."

Huffman figured that the Turkish navy was scrambling to get its German-designed Type 214 subs out to sea. The

Type 214 was a good boat with a half-dozen satisfied cus-
tomers from South Korea to Portugal. However, it could
not match Iran's Russian-built subs in displacement or
armament.

The admiral leaned back in his chair and considered
what the U.S. 6th Fleet had looked like when it had teeth.
Like in 1956 when the 6th Fleet rescued 3,000 Americans,
UN personnel, and foreigners as the Suez crisis brewed.
Huffman could not help comparing this to 2011, when
U.S. citizens had to be evacuated by a chartered Maltese
ferry during Qaddafi's violent overthrow.

He thought about how the 6th Fleet's presence and
amphibious forces put a lid on the armed dispute between Lebanon's Maronite Christians and Muslims as
Soviet forces maneuvered to exploit the civil conflict
in 1958.

Huffman's second-year history class at the Naval
Academy offered as a case study the 6th Fleet's success in
deterring Soviet naval forces that aimed to interrupt the
life-sustaining flow of U.S. military equipment to Israel
in the 1973 Yom Kippur War. He remembered the old
professor who had been the operations officer aboard
the carrier USS *Independence*. The ship was part of a chain
of U.S. carriers used as refueling and crew rest stops for
American combat aircraft sent to replenish Israeli air
force tactical jets.

The United States had long since lost the ability to use
hard power to influence events similarly in the Mediterranean. George Huffman figured that it was a question
of time until his countrymen fully understood the consequences of this loss. He put aside his thoughts and concentrated on the briefer.

"What do you guys think?" asked the admiral. "Are

those Iranian subs there on a Turkey shoot? And what do you make of the Turkish surface ship deployments?"

The Cypriot government was asking the same question about Turkish naval movements. Besides very limited coastal patrol vessels, Cyprus had no navy or air force. Nicosia depended on Athens for its defense just as Northern Cyprus—recognized as a sovereign state only by Ankara—depended on Turkey. The Cypriot government believed that Turkey could indeed use force as the date of the first shipment of natural gas from Cyprus's offshore rigs approached.

Turkey's military was stronger, bigger, and better equipped than that of Greece, which was an economic basket case without a handle. If Erdogan attacked Cyprus because it had started shipping natural gas that Turkey believed it owned, Greek forces were unlikely to prevail. The Cypriot national security council debated asking for NATO assistance. Its members chose not to do so. They decided that, for want of available American and European combat ships, the answer was a foregone conclusion.

However, Russia was another matter. Relations between Russia and Cyprus had experienced the occasional bump over time but were fundamentally sound. Russian tourists came to Cyprus for the sun and beaches. As a result of agreements signed a decade earlier, Russian naval vessels called at Limassol and Larnaca, where they refueled, repaired, and sent their crews off on liberty. Wealthy Cypriots had become an important source of direct foreign investment in Russia. Moscow's access to Syrian naval facilities helped establish Russia as a Mediterranean power. Vladimir Putin was pleased to add Cypriot ports to his fleet's expanding influence.

As the Turkish flotilla gathered in the Sea of Marmara in advance of Cyprus's first shipment of natural gas abroad, the Cypriot foreign minister flew to Moscow. There, he offered Russian air and naval forces unrestricted access to Cypriot military and naval facilities. This included an invitation to place Russian troops and equipment on the ground in Cyprus. The Cypriots had grown weary of being rebuffed in gaining access even to NATO's program for states that wanted to join. Moscow would be able to add more forces to the region and did not have to be implored. In return for access, Russia would "supplement" Greece's defense of Cyprus.

From a high-priority message relayed by DIA that had originated with the Israeli Defense Force's (IDF) directorate of military intelligence, Vice Admiral Huffman learned of the Russia-Cyprus agreement the day after his intelligence officer briefed him on Turkey's Aegean-bound flotilla.

He was not surprised. Russia and Turkey had a long and disagreeable relationship. It preceded the nineteenth-century war over the Crimea that pitted the Ottoman against the Russian empire. Athens would wrinkle its brow at Russia's strategic gain so close to home, but Greek leaders would lose no sleep over the prospect that Moscow might take Ankara down a notch or two. Besides, maybe the Greeks, as a maritime state, should be thinking about a similar deal. NATO had nothing to offer them anymore now that Russia was the major external seapower in the Mediterranean.

The DIA message had an addendum, also provided by the IDF.

Captain Sloss, the admiral's intelligence officer, briefed it rather than send it in to Huffman with other reports.

"Sir, do you remember the Greek- and Bulgarian-owned ships whose courses intersected off Malta?"

"Yes, Bob. Why?"

"Before departing for New Orleans, *Callixtus* came out of a Piraeus repair facility after having her electrical system, main engine, fuel pumps, and steering gear completely replaced."

"Ships need maintenance, Bob."

"Yes sir. But *Callixtus* was launched six years ago—a bit soon for a major overhaul, don't you think?

"Bob, draft a flash message from me to General Christensen (the director of DIA). I want immediate authority to communicate directly with the IDF intel chief."

"DIRLAUTH approved," came back the response an hour later. Direct Liaison Authorized.

Huffman was on the secure phone with Rear Admiral Ezrachi a few minutes later.

"What's going on, Benny?" Huffman asked. The two men had known each other since attending the same class at the Naval War College in Newport, Rhode Island, several years earlier.

"I'm not certain, but I think we need to know more. We looked into *Callixtus*'s ownership. It's quite muddy. The owner of record is a small Greek firm, but the main partners' offices are in Athens, Beirut, Istanbul, and Riyadh."

"What do you make of that?"

"Only the Athens address checks out. The addresses in the other cities are either private residences or else buildings with fabricated numbers that do not exist."

"This is not good," said the American admiral. "A virtually new ship with no record of damage or accident doesn't need its guts replaced."

"No," answered General Ezrachi. "Not unless its owners wanted to be as sure as possible that it would operate flawlessly."

"But that's not all," he continued. "Did your people see that *Callixtus* and another merchant ship, the Liberian-registered *Voronezh*, crossed paths at the same time three days ago?"

"Yes."

"*Voronezh* put in at Bandar Abbas before what may have been a rendezvous with *Callixtus*."

Huffman sat down. "We have no record of this. Its last port of call was Qatar."

"Its last *official* port of call was Qatar. But it made a short unscheduled stop in Bandar Abbas to off-load a crew member who was diagnosed with appendicitis. I have the recording of the comms between the ship, its operations center in Sofia, and the port authorities in Iran."

"All right," said Huffman. "Something's wrong here."

"Very wrong," said Ezrachi. "There's no record of anyone being admitted to the Hadish naval hospital in Bandar Abbas that evening, except for a couple of kids with bruises from a minor motor scooter accident."

"Thanks, Benny. I'll talk with my people in Washington."

"Sure, let us know if we can help."

Huffman hung up and thought about the T-shirt he'd seen for sale in Jerusalem's Old City: "Don't Worry, America. Israel Has Your Back."

He put in a call to the J-3, the operations directorate chief at the Joint Staff in the Pentagon, and explained what he knew.

The Joint Chiefs met that same hour. There was no evidence of hostile intent, and the intel folks could sort out later whether this was a rogue military officer's plan, an IRGC matter, or if Tehran knew anything of what was going on—or if in fact anything was going on. For the moment, the chiefs had to consider that a weapon of mass destruction had been placed aboard a ship whose destination was the United States.

The *Callixtus* had already steamed into the West Atlantic. The chiefs agreed they had to assume that the merchant ship's stop in Bandar Abbas had allowed a nuclear, chemical, or biological device to be loaded aboard, perhaps in the nosecone of a missile mounted inside a freight container. Iran possessed cruise missiles that could be launched from a ship against a land target. The Meshkat had a range of over 2,000 kilometers. As it continued on its west-southwest course, the *Callixtus* had already come within launching range of the continental United States.

The greater concern was a dirty bomb or actual nuclear device that could be detonated in a U.S. port. A missile attack could already have been initiated. Also, launching a cruise missile would provide flight data that directly implicated Iran. Moreover, the entire crew would know what had happened. Finally, the United States had recently fielded airborne lasers that could detect and destroy a cruise missile from above. As a precaution, the Americas Command was ordered to locate and maintain twenty-four-hour surveillance of the *Callixtus* using specially equipped C-17s, called Apollos, that carried high-powered lasers. So far, the U.S. Air Force had taken delivery of four Apollos. All of these would be needed to maintain a single plane's continual coverage several miles above the ship.

The immediate task was to find out what was aboard the *Callixtus*. For the past several days, the ship had been sailing through the U.S. European Command's area of responsibility (AOR). When it passed 40 degrees west longitude, it entered the U.S. Northern Command's AOR. Neither combatant commander, said the operations directorate chief, still possessed ships that could reach the *Callixtus* as she continued to approach the East Coast.

The J-3, Lieutenant General Jim Kojak (USMC) called the Americas Command deputy, Vice Admiral Kevin Trout, also a three-star officer.

"Kevin," said General Kojak, "the chiefs are meeting right now, but I wanted to get your read on the situation with the merchant ship *Callixtus*."

"We've sent out the warning order and we'll have the first bird over the ship in 24 hours."

"Ok."

"I assume you're calling about interdicting the ship."

"That's it. We need to find out what's aboard it."

"There's one cutter that pulled into Veracruz last night with its main shaft off kilter. I'm waiting for a sitrep (situation report). Another cutter's on a counter-drug patrol in the Leeward Islands. We've got a destroyer on a port visit in Cartagena. Otherwise, that's it."

Admiral Trout added, "The soonest the destroyer can reach the Keys is 65 hours from receiving orders. And that's cutting it pretty close."

"Other options?" asked General Kojak. "That ship cannot be allowed to approach a U.S. port before we know what she's carrying."

"Jim, we're talking with SOCOM (U.S. Special Operations Command) right now. Give me a half hour and I'll have an answer."

Vice Admiral Trout called the commander of the Naval

Special Warfare Development Group (DEVGRU), better known as SEAL Team Six. A few minutes later, he was back on the secure line with the J-3.

"Jim, there's one assault unit in Virginia Beach. The rest are deployed in the Middle East and Africa. They can be over target 24 hours after the warning order."

"That will have to do, Kevin. But this has to be a night operation. If the ship is carrying a nuclear device I don't want it detonated—anywhere."

"They don't need to be told. They're already planning a night operation from a C-17. They'll drop three Mk1 boats that will marry up with the DEVGRU guys 10 miles astern *Callixtus* and then go board her under way. I'll have the DEVGRU CO brief you."

In fact, the Joint Chiefs asked the DEVGRU commanding officer to brief them that same afternoon. There was some haggling over the rules of engagement if crew members resisted. But the possibility that the vessel approaching New Orleans might have a nuclear weapon aboard silenced all concerns.

Three C-17s lifted off from Naval Air Station Oceana in Virginia Beach late in the afternoon the next day. The sailors, including two explosives ordnance disposal (EOD) senior chief petty officers, and boats were parachuted an hour after nightfall. DEVGRU team members boarded the ship and took over the bridge without opposition. The ship's master pleaded ignorance, but was alarmed by the Americans' suddenness and abundant force. When asked, he pointed to the container that his ship had taken on at sea in the Mediterranean. "Drugs," he thought. "Not rugs." Detection devices located the nuclear device and the EOD men removed the detonator and radio receiver.

The developing crisis in the Eastern Med did not turn out as well. Russian warships placed themselves between Cyprus and the approaching Turkish flotilla. When Sultan Erdogan ordered his navy to put troops ashore in Turkish-controlled northern Cyprus, Russian subs sank the escorting Turkish submarines and torpedoed the Turkish amphibious ships as they conducted an unopposed landing. Iranian submarines operated together with the Russian navy in the same operation.

Turkey invoked NATO's Article 5. In response, the other NATO members offered to send reconnaissance aircraft, a gesture intended to demonstrate a concerned but watered-down faithfulness to Article 5. The fig leaf did not cover the disunity within the Atlantic alliance between the French, who wanted to fight, and the Americans, who were stretched too thin to provide a timely response. Vice Admiral Huffman's four littoral combat ships—which had been upgraded almost enough to call them "frigates"—would not be sent to engage the Russia-Iran Axis. American naval dominance in the Med, which had begun in 1945 and whose roots stretched back to the wars against the Barbary pirates, ended.

Russia and Iran had no interest in controlling the migrant tides from North Africa into Europe. These flows now included millions from south of the Maghreb, where sickness, famine, war, and terror were depopulating entire states. Chaos in Europe drove up energy prices and generated political crises. It rattled what was left of the European Union and shattered such trans-Atlantic cohesion as remained after NATO's demise.

The outcome was as unnecessary as it had been avoidable. Cyprus had sought to join NATO for over a decade. Had NATO relented, the Russians would have received no invitation to increase their naval and military presence on the strategically placed island. Russia had become a Mediterranean naval power during the Syrian civil war, nearly a decade and a half earlier. When Iran drove ISIS from its Libyan perch, Russia expanded its naval presence to the middle of the Mediterranean. Meanwhile, China bought major port facilities from Piraeus to Algeciras. Russian ships were welcomed here for repairs and provisioning.

No one forced the United States to relinquish its position as the inland sea's dominant naval power. The abdication was entirely self-willed. U.S. naval shipbuilding budgets stayed anemic. Without substantive relief, the Navy absorbed the enormous expense of modernizing its ballistic-missile fleet, thus forgoing other combatants, such as destroyers and attack submarines, whose deployment to the Mediterranean would have maintained America's presence, influence, deterrence, and warfighting abilities.

But the ballistic-missile fleet modernization issue was more symptom than cause. A sustained 12 percent per year increase in the Navy's shipbuilding budget over the proposed 2017 amount, $18.4 billion, would have ensured U.S. naval superiority globally. It would also have put enough major combatants to sea to reestablish American naval dominance in the Mediterranean by 2025. The decision to keep shipbuilding budgets flat as the cost of ships rose was a failure of political will.

CHAPTER XIII

THE MORALITY OF DEFENSE

American exceptionalism became a debated topic early in the Obama administration when the president compared Americans' belief in their country's unique quality to the views of citizens of other states of their own exceptional qualities. What began in speech continued in policy as the new president sought to reduce American engagement in the Middle East, establish a new relationship with a revanchist Russian government, appease Iran's theocracy, avoid seriously contesting China's claims to sovereignty over the international waters of the West Pacific, and reduce the size and capability of U.S. armed forces.

These policies did not grow out of bad intentions. They are, rather, consistent with long-held American leftist opinion that the United States has much for which to apologize: slavery and segregation, the wrongful treatment of Native American peoples, the Mexican War, the Vietnam War, and continued economic inequality, to name a few. America is not perfect. But despite its imperfections, it is exceptional in an admirable way that is worth the price Americans have paid since our founding. Or so the generations of citizens who have fought and died for the nation believed.

We are unique because, up until now, our basic principles conform to the most important political idea of modern times: natural rights. All humans possess natural rights because they share the desire to live, to be free, and to lead more prosperous lives. Government, Americans believe, exists to protect these rights, which are called "natural" because all of humankind shares the same desires. This is the heart of American exceptionalism. It is the foundation of the Declaration of Independence, which justifies the political independence of the American people by an appeal to the natural rights of all human beings. Thomas Jefferson, the author, and the other signatories of the Declaration, argued that the truth of the teaching about natural rights is self-evident. In the same document, the signers said that the vindication of those rights nevertheless requires a pledge of life, fortune, and sacred honor.

Americans have been asked to defend the nation since it was founded. Besides free enterprise, political stability, and the nation's unsought position as leader of the free world, the sum and frequency of conflicts helps explain why America possesses the most powerful armed forces in history. In each generation, people have had to decide what defense policy is prudent and honorable. The need for defense is obvious in war. It is less clear in peace, when safety can be—and has traditionally been—taken for granted. But what happens in peacetime affects war when it comes.

War is part of man's political nature. It takes its meaning from its purpose; in the specific case of the United States, that is the freedom to govern ourselves, which was the object in 1776. War is a contest of right, not merely of might. Alexander Hamilton, who fought with distinction in the Revolution, is firmly for civil rule over the military. The most powerful, those who have armies at their command, do not have the right to deny people's natural rights. Hamilton places the importance of framing a constitution for the government of America on a moral level. The most powerful or most successful do not rule. The people do.

Hamilton points out, by his insistence on reflection and choice, that Americans are to be guided by morality, not solely by expedience. The moral quality of political debate, aside from the prudential character of defense, is tied to reflection on the proper course of action and on the claim that various options exist among which the people and the government must choose. Whenever Americans defend themselves they must first deliberate, guided by their natural rights, in order to decide on a course of action. In doing so, they also defend the moral dignity implied in the idea of natural rights, not merely their lives.

Gouverneur Morris emphasized the special importance of defense in the Preamble to the Constitution. The Constitution is the instrument created by the founders and ratified by the American people to achieve the Declaration's objective, the securing of natural rights. The Preamble enumerates five ends of government, the successful pursuit of which would constitute a more perfect union than the one for which the Articles of Confederation provided.

Those ends are establishing justice, insuring domestic tranquility, providing for the common defense, promoting general welfare, and securing the blessings of liberty, not just for the generation that parted ways with Britain, but for posterity.

Central among these ends is the common defense. Without it, the other goals are beyond reach. This is also the only one of the five ends of national government that is the exclusive duty of the executive branch. In other objects of government, self-rule is wholly compatible with tension between and among the executive, legislative, and judicial branches as well as between and among federal, state, and local jurisdictions. War is an exception. If defense suffers either from bipartisan inattention or partisan dispute, it is hobbled. A country divided by faction could not successfully defend itself. History, which the American founders knew well, demonstrates this. Athens' war with Sparta lasted twenty-seven years. In the twentieth year of the conflict, internal dissension over the conduct of the war and the burden of taxation led to a revolt in which an oligarchy replaced Athens' democracy. This ended neither military misfortune nor civil division, and Athens surrendered seven years later.

The concern of the first generation of Americans for a common defense was legitimate—as was their understanding that political unity was central to the preparations that are key to war's prevention. As the otherwise undistinguished Roman writer Publius Flavius Vegetius wrote during imperial times, "Si vis pacem, para bellum." If you want peace, prepare for war. George Washington's first annual message, in 1790, said as much: "To be prepared for war is one of the most effectual means of preserving peace."[1] Washington's quote is equally true when its Latin structure is reversed: "Si vis bellum, para pacem"—if you want war, prepare for peace.

The right to life that the European enlightenment thinkers identified implies a right of self-defense to preserve life. This right is also a duty of self-defense, as the Declaration states. There is no right not to defend oneself. There is no choice concerning whether to defend oneself. The single option is how best to defend oneself. Defense is a moral imperative and is codified in the Constitution in the very oath of office required of the president in Article II, Section 1, Clause 8:

> Before he enter on the Execution of his Office, he shall take the following Oath or Affirmation:—"I do solemnly swear (or affirm) that I will faithfully execute the Office of President of the United States, and will to the best of my Ability, preserve, protect and defend the Constitution of the United States."

The Constitution also underscores the importance of political debate and defense in the Bill of Rights. The First Amendment is first because it protects the free speech on which self-rule depends and establishes the separation between Church and State, whose conflation had proven so deadly elsewhere. The Second Amendment declares the government cannot dilute the natural right to self-defense and connects it to the militia, which, when called to action, is commanded by the president as commander-in-chief. These rights belong to the people and are necessary for government to function. If Americans do not understand or cease to concern themselves with self-defense and political debate, they will lose their freedom.

When the founders created American political institutions to defend natural rights, they set a higher standard than the one that existed at the time: protecting a state's self-interest. This added honor to what the American state was obliged to defend. American citizens regarded the Barbary pirates' predations as an insult to national honor. They held the same view when Britain boarded American ships on the high seas and kidnapped members of their crew. In his June 1, 1812, report to Congress on Britain's threat to American merchant shipping, President Madison urged a decision that was consistent with "the rights, the interests, and the honor of our country."[2]

Today, public debate has changed the terms of reference. "Human rights" have replaced natural rights. To note one prominent example, a significant portion of public opinion, influenced by judicial findings, believes that the Constitution intended to allow the termination of unborn life. This issue remains unresolved and hinges on a clash between liberty and the right to life, both of which the Constitution protects. National defense raises similar tensions in arguments about the affordability of weapons, national debt, and the character of threats to the United States. Partisan strife has characterized American political life since the beginning of the republic. But this strife cannot be allowed to supersede the moral imperative of defense and the immorality of defenselessness. The major parties that govern America with popular consent are equally obliged to defend Americans. There is today, however, growing uncertainty about what is required for defense.

This confusion is the consequence of defense policies whose results, since the end of the Cold War, are unclear. Political leaders point with pride to such accomplishments as the killing of Osama bin Laden and other radical jihadist terrorists. At the same time, American leaders of both parties have used the rhetoric of weariness and exhaustion to explain *de minimis* policy in the South China Sea, Ukraine, Syria, and Iran. Americans do not know whether their country is at war or somewhat at war or at peace. The same opacity blankets the government's plans to defend the nation. Major weapons programs are canceled or truncated. Defense budgets are subject to similar pressure. The clarity that in the past distinguished one political party's vigorous support for a strong defense from its opponent's reasonable skepticism has disappeared.

The tentacles of the resulting confusion reach into the theoretical basis of defense and foreign policy. In foreign affairs, this means growing uncertainty about whether it is justified to go to war, not merely whether it is prudent. A president draws a "red line" against Syria's use of chemical weapons and then allows it to be crossed. Our leaders constantly remind citizens of war weariness while the vast preponderance of Americans do not serve in the military, do not know anyone who does, and have not seen their taxes rise to pay for war since Vietnam.

Notwithstanding the fact that most contemporary American military interventions have achieved their objectives—as in the removal of a Panamanian dictator, the expulsion of a communist government from Grenada, and of Saddam Hussein's army from Kuwait—Americans today increasingly doubt the prudential use of force to achieve legitimate reasons of state. These doubts encourage isolation, and isolation is not selective. It falls on prudential and moral considerations alike. This muddies our ideas about war and peace, and calls for a clearer justification of defense.

It is important to see what still divides popular opinion about defense and foreign policy generally. No less important is the caution that the Cold War's end and the events that followed blur distinctions that, although subject to bitter partisan debate, were once clearer. One party could be called idealistic and the other realist. From a partisan perspective, the parties might dismiss each other, the one as too naïve, and the other as too suspicious. The differing principles that partisans ascribe to themselves are hope and prudence.

Each principle carries the risk of incubating what it seeks to avoid. President George W. Bush's prudential concern that Iraq might become a nuclear power led to military action that upset an uneasy balance between competing wings of Islam, with results that continue to roil the Middle East.

A Wilsonian-like duty to mankind was invoked as an argument against missile defense during the Cold War. Opposition to developing a missile that could defend against an enemy's ballistic missiles began over a half century ago, as the technology to hit one missile with another came within reach. It rose again to the level of a national debate when President Reagan argued that an effective defense against ballistic-missile attack was morally superior to the doctrine known as mutual assured destruction (MAD). MAD, some believed, prevented nuclear conflagration through the assurance that the United States and the USSR could damage each other so grievously that neither would initiate a nuclear attack.

The moral question that Reagan's strategic defense initiative raised may not have been answered to universal satisfaction. But the United States developed ballistic-missile defenses and now routinely deploys them to defend America and its allies. Although Russia and China modernize and add to their nuclear weapons arsenal, MAD has no serious contemporary proponents. The immorality of resting our defense solely on the threat of destroying millions is today accepted. The moral objective of preventing a global catastrophe by assuring total annihilation initially led some—much of the Democratic Party in fact—to oppose what has proved to be effective defenses against missile-borne nuclear weapons.

Carrying this idea to its extremity, no justification exists for going to war, because all war is potentially nuclear war. It is not possible to predict the outcome of any conflict, and experience shows that conflicts can escalate far beyond what any of the belligerent parties envision. Is this not a reasonable argument for reducing America's defenses to the levels advocated by some presidential candidates in the 2016 election? The Vermont senator who was defeated for the Democratic nomination had previously supported cutting defense spending by one half. The Libertarian candidate advocated cutting defense expenditures by 43 percent. Either measure would have ended the ability of the United States to deter war at a distance from our borders.

However, if a moral duty exists to prevent war and possible annihilation, is this duty more compelling than to

national organizations, used diplomacy, threats, and embargoes to attempt to prevent Pyongyang from developing nuclear weapons. Over time, the ineffectiveness of these measures succeeded only in persuading North Korea that there would be no serious consequences for building and testing weapons along with the missiles that can deliver them.

Similar diplomatic means were directed against Iran, which is now a "nuclear threshold" state. In March 2016, a letter to then–U.N. Secretary General Ban Ki-moon signed by American, British, French, and German representatives stated that ballistic-missile tests conducted earlier that month were "inconsistent with" and "in defiance of" Security Council resolution 2231. Who doubts that, as Iran continues to amplify the range and accuracy of its ballistic missiles, the country will become a nuclear power? Who expects that the United Nations will do anything more to prevent this than issue statements?

The rise of new powers, the resuscitation of old ones, and the certainty of increasing strategic competition underscore the importance of examining the view that America has a duty to mankind. This idea, however, as expressed by the left's willingness to cede issues of sovereign defense to international judgment, argues that the United States has a higher responsibility than to protect its own citizens. Skepticism about this notion is understandable. The foremost international organization, the United Nations, has a poor record in instances where it tried to restore peace or prevent violence. Two permanent members of the U.N.'s Security Council, Russia and China, violate its Universal Declaration of Human Rights as a matter of policy.

In its extreme form, the opinion that America is free of duty to mankind offers no good answer either. The power of moral principles causes disdain toward those who profess human rights but do nothing to stop their widespread violation. When we see a Syrian boy in shock following a military attack, we are repelled by the sight and discomfited by the failure of those who profess respect for human rights to protect him and other innocents from even worse.

The right to life and liberty entails a right to defend one's life. Not to defend oneself would be to alienate the right to life—which Jefferson wrote was unalienable. But the right to defense can make men dangerous to each other. When was the last time that an international outlaw failed to claim "self-defense" as a justification for aggression? Self-defense raises the possibility, as the political thinkers of the European Enlightenment observed, of a war of all against all, caused by suspicion and the fear of violent death. Self-interest, to be able to secure the good things it seeks, would have to be, as Alexis de Tocqueville put it, "rightly understood," or connected to doing the right thing.

Or have we decided that in international affairs might makes right? There is no government among nations and no authority that can enforce punishment for attacks on natural rights. Could America retain its character while admitting that power alone enforces the self-interest of the powerful, so that the weak suffer without hope? That would require Americans to ignore the difference between the victims of aggression and those who commit such atrocities, instead considering only who has more power.

Should U.S. policy have ignored the Serbs who killed more than 8,000 men and boys at the Bosnian town of Srebenica in the summer of 1995? Certainly the United States had an economic and political interest when Saddam Hussein invaded Kuwait in 1990, but Iraq's military action also violated the international proscription against using force to seize another state. If the moral argument carried no weight, what does that mean? But the moral argument did weigh. Congress's authorization of the George H. W. Bush administration's use of force demanded that Kuwait's "independence and legitimate government be restored." It called Iraq's occupation of Kuwait "illegal." The president and a majority in Congress agreed that Saddam Hussein had acted wrongfully and against civilized mores.

Saddam wasn't the first. Hitler lacked the raw materials to transform the Wehrmacht into a large military threat until he began to annex, conquer, and subjugate neighboring states that possessed more steel, coal, and raw materials than Germany. It is difficult to see how Americans can ignore the voice of conscience and prudence and expect at the same time to be left alone.

Can a people who believe in an order grounded in the right to life survive in a world where there is neither reason nor right, but only arbitrary rule by the powerful? If Americans concede the moral equivalent of aggressor and victim, they condemn themselves ultimately to become victims themselves—or aggressors.

Here again is the extreme consequence of the argument that ideas and ideologies do not weigh in the conduct of foreign policy. Had Japan not attacked Pearl Harbor, the isolationism that Franklin Roosevelt opposed could well have resulted in a world that monsters ruled.

The radical elevation of self-interest to a nation's sole guiding principle leads nowhere better. The practical goal of keeping the Union intact was Lincoln's first priority, but he knew that the nation could not measure up to the Declaration's moral standard were it to be preserved with slavery intact. America's Cold War presidents understood that the existential threat of Soviet communism included the triumph of its values as well as the danger of its nuclear-tipped missiles.

The current threat to America is neither China's growing military nor the chance that Iran will become a nuclear power, but rather the combination of these physical dangers with the authoritarianism of the former and the theological radicalism of the latter. Compromising the moral quality of a constitutionally ordered republic that American leaders are sworn to defend leaves nothing to protect except the forms of our government. The forms were created to protect natural rights. Remove the safeguarding of natural rights as an essential part of our foreign policy, and the nation's core goes with it.

Neither a policy based solely on self-interest nor one set exclusively upon principle can successfully defend the United States. The two extremes expose the fissures in current American political thinking. The left is more unified than the right: it demands that international bodies sanction the use of American force. Some on the right look askance at the defense budget because of its cost. Others are increasingly skeptical about engagement itself. Still others hold to the traditional view that active participation by the United States beyond its borders is required to advance our principles and defend our interests. Agreement on foreign policy has not yet splintered into the shards of identity politics. But such agreement about the common good that once offered a middle ground is scarce.

The middle ground would reconcile the advancement of American interests with an understanding of the responsibility that accompanies the humanity that Americans share with others. The object is greater political agreement about the character and level of defense needed to protect Americans' natural rights.

The departure point is the founders' sophisticated understanding of America's place in the world. They believed that there is a coherence in human affairs that extends to mankind in general. They observed that human beings are always organized into nations. The right to life, understood as a limitation on one's actions with respect to others, cannot create a proscription against self-defense or a moral argument for the slow drip of disarming a nation. Neither disengagement nor disarmament protects individuals from war. It gives some nations more power over others. Recognition of humanity's common nature leads straight to a moral understanding: no one should harm others.

But they do. The character of America's enemies is that they conquer, kill, and deny human rights to many people, indeed, to entire peoples. The Cuban dictatorship is a good example of the latter. The Castro regime's nearly sixty-year-old violation of human rights is incompatible with freedom. In finding such regimes illegitimate, Americans connect themselves with the founders. The founders connected themselves with moral questions, not merely with questions of interest. The Declaration of Independence accused George III of "repeated injuries and usurpations." It was, said Jefferson, "their [i.e., Americans'] right, it is their duty to throw off" a government that committed the abuses listed in the Declaration. The founders considered despots wrong even if they were strong. So should we.

Americans are also skeptical about those who do not defend themselves, particularly states that neglect political facts and events. U.S. criticism of NATO members for contributing insufficiently to the alliance's defenses did not begin with the 2016 presidential election. Former Senator Sam Nunn (D-GA) proposed legislation in 1984 that would have removed nearly a third of U.S. troops from Europe if NATO members refused to increase their alliance defense spending. Nunn's measure failed, although U.S. irritation moved alliance members to contribute more.[6] The character of a nation is called into question by weakness. Moral action requires resolve. Successful self-defense demonstrates resolve.

Resolve includes the moderation necessary to defend the United States without being distracted by other claimants to federal revenues. This statement is not a justification for a blank check to the Defense Department, but rather a reminder that other priorities Americans seek through government can only be achieved if the nation is secure. Self-restraint—in allocating and spending revenue and in crafting and executing foreign and security policy—is required. The duty not to harm others through misjudgment or broken assurances of security corresponds to the duty not to harm oneself by weakness. The one who cannot honor a promise to help others is unlikely to keep from injuring himself.

Defense has a double character, as right and as duty. The link between rights and duties parallels the connection between self-defense and self-government. Those who cannot control themselves cannot lead others. But the American polity stands on the right to govern and be governed by other Americans.

Besides protecting life and liberty, the moral imperative of self-defense supports other peaceful nations. In this way, American self-interest includes a concern for the good of friends and allies. U.S. defense cooperation with Taiwan, Japan, and other treaty allies in the region supports their democratic political systems as it seeks to constrain China and North Korea, whose regional ambitions threaten international order. If other nations disregard morality in conducting their foreign affairs, this has no bearing on the effectiveness or necessity of a moral American foreign policy. The imperative of defense cannot be separated from our—or any people's—natural right to life.

Americans are exceptional in having built a nation on ideas rather than ethnicity, ties to the soil, or religion. But the idea that all men possess natural rights binds us to the rest of humanity. This bond requires Americans to live up to the foundational teaching about natural rights. This does not require us to act wherever in the world natural rights are at risk. It does mean that the defense of natural rights should be included in our calculations of interest. Today, these calculations have become flaccid. Russia,

China, Iran, and North Korea are increasing their military capability while we are shrinking ours. In this gap lies not only physical danger but also the moral obligation of the United States to protect and defend its people's natural rights.

Large and difficult questions must be answered as the new administration rebuilds the U.S. military. What strategy should guide U.S. defense policy as adversaries modernize and grow their forces? How best can the United States marshal its resources to defeat the asymmetric challenges of China, Russia, and Iran while at the same time prosecuting the Long War against radical Islamic jihadists? For American seapower in particular, what strategy is best suited as threats multiply around the globe? How can such a strategy be explained to a public that assumes the permanence of our dominant global seapower? What kinds of ships and planes are required to transform this strategy into an effective defense against increasing risk? How can the Defense Department's management be reordered to save money and increase its ability to supply the right weapons and platforms more quickly? What organizational changes are needed to improve the nation's defenses against cyber attacks?

The question that should not burden national leadership is whether this undertaking is feasible given the political, financial, and intellectual problems of restoring the nation's defenses. The question answers itself. We are morally bound to defend ourselves.

NOTES

CHAPTER I. WHAT IS A HOLLOW MILITARY?

1. Major General Robert H. Scales Jr., *Certain Victory: The U.S. Army in the Gulf War* (Washington, D.C.: Brassey's, 1994), 15.

2. Andrew Feickert and Stephen Daggett, *A Historical Perspective on "Hollow Forces"* (Congressional Research Service, January 31, 2012), 5, https://fas.org/sgp/crs/natsec/R42334.pdf.

3. Ibid.

4. Scales, *Certain Victory*, 16.

5. George W. Baer, *One Hundred Years of Sea Power: The U.S. Navy, 1890–1990* (Stanford, Calif.: Stanford University Press, 1993), 413.

6. Christopher Chantrill, USGovernmentSpending.com, http://www.usgovernmentspending.com/defense_spending.

7. Thaleigha Rampersad, "The History of Defense Spending in One Chart," *The Daily Signal*, February 14, 2015, http://dailysignal.com/2015/02/14/history-defense-spending-one-chart/.

8. John F. Lehman Jr., *Command of the Seas* (New York: Charles Scribner's Sons, 1988), 163.

9. Paul B. Ryan, *First Line of Defense: The U.S. Navy Since 1945* (Stanford, Calif.: Hoover Institution Press, 1981), 179.

10. Lehman, *Command of the Seas*, 163.

11. Ryan, *First Line of Defense*, 179.

12. Lehman, *Command of the Seas*, 163.

13. Lawrence Korb, "The Erosion of American Naval Preeminence," in *In Peace and War: Interpretations of American Naval History, 1775–1984*, edited by Kenneth J. Hagan, 2nd ed. (Westport, Conn., and London: Greenwood Press, 1984), 333.

14. *Understanding Soviet Naval Developments* (Washington, D.C.: Office of the Chief of Naval Operations, April 1975), 12. Quoted in Korb, "The Erosion of American Naval Preeminence," 336.

15. Marcus Weisgerber, "Panetta Raises Specter of Hollow Force," *Defense News*, August 16, 2011.

16. Phil Stewart, "Gates Warns Against Deep Military Cuts," *Washington Post*, May 22, 2011, http://www.washingtonpost.com/politics/gates-warns-against-deep-military-cuts/2011/05/22/AFKMjL9G_story.html.

17. Reid Pillifant, " 'A formula for chaos and anarchy': Robert Gates on Snowden, Syria, and Obama," *Politico*, June 24, 2013, http://www.capitalnewyork.com/article/politics/2013/06/8531240/formula-chaos-and-anarchy-robert-gates-snowden-syria-and-obama.

18. Lolita C. Baldor, "U.S. to Beef Up Military Presence in Eastern Europe," *Military Times*, March 30, 2016, http://www.militarytimes.com/story/military/2016/03/30/us-beef-up-military-presence-eastern-europe/82416066/.

19. General Daniel Allyn, Vice Chief of Staff, United States Army, "Current State of Readiness of the U.S. Forces in Review of the Defense Authorization Request for Fiscal Year 2017 and the Future Years Defense Program," Statement before the Senate Armed Services Committee Subcommittee on Readiness and Management Support, Second Session, 114th Congress, March 15, 2016, http://www.armed-services.senate.gov/imo/media/doc/Allyn_03-15-16.pdf.

20. "Air Force Budget Request for Fiscal Year 2017," video with transcripts, C-SPAN, February 12, 2016, https://www.c-span.org/video/?404637-1/hearing-fiscal-year-2017-air-force-budget.

21. Stephanie Gaskell, "Hagel's Korean War Lesson from a Hollow Force," *Defense One*, July 22, 2013, http://www.defenseone.com/threats/2013/07/history-lessons-hollow-force/67223/.

22. Alfred Thayer Mahan, *The Influence of Sea Power upon History*, 2nd ed. (Boston, Mass.: Little, Brown, and Company, 1891), 41, https://books.google.com/books?id=yzdJAAAAYAAJ&printsec=frontcover#v=onepage&q&f=false.

23. Robert Hutchinson, *The Spanish Armada* (New York: Thomas Dunne Books, St. Martin's Press, 2013), 98.

24. Robert Hutchinson, "How the Spanish Armada Was Really Defeated," *The History Reader*, May 30, 2014, http://www.thehistory reader.com/modern-history/spanish-armada-really-defeated/.

25. Chiyo Ishikawa, *Spain in the Age of Exploration, 1492–1819* (Lincoln: University of Nebraska Press, 2004), 69.

26. David Goodman, *Spanish Naval Power, 1589–1665: Reconstruction and Defeat* (Cambridge, UK: Cambridge University Press, 1997), 40.

27. Ibid.

28. Ibid., 46.

29. Ibid.

30. Mahan, *The Influence of Sea Power upon History*, 41.

31. "US Ship Force Levels: 1886–Present," *Naval History and Heritage Command*, last updated December 6, 2016, https://www.history.navy .mil/research/histories/ship-histories/us-ship-force-levels.html.

32. Ibid.

33. Peter D. Haynes, *Toward a New Maritime Strategy: American Naval Thinking in the Post–Cold War Era* (Annapolis, Md.: Naval Institute Press, 2015), 149.

34. 2001 Quadrennial Defense Review, quoted in Haynes, *Toward a New Maritime Strategy*, 149.

35. Ibid.

36. Ibid.

37. Zachary Keck, "America's New Aircraft Carriers Will Use Lasers to Annihilate Missiles," *The National Interest*, June 18, 2015, http:// nationalinterest.org/blog/the-buzz/americas-new-aircraft-carriers-will -use-lasers-annihilate-13140.

38. Sam LaGrone, "Navy Planning on Not Buying More LRLAP Rounds for Zumwalt Class," *USNI News*, November 7, 2016, https:// news.usni.org/2016/11/07/navy-planning-not-buying-lrlap-rounds.

39. Megan Eckstein, "Ford Carrier Delayed Again Due to 'First-of-Class-Issues,'" *USNI News*, July 12, 2016, https://news.usni.org /2016/07/12/cvn-78-delivery-pushed-back-due-first-class-issues.

40. Sam LaGrone, "Navy Requires $450 Million More to Complete Zumwalt-Class Due to Shipyard Performance," *USNI News*, April 6, 2016, https://news.usni.org/2016/04/06/navy-requires-450-million -more-to-complete-zumwalt-class-due-to-shipyard-performance.

41. Stephen Moore, "No, Bill Clinton Didn't Balance the Budget," *Cato Institute*, October 8, 1998, https://www.cato.org/publications /commentary/no-bill-clinton-didnt-balance-budget.

42. Haynes, *Toward a New Maritime Strategy*, 149–150.

43. Ibid., 151–152.

44. Ibid., 165–167.

45. Jordan Crucchiola, "The New $3B *USS Zumwalt* Is a Stealthy Oddity That May Already Be a Relic," *Wired*, December 10, 2015, https://www.wired.com/2015/12/the-new-3b-uss-zumwalt-is-a-stealthy -oddity-that-may-already-be-a-relic/.

46. LaGrone, "Navy Planning on Not Buying More LRLAP Rounds for Zumwalt Class."

47. Sam LaGrone, "SECDEF Carter Directs Navy to Cut Littoral Combat Ship Program to 40 Hulls, Single Shipbuilder," *USNI News*, December 17, 2015, https://news.usni.org/2015/12/16/secdef-carter -directs-navy-to-cut-littoral-combat-ship-program-to-40-hulls-single -shipbuilder.

48. Andrea Drusch, "Fighter Plane Cost Overruns Detailed," *Politico*, February 16, 2014, http://www.politico.com/story/2014/02/f-35 -fighter-plane-costs-103579.

49. Admiral Thomas Hayward, Oral History, Interview #7, June 7, 2002 (Operational Archives, Naval History and Heritage Command, Washington, D.C.), 329; quoted in Commander Guy M. Snodgrass (USN), "Keep a Weather Eye on the Horizon: A Navy Officer Retention Study," *Naval War College Review* 67, no. 4 (2014): 64, https://www .usnwc.edu/getattachment/66837e4f-702f-4293-b653-cfa9dd4df1ab /Keep-a-Weather-Eye-on-the-Horizon--A-Navy-Officer-.aspx.

50. Snodgrass, "Keep a Weather Eye on the Horizon," 64.

51. Ibid., 65.

52. Ibid.

CHAPTER II. WHY SEAPOWER?

1. Quoted by Admiral Lord Jacky Fisher, *Memories* (London: Hodder and Stoughton, 1919), 18.

2. Greg Jaffe and Griff Witte, "A Cold-Eyed View of Allies Has Left Obama with Few Overseas Friends," *Washington Post*, April 18, 2016, https://www.washingtonpost.com/politics/a-cold-eyed-view-of-allies

-has-left-obama-with-few-overseas-friends/2016/04/18/49d5e3ce-0195
-11e6-9203-7b8670959b88_story.html.

3. Conversation of George W. Bush administration Middle East
policy adviser with the author, Summer 2003.

4. John Kerry, "Message to the Iranian People on Nowruz,"
March 20, 2013, https://2009-2017.state.gov/secretary/remarks/2013
/03/206474.htm.

5. Amir Vahdat, "Iranian Commander Threatens to Close Strait
of Hormuz to US," *Associated Press*, May 4, 2016, https://apnews.com
/33852dd77f4c45989e3cbebf6b3e24a1/iranian-commander-threatens
-close-strait-hormuz-us.

6. Przemyslaw Grudzinski, former ambassador of Poland to the
United States, in conversation with the author.

7. James Harvey Robinson, *Readings in European History*, vol. 2
(Boston, Mass.: Ginn & Company, 1906), 207.

CHAPTER III. SINEWS CHALLENGED: RUSSIA

1. Jessica Huckabey, "The Paradox of Admiral Gorshkov," *Center
for International Maritime Security*, October 1, 2014, http://cimsec.org
/paradox-admiral-gorshkov/13197.

2. Donald Chipman, "Admiral Gorshkov and the Soviet Navy,"
Air University Review (July–August 1982), http://www.au.af.mil/au/afri
/aspj/airchronicles/aureview/1982/jul-aug/chipman.html.

3. Ibid.

4. Ibid.

5. Ibid.

6. Ibid.

7. Ibid.

8. Ibid.

9. Ibid.

10. Major Noel Hidalgo, USAF, "Soviet Military Assistance to Latin
America," *Defense Institute of Security and Assistance Management Publications*
(1984), http://www.disam.dsca.mil/pubs/Vol%207-2/Hidalgo.pdf.

11. Ibid.

12. Daniel Southerland, "Why Soviets May Be Wary of Deeper
Involvement in Nicaragua," *Christian Science Monitor*, March 23, 1981,
http://www.csmonitor.com/1981/0323/032345.html.

13. Hidalgo, "Soviet Military Assistance to Latin America."

14. Ibid.

15. Ibid.

16. Jeremy Bervoets, "The Soviet Union in Angola: Soviet and African Perspectives on the Failed Socialist Transformation," *Vestnik, The Journal of Russian and Asian Studies*, May 11, 2011, http://www.sras.org /the_soviet_union_in_angola.

17. Ibid.

18. Peter Vanneman, *Soviet Strategy in Southern Africa: Gorbachev's Pragmatic Approach* (Stanford, Calif.: Hoover Institution Press, 1990), 85.

19. Ibid.

20. "Russian Military Budget," *Global Security.org*, http://www.global security.org/military/world/russia/mo-budget-1996-99.htm.

21. Stockholm International Peace Research Institute, chart of Russian military spending, 1992–2012, https://en.wikipedia.org/wiki /Military_budget_of_the_Russian_Federation#/media/File: Russian_Military_Spending_1992-2012_SIPRI.jpg.

22. William C. Fuller, Jr., *Strategy and Power in Russia, 1600–1914* (New York: The Free Press, 1992), 60.

23. Leo Tolstoy, "Famine or Not Famine," in *Essays, Letters, Miscellanies* (New York: Charles Scribner's Sons, 1922), 285.

24. Karl Soper, "Russia Confirms Higher Level of Submarine Patrol Activity," *IHS Jane's Defence Weekly*, March 23, 2016; see complete article at http://www.matthewaid.com/post/141539776591/russia-confirms-higher-level-of-submarine-patrol.

25. Ibid.

26. Nicholas de Larrinaga, "Russian Submarine Activity Topping Cold War Levels," *IHS Jane's Defence Weekly*, February 2, 2016; see Australian Naval Institute, February 13, 2016, http://navalinstitute.com .au/russian-submarine-activity-topping-cold-war-levels/.

27. Dave Majumdar, "The U.S. Navy's Worst Nightmare: Super Advanced Russian Submarines," *The National Interest*, October 29, 2015, http://nationalinterest.org/blog/the-buzz/the-us-navys-worst-night mare-super-advanced-russian-14203.

28. Vice Admiral James Foggo III and Alarik Fritz, "The Fourth Battle of the Atlantic," *Proceedings Magazine* (June 2016), https://www .usni.org/node/87164.

29. Vladimir Putin, quoted in "Putin: Soviet Collapse a 'Genuine

Tragedy,'" Associated Press, April 25, 2005, http://www.nbcnews.com /id/7632057/ns/world_news/t/putin-soviet-collapse-genuine-tragedy /#.WU27gYVkB-J.

30. Magnus Nordenman, "Larger NATO Baltic Sea Exercise Sends Important Message to Russia," *USNI News*, June 1, 2016, https://news .usni.org/2016/06/01/highend_baltic_ex_message_to_russia.

31. Matthew Bodner, "Massive Leadership Cull in Russia's Baltic Sea Fleet," *Defense News*, July 1, 2016, http://www.defensenews.com /story/defense/2016/07/01/massive-leadership-cull-russias-baltic-sea -fleet/86595472/.

32. Dmitry Rogozin, remarks on a draft of the Russian Federation Marine Doctrine, in "Russian Federation Marine Doctrine," President of Russia, July 26, 2015, http://en.kremlin.ru/events/president /news/50060.

33. Ibid.

34. Kenneth J. Bird, Ronald R. Charpentier, et al., "Circum-Arctic Resource Appraisal: Estimates of Undiscovered Oil and Gas North of the Arctic Circle," U.S. Geological Survey, Fact Sheet 2008-3049, July 23, 2008, http://pubs.usgs.gov/fs/2008/3049/.

CHAPTER IV. FAILURE OF IMAGINATION

1. Brayton Harris, *Admiral Nimitz: The Commander of the Pacific Ocean Theater* (New York: St. Martin's Press, 2011), 33.

2. Roberta Wohlstetter, *Pearl Harbor: Warning and Decision* (Stanford, Calif.: Stanford University Press, 1962), 43.

3. Ibid., 53.

4. Ibid., 393.

5. *Final Report of the National Commission on Terrorist Attacks Upon the United States*, Thomas H. Kean and Lee H. Hamilton, July 22, 2004, 345. Note: Omar Abdel-Rahman, known as "the Blind Sheikh," is currently serving a life sentence plus fifteen years following a 1995 conviction on charges of seditious conspiracy for, among other things, his role in planning the 1993 World Trade Center bombings.

6. Ibid., 345.

7. Admiral Harry B. Harris, Commander U.S. Pacific Command, before the House Armed Services Committee, April 26, 2017, 3.

8. Holly Ellyatt, "Putin 'Weaponizing' Migrant Crisis to Hurt

Europe," CNBC, March 2, 2016, http://www.cnbc.com/2016/03/02
/putin-weaponizing-migrant-crisis-to-hurt-europe.html?view=story
&%24DEVICE%24=native-android-mobile.

CHAPTER VI. SINEWS CHALLENGED: CHINA

1. Dennis J. Blasko, quoted by Bernard D. Cole, *China's Quest for Great Power: Ships, Oil, and Foreign Policy* (Annapolis, Md.: Naval Institute Press, 2016), 56.

2. "Military Expert: China May Have 3 Aircraft Carrier Battle Groups," *People's Daily Online*, January 5, 2017, http://en.people.cn /n3/2017/0105/c90000-9163355.html.

3. *2014 Report to Congress of the U.S.-China Economic and Security Review Commission*, 12, https://www.uscc.gov/sites/default/files/annual_ reports/Executive%20Summary.pdf.

4. "Gross Savings (% of GDP)," 2014, The World Bank, http:// data.worldbank.org/indicator/NY.GNS.ICTR.ZS?view=chart.

5. David P. Goldman, "Chicken Little Does China," *Asia Times*, February 22, 2016, http://www.atimes.com/chicken-little-does-china/.

6. Andrew S. Erickson, Testimony before the House Committee on Foreign Affairs, Subcommittee on Asia and the Pacific, Hearing on "America's Security Role in the South China Sea," July 23, 2015, http://www.andrewerickson.com/2015/07/my-testimony-before-the -house-committee-on-foreign-affairs-subcommittee-on-asia-and-the -pacific-hearing-on-americas-security-role-in-the-south-china-sea/.

7. Paul S. Giarra, "Book Review: "The Perils of Proximity—China/ Japan Security Relations," *The Diplomat*, August 3, 2012, http://the diplomat.com/2012/08/book-review-the-perils-of-proximity-china -japan-security-relations/.

8. Jordan Wilson, "China's Expanding Ability to Conduct Conventional Missile Strikes on Guam," U.S.-China Economic and Security Review Commission (established by Congress in 2000), May 10, 2016, https://www.uscc.gov/sites/default/files/Research/Staff%20Report _China%27s%20Expanding%20Ability%20to%20Conduct%20Con ventional%20Missile%20Strikes%20on%20Guam.pdf.

9. Franz-Stefan Gady, "China and Russia Conclude Naval Drill in Mediterranean," *The Diplomat*, May 22, 2015, http://thediplomat.com /2015/05/china-and-russia-conclude-naval-drill-in-mediterranean/.

10. "Annual Report to Congress: Military and Security Develop-

ments Involving the People's Republic of China 2016," Office of the Secretary of Defense, 69, http://www.defense.gov/Portals/1/Docu ments/pubs/2016%20China%20Military%20Power%20Report.pdf.

11. Vijay Sakhuja, "Chinese Submarines in Sri Lanka Unnerve India: Next Stop Pakistan?" *China Brief* (The Jamestown Foundation), May 29, 2015, http://www.jamestown.org/programs/chinabrief/single /?tx_ttnews%5Btt_news%5D=43960&cHash=a78005ce4ef4d128216bf3 c97b8b9fbe#.V5op2vkrLcs.

12. Shannon Tiezzi, "Chinese Company Wins Contract for Deep Sea Port in Myanmar," *The Diplomat*, January 1, 2016, http:// thediplomat.com/2016/01/chinese-company-wins-contract-for-deep -sea-port-in-myanmar/.

13. Aung Hla Tun and Timothy McLaughlin, "China's CITIC Wins Projects to Develop Myanmar Economic Zone," *Reuters*, December 31, 2015, http://www.reuters.com/article/myanmar-citic-project-idUSL3N 14K1D720151231.

14. Wade Shepard, "China Requests 15,000 Acres of Land in Sri Lanka to Create a Million Jobs," *Forbes*, July 27, 2016, http://www .forbes.com/sites/wadeshepard/2016/07/27/china-just-asked-for-15000 -acres-of-land-in-sri-lanka-for-a-million-worker-sez/#f7c853531cf5.

15. Ankit Panda, "China's Sri Lankan Port Ambitions Persist," *The Diplomat*, July 27, 2015, http://thediplomat.com/2015/07/chinas-sri -lankan-port-ambitions-persist/.

16. "China's Gwadar Port Nears Completion," *Maritime Executive*, March 14, 2016, http://www.maritime-executive.com/article/chinas -gwadar-port-nears-completion.

17. Ibid.

18. Ankit Panda, "Chinese State Firm Takes Control of Strategi- cally Vital Gwadar Port," *The Diplomat*, November 13, 2015, http://the diplomat.com/2015/11/chinese-state-firm-takes-control-of-strategically -vital-gwadar-port/.

19. Suez Canal Traffic Statistics, http://www.suezcanal.gov.eg /TRstat.aspx?reportId=1.

20. Claudette Roulo, "Technology Gap Closing, Top Acquisitions Official Warns," *DoD News*, November 5, 2014, http://archive.defense .gov/news/newsarticle.aspx?id=123570.

21. Ibid.

22. "Top 15 Defence Budgets 2015," International Institute for

Strategic Studies, London, https://www.iiss.org/-/media//images /publications/the%20military%20balance/milbal2016/mb%202016 %20top%2015%20defence%20budgets%202015.jpg?la=en.

23. Robert Johnson, "China Successfully Tests 'Carrier Killer' Missile in the Gobi Desert," *Business Insider*, January 25, 2013, http:// www.businessinsider.com/chinas-carrier-killer-missile-test-proves-df -21d-lives-up-to-name-2013-1.

24. Yoichi Kato, "U.S. Commander Says China Aims to Be a 'Global Military' Power," *Asahi Shimbun*, December 28, 2010, quoted in Andrew S. Erickson, "Admiral Willard, COMPACOM, Tells Asahi Shimbun's Yoichi Cato That China's Anti-Ship Ballistic Missile (ASBM) Has Reached Equivalent of 'Initial Operational Capability' (IOC)," *China Analysis from Original Sources* (blog), December 27, 2010, http://www.andrewerickson.com/2010/12/admiral-willard-compacom -tells-asahi-shimbun%E2%80%99s-yoichi-kato-that-china%E2%80% 99s-anti-ship-ballistic-missile-asbm-has-reached-equivalent-of-%E2%80 %9Cinitial-operational-capability%E2%80%9D/.

25. Lyle Goldstein and Shannon Knight, "Wired for Sound in the 'Near Seas,'" *Proceedings Magazine* (U.S. Naval Institute) (April 2014), http://www.usni.org/magazines/proceedings/2014-04/wired-sound -near-seas.

26. Lyle J. Goldstein, "China's 'Undersea Great Wall,'" *The National Interest*, May 16, 2016, http://nationalinterest.org/feature/chinas-under sea-great-wall-16222.

27. Jane Perlez, "Tribunal Rejects Beijing's Claims in South China Sea," *New York Times*, July 12, 2016, http://www.nytimes.com/2016/07 /13/world/asia/south-china-sea-hague-ruling-philippines.html.

28. Ibid.

29. John Pomfret, "U.S. Takes a Tougher Tone with China," *Washington Post*, July 30, 2010, http://www.washingtonpost.com/wp-dyn /content/article/2010/07/29/AR2010072906416.html.

30. Shi Yinhong, "Major Strategic Issues of Chinese Foreign Policy in the Short Run—and Basic Strategic Opportunities in the Long Run," *Zhanlue Yu Guanli* [*Strategy and Management*] (November 2003): 21–25, quoted in Aaron L. Friedberg, *A Contest for Supremacy: China, America, and the Struggle for Mastery in Asia* (New York: W. W. Norton, 2011), 165.

31. Officially, the Central Party School of the Communist Party of China; a Beijing training facility for communist party officials.

32. Men Honghua, "Expansion of China's National Strategic Interest," *Zhanlue Yu Guanli* [*Strategy and Management*] (March 2003): 83–89, quoted in Friedberg, *A Contest for Supremacy*, 165.

33. Chris Buckley, "China PLA Officer Urges Challenging U.S. Dominance," *Reuters*, February 28, 2010, http://www.reuters.com /article/us-china-usa-military-exclusive-idUSTRE62OOP620100301, quoted in Friedberg, *A Contest for Supremacy*, 165.

34. Graham Allison, "Thucydides' Trap Has Been Sprung in the Pacific," *Financial Times*, August 21, 2012, https://www.ft.com/content /5d695b5a-ead3-11e1-984b-00144feab49a.

35. Thucydides, *History of the Peloponnesian War*, translated by Richard Crawley, published in *The Landmark Thucydides: A Comprehensive Guide to the Peloponnesian War*, edited by Robert B. Strassler (New York: Simon & Schuster, 1996), 42.

36. Ibid., 45.

CHAPTER VIII. BUDGET APOCALYPSE

1. "Table 6-10: Department of Defense Budget Authority by Military Department," in *National Defense Budget Estimates for FY 2016* (Office of the Under Secretary of Defense [Comptroller], March 2015), 147–153, available at: http://comptroller.defense.gov/Portals/45 /Documents/defbudget/fy2016/FY16_Green_Book.pdf.

2. Thom Shanker and Christopher Drew, "Pentagon Expects Cuts in Military Spending," *New York Times*, November 2, 2008, http://www .nytimes.com/2008/11/03/washington/03military.html?_r=0.

3. Robert M. Gates, *Duty: Memoirs of a Secretary at War* (New York: Knopf, 2014), 314–318.

4. "Table 6-10: Department of Defense Budget Authority by Military Department," 142.

5. Charles Hoskinson and Josh Gerstein, "Obama: Cut $400B from Security," *Politico*, April 14, 2011, http://www.politico.com/story/2011 /04/obama-cut-400b-from-security-053159.

6. Mackenzie Eaglen, "Military Already Being Cut, but Obama Makes It Official," *Daily Signal*, April 13, 2011, http://dailysignal.com /2011/04/13/military-already-being-cut-but-obama-makes-it-official/.

7. Hoskinson and Gerstein, "Obama."

8. Robert Gates, "At War with al Qaeda, At War with Washington," speech given to the Los Angeles World Affairs Council, January 30, 2014, http://www.lawac.org/speech-archive/pdf/2014/Gates_1666.pdf.

9. Karen L. Haas, *Statistics of the Congressional Election of November 2, 2010* (Washington, 2011), http://clerk.house.gov/member_info/election Info/2010election.pdf.

10. "Election 2010: Senate Map," *New York Times*, http://elections.nytimes.com/2010/results/senate.

11. Dan Balz and William Branigin, "After Midterm Wins, GOP Vows to Block Obama's Agenda," *Washington Post*, November 3, 2010, http://www.washingtonpost.com/wp-dyn/content/article/2010/11/02/AR2010110207506.html?sid=ST2010110201489.

12. Jackie Calmes and Carl Hulse, "Debt Ceiling Talks Collapse as Boehner Walks Out," *New York Times*, July 22, 2011, http://www.nytimes.com/2011/07/23/us/politics/23fiscal.html.

13. "The Sequester Explained," Bipartisan Policy Center, May 27, 2012, bipartisanpolicy.org/wp-content/uploads/sites/default/files/BCA%20Sequester%20Fact%20Sheet.pdf.

14. Molly Ball, "Here's Who Is Really to Blame for Sequestration," *The Atlantic*, February 28, 2013, http://www.theatlantic.com/politics/archive/2013/02/heres-who-is-really-to-blame-for-sequestration/273587/.

15. Ibid.

16. Lynn M. Williams, *The Budget Control Act and the Defense Budget: Frequently Asked Questions*, Congressional Research Service, April 21, 2017, https://www.fas.org/sgp/crs/natsec/R44039.pdf; and personal calculations.

17. "Trump Outlines Plan to Build 350 Ship Navy and Revitalize America's Infrastructure," press release, October 21, 2016, https://votesmart.org/public-statement/1139001/trump-outlines-plan-to-build-350-ship-navy-and-revitalize-americas-infrastructure#.WUcYN4VkB-I.

18. Kyle Mizokami, "What Would Trump's 350-Ship Navy Look Like?," *Popular Mechanics*, December 13, 2016, http://www.popularmechanics.com/military/navy-ships/a24284/trump-350-ship-navy/.

19. David B. Larter, "Donald Trump Wants to Start the Biggest

Navy Build-Up in Decades," *Navy Times*, November 15, 2016, https://www.navytimes.com/articles/donald-trumps-navy-bigger-fleet-more-sailors-350-ships.

20. Ibid.

21. "Secretary of the Navy Announces Need for 355-Ship Navy," America's Navy, December 16, 2016, http://www.navy.mil/submit/display.asp?story_id=98160.

22. Sam LaGrone and Megan Eckstein, "Navy Wants to Grow Fleet to 355 Ships; 47 Hull Increase Adds Destroyers, Attack Subs," *USNI News*, December 16, 2016, https://news.usni.org/2016/12/16/navy-wants-grow-fleet-355-ships-47-hull-increase-previous-goal.

23. Charles Tiefer, "President Trump Is Likely to Boost U.S. Military Spending by $500 Billion to $1 Trillion," *Forbes*, November 9, 2016, http://www.forbes.com/sites/charlestiefer/2016/11/09/president-trump-is-likely-to-boost-u-s-military-spending-by-500-billion-to-1-trillion/2/#6d15e2ed66bf.

24. Harper Neidig, "Trump to Call for End of Military Sequestration," *The Hill*, September 6, 2016, http://thehill.com/blogs/ballot-box/presidential-races/294731-trump-to-call-for-end-of-military-sequestration.

25. "DoD Fiscal 2013 Budget Proposal Released," America's Navy, February 13, 2012, http://www.navy.mil/submit/display.asp?story_id=65326.

26. See documents for budget requests for Fiscal Years 2010–2016 at http://comptroller.defense.gov/budgetmaterials/budget2016.aspx, http://comptroller.defense.gov/budgetmaterials/budget2015.aspx, http://comptroller.defense.gov/Portals/45/Documents/defbudget/fy2014/FY2014_Budget_Request.pdf, http://comptroller.defense.gov/Portals/45/Documents/defbudget/fy2013/FY2013_Budget_Request.pdf, http://comptroller.defense.gov/Portals/45/Documents/defbudget/fy2012/FY2012_BudgetBriefing.pdf, http://comptroller.defense.gov/Portals/45/Documents/defbudget/fy2011/FY2011_BudgetBriefing.pdf, and http://comptroller.defense.gov/Portals/45/Documents/defbudget/fy2010/fy2010_BudgetBriefing.pdf.

27. Rear Admiral William K. Lescher, "Department of the Navy FY 2016 President's Budget," February 2, 2015, http://www.secnav.navy.mil/fmc/fmb/Documents/16pres/DON_PRESS_BRIEF.pdf.

28. Office of the Under Secretary of Defense, "Fiscal Year 2011

Budget Request," February 2010, http://comptroller.defense.gov/Por
tals/45/Documents/defbudget/fy2011/FY2011_BudgetBriefing.pdf.

29. Office of the Under Secretary of Defense, "Fiscal Year 2012
Budget Request," February 2011, http://comptroller.defense.gov/Por
tals/45/Documents/defbudget/fy2012/FY2012_BudgetBriefing.pdf.

30. Office of the Under Secretary of Defense, "Fiscal Year 2013
Budget Request," February 2012, http://comptroller.defense.gov/Por
tals/45/Documents/defbudget/fy2013/FY2013_Budget_Request.pdf.

31. Office of the Under Secretary of Defense, "Fiscal Year 2016
Budget Request: Overview," February 2015, http://comptroller
.defense.gov/Portals/45/Documents/defbudget/fy2016/FY2016
_Budget_Request_Overview_Book.pdf.

32. Transcript, "Hearing to Receive Testimony on the Posture of
the Department of the Navy in Review of the Defense Authorization
Request for Fiscal Year 2017 and the Future Years Defense Program,"
U.S. Senate Committee on Armed Services, March 15, 2016, 13, http://
www.armed-services.senate.gov/imo/media/doc/16-31_3-15-16.pdf.

33. Statement of Admiral Jonathan Greenert, U.S. Navy Chief of
Naval Operations, before the Senate Armed Services Committee on
the Impact of Sequestration on National Defense, January 28, 2015,
http://www.navy.mil/navydata/people/cno/Greenert/Testimony
/150128%20Chief%20of%20Naval%20Operations%20(CNO)%20
Adm.%20Greenert%20Statment%20and%20Slides%20before%20
Senate%20Armed%20Services%20Committee.pdf.

34. "Department of the Navy FY 2012 Budget Estimates, Budget
Data Book," April 2011, http://www.secnav.navy.mil/fmc/fmb
/Documents/12Pres/FY12_Data_Book.pdf.

35. "Chief of Naval Operations Confirmation Hearing," C-Span,
July 30, 2015, http://www.c-span.org/video/?327404-1/chief-naval
-operations-confirmation-hearing.

36. "Sequestration: Comprehensive and Updated Cost Savings
Would Better Inform DOD Decision Makers If Future Civilian Furloughs Occur," U.S. Government Accountability Office, Report to
Congressional Committees, June 2014, http://www.gao.gov/assets
/670/664142.pdf.

37. Admiral Jonathan Greenert, "Hearing on President Obama's
Fiscal 2016 Budget Request for the Navy," House Appropriations
Subcommittee on Defense, February 26, 2015, http://www.navy.mil

/navydata/people/cno/Greenert/Testimony/150226%20HAC-D%20
Navy%20Budget%20Hearing.pdf.

38. Matt Burke, "Budget Cuts Cancel Deployments of More Navy
Ships," *Stars and Stripes*, March 26, 2013, http://www.stripes.com/news
/budget-cuts-cancel-deployments-of-more-navy-ships-1.213540.

39. Statement of Admiral Jonathan Greenert, U.S. Navy Chief of
Naval Operations, before the Senate Armed Services Committee on
the Impact of Sequestration on National Defense, January 28, 2015,
http://www.navy.mil/navydata/people/cno/Greenert/Testimony
/150128%20Chief%20of%20Naval%20Operations%20(CNO)%20Adm
.%20Greenert%20Statment%20and%20Slides%20before%20Senate
%20Armed%20Services%20Committee.pdf.

40. Mike Hixenbaugh, "Navy Falls Behind on Maintenance,
Deployments," *Virginian-Pilot*, October 27, 2014, http://pilotonline
.com/news/military/navy-falls-behind-on-maintenance-deployments
/article_45ce8855-c65c-5fcf-bd64-cofee1058c06.html.

41. Sydney J. Freedberg Jr., "Navy Will Cancel Maintenance on
23 Ships on Feb. 15; Small Shipyards, Readiness at Risk," *Breaking
Defense*, February 1, 2013, http://breakingdefense.com/2013/02/navy
-will-cancel-maintenance-on-23-ships-on-feb-15-small-shipy/.

42. Sydney J. Freedberg Jr., "Navy Strains to Handle Both China
and Iran at Once," *Breaking Defense*, May 21, 2012, http://breaking
defense.com/2012/05/navy-strains-to-handle-both-china-and-iran-at
-once/.

43. Admiral Jonathan Greenert, "Hearing on President Obama's
Fiscal 2016 Budget Request for the Navy," House Appropriations
Subcommittee on Defense, February 26, 2015, http://www.navy.mil
/navydata/people/cno/Greenert/Testimony/150226%20HAC-D%20
Navy%20Budget%20Hearing.pdf.

44. Ibid.

45. Admiral Jonathan Greenert, "Document: Greenert Letter to
Thornberry on Cruiser Modernization," *USNI News*, April 29, 2015,
https://news.usni.org/2015/04/29/document-greenert-letter-to
-thornberry-on-cruiser-modernization.

46. Megan Eckstein, "Gen. Paxton: Some Marine Units Operating
at Less Than 1:2 Deployment-to-Dwell Ratio," March 27, 2015, http://
news.usni.org/2015/03/27/gen-paxton-some-marine-units-operating-at
-less-than-12-deployment-to-dwell-ratio.

47. David Barno, Nora Bensahel, and M. Thomas Davis, *The Carrier Air Wing of the Future*, white paper (Washington, D.C.: Center for a New American Security, February 2014), https://s3.amazonaws.com/files .cnas.org/documents/CNAS_CarrierAirWing_white.pdf.

48. "Military Readiness: Progress and Challenges in Implementing the Navy's Optimized Fleet Response Plan," Government Account-ability Office, May 2, 2016, 1, http://www.gao.gov/assets/680/676904 .pdf.

49. Mike Hixenbaugh, "Navy Falls Behind on Maintenance, Deployments."

50. U.S. Government Accountability Office, "Military Readiness: Progress and Challenges in Implementing the Navy's Optimized Fleet Response Plan," GAO-16-466R, May 2, 2016, 7, http://www.gao.gov /assets/680/676904.pdf.

51. Ibid., 13.

52. Ibid., 15.

53. Ibid., 16.

54. Ibid.

55. Ibid., 23.

56. Department of the Navy, "Fiscal Year (FY) 2011 Budget Estimates, Justification of Estimates: Procurement, Marine Corps," February 2010, http://www.secnav.navy.mil/fmc/fmb/Documents /11pres/PMC_Book.pdf.

57. Department of Defense, "Fiscal Year (FY) 2017 President's Budget Submission: Navy, Procurement, Marine Corps," February 2016, http://www.secnav.navy.mil/fmc/fmb/Documents/17pres/PMC _Book.pdf.

58. Andrew deGrandpre, "General: With Cuts, Marine Corps Will 'Cut into Bone,' " *USA Today*, March 3, 2013, http://www.usa today.com/story/news/nation/2013/03/03/marine-corps-amos-letter -sequester/1961117/.

59. "U.S. Marine Corps," 2016 Index of U.S. Military Strength, http://index.heritage.org/military/2016/assessments/us-military -power/us-marine-corps/.

60. Ibid.

61. Ibid.

62. Ibid.

63. General Joseph Dunford, in Admiral Jonathan Greenert,

"Hearing on President Obama's Fiscal 2016 Budget Request for the Navy," House Appropriations Subcommittee on Defense, February 26, 2015, http://www.navy.mil/navydata/people/cno/Greenert /Testimony/150226%20HAC-D%20Navy%20Budget%20Hearing.pdf.

64. *Marine Aviation Plan 2016*, https://marinecorpsconceptsandpro grams.com/sites/default/files/files/Marine%20Aviation%20Plan%20 2016%20FINAL.pdf.

65. Ibid.

66. Jesse Sloman, "Demands on the Marine Corps Are Slowly Breaking Marine Aviation," *War on the Rocks*, February 10, 2016, http:// warontherocks.com/2016/02/demands-on-the-marine-corps-are-slowly -breaking-marine-aviation/.

67. Jeff Schogol, "The Marine Corps' Aviation Fleet Is in Peril," *Marine Corps Times*, April 26, 2016, https://www.marinecorpstimes.com /story/military/2016/04/26/fleet-peril-how-congressional-budget-cuts -are-crippling-the-marines-air-power/81974498/.

68. Zachary Cohen, "Desperate for Planes, Military Turns to the 'Boneyard,'" CNN, July 14, 2016, http://www.cnn.com/2016/07/13 /politics/military-aircraft-boneyard/index.html.

69. Leo Shane III, "Congressional Failures Just Forced the Marines to Raid a Museum for Aircraft Parts," *Military Times*, March 30, 2016, http://www.militarytimes.com/story/military/2016/03/30 /marine-corps-broke-plane-parts-museum-raid-aviation-thornberry /82416918/.

70. "U.S. Marine Corps," 2016 Index of U.S. Military Strength, http://index.heritage.org/military/2016/assessments/us-military -power/us-marine-corps/.

71. Lance M. Bacon, "Here's How Marines Are Using 3-D Printing to Make Their Own Parts," *Marine Corps Times*, April 30, 2016, https:// www.marinecorpstimes.com/story/military/2016/04/30/heres-how -marines-using-3-d-printing-make-their-own-parts/83544142/.

72. "U.S. Marine Corps," 2016 Index of U.S. Military Strength, http://index.heritage.org/military/2016/assessments/us-military -power/us-marine-corps/.

73. Jeff Schogol, "The Marine Corps' Aviation Fleet Is in Peril," *Marine Corps Times*, April 26, 2016, http://www.marinecorpstimes.com /story/military/2016/04/26/fleet-peril-how-congressional-budget-cuts -are-crippling-the-marines-air-power/81974498/.

74. Gina Harkins and Andrew deGrandpre, "Marines Fired Commander Days before Deadly Helicopter Crash in Hawaii," *Marine Corps Times*, January 28, 2016, https://www.marinecorpstimes.com/story /military/2016/01/28/marines-fired-commander-days-before-deadly -helicopter-crash-hawaii/79486936/.

75. James K. Sanborn, "Marine Aviation Deaths Hit 5-Year High," *Marine Corps Times*, September 6, 2015, https://www.marinecorpstimes .com/story/military/2015/09/06/marine-aviation-deaths-hit-5-year -high/71665398/.

76. Hope Hodge Seck, "Navy Air Boss: Fighter Readiness Not in Crisis," Military.com, August 22, 2016, http://www.military.com /daily-news/2016/08/22/navy-air-boss-fighter-readiness-not-in-crisis .html?utm_source=Sailthru&utm_medium=email&utm_campaign =Military%20EBB%208-23-16&utm_term=Editorial%20-%20Military %20-%20Early%20Bird%20Brief.

77. Mike Hixenbaugh, "Inquiry: Frayed Wire Led to Fatal Navy Helicopter Crash," *Virginian-Pilot*, September 7, 2014, http://pilot online.com/news/military/inquiry-frayed-wire-led-to-fatal-navy-heli copter-crash/article_2ef12ff9-b89f-5d36-a020-d61009b4f03b.html.

78. Navy Retention Study: Results, http://www.dodretention.org /results/.

79. Ibid.

80. Chris Church, "As USS Theodore Roosevelt Exits, US Has No Carriers in Persian Gulf," *Stars and Stripes*, October 9, 2015, http:// www.stripes.com/news/as-uss-theodore-roosevelt-exits-us-has-no -carriers-in-persian-gulf-1.372488; U.S. Navy, "USS Harry S. Truman Strike Fighters Sortie in Support of Operation Inherent Resolve," YouTube video, December 29, 2015, https://www.youtube.com/watch ?v=gfC9eLMbECM.

81. Sam LaGrone, "Harry S. Truman Strike Group Returns from Extended Deployment," *USNI News*, July 13, 2016, https://news.usni .org/2016/07/13/harry-s-truman-extended-deployment.

82. David Larter, "Carrier Scramble: CENTCOM, PACOM Face Flattop Gaps This Spring amid Tensions," *Navy Times*, January 7, 2016, http://www.navytimes.com/story/military/2016/01/07/carrier-scramble -centcom-pacom-face-flattop-gaps-spring-amid-tensions/78426140/.

83. Megan Eckstein and Sam LaGrone, "Carrier Ford's Maiden Deployment Could Face 2-Year Delay Due to Shock Trials," *USNI*

News, September 11, 2015, http://news.usni.org/2015/09/10/carrier-fords-maiden-deployment-could-face-2-year-delay-due-to-shock-trials.

84. Statement of Admiral Jonathan Greenert, U.S. Navy Chief of Naval Operations, before the Senate Armed Services Committee on the Impact of Sequestration on National Defense, January 28, 2015, http://www.navy.mil/navydata/people/cno/Greenert/Testimony/150128%20Chief%20of%20Naval%20Operations%20(CNO)%20Adm.%20Greenert%20Statment%20and%20Slides%20before%20Senate%20Armed%20Services%20Committee.pdf.

85. Secretary of the Navy Raymond Mabus, in Admiral Jonathan Greenert, "Hearing on President Obama's Fiscal 2016 Budget Request for the Navy," House Appropriations Subcommittee on Defense, February 26, 2015, http://www.navy.mil/navydata/people/cno/Greenert/Testimony/150226%20HAC-D%20Navy%20Budget%20Hearing.pdf.

86. Statement of Admiral Jonathan Greenert, U.S. Navy Chief of Naval Operations, before the Senate Armed Services Committee on the Impact of Sequestration on National Defense, January 28, 2015, http://www.navy.mil/navydata/people/cno/Greenert/Testimony/150128%20Chief%20of%20Naval%20Operations%20(CNO)%20Adm.%20Greenert%20Statment%20and%20Slides%20before%20Senate%20Armed%20Services%20Committee.pdf.

87. Testimony of Chief of Naval Operations Admiral Jonathan Greenert, House Appropriations Subcommittee on Defense, Hearing on President Obama's Fiscal 2016 Budget Request for the Navy, February 26, 2015, http://www.navy.mil/navydata/people/cno/Greenert/Testimony/150226%20HAC-D%20Navy%20Budget%20Hearing.pdf.

88. Ronald O'Rourke, *Navy Force Structure and Shipbuilding Plans: Background and Issues for Congress*, Congressional Research Office, June 7, 2017, 21–22, https://www.fas.org/sgp/crs/weapons/RL32665.pdf.

CHAPTER X. REBUILDING AMERICAN SEAPOWER

1. Carrie Booze, "Historic Battle of 'Chapultepec' Remembered," Marines, September 14, 2007, http://www.mcrc.marines.mil/News/News-Article-Display/Article/519657/historic-battle-of-chapultepec-remembered/; and Don Burzynski, *The First Leathernecks: A Combat History of the U.S. Marines from Inception to the Halls of Montezuma*, Ebook edition (Open Road Media, 2013), https://books.google.com/books/about/The_First_Leathernecks.html?id=nbqZxWmRMQwC.

2. David M. White, "The War of 1812 and the Battle of New Orleans," Marines, January 8, 2015, http://www.quantico.marines.mil /News/News-Article-Display/Article/559876/the-war-of-1812-and-the -battle-of-new-orleans/.

3. Richard F. Grimmett, "Instances of Use of United States Armed Forces Abroad, 1798–2009," Congressional Research Service, January 27, 2010, http://www.au.af.mil/au/awc/awcgate/crs/rl32170.pdf.

4. *2nd Battalion, 5th Marines at Belleau Wood—A Pocket History*, Project Leatherneck, June 6, 1994, http://www.2ndbn5thmar.com/history /25belleau1918.pdf.

5. Alan R. Millett, *Semper Fidelis: The History of the United States Marine Corps* (New York: The Free Press, 1980), 325.

6. Lieutenant Colonel LeRoy D. Stearns, *U.S. Marines in the Persian Gulf, 1990–1991: The 3d Marine Aircraft Wing in Desert Shield and Desert Storm* (Washington, D.C.: USMC History and Museums Division, 1999), http://www.marines.mil/Portals/59/Publications/U.S.%20Marines %20in%20the%20Persian%20Gulf%2090-91%20The%203D%20 MARINE%20AIRCRAFT%20WING%20%20PCN%2019000314900 _1.pdf?ver=2012-10-11-164209-947, and http://www.marines.mil/Portals /59/Publications/U.S.%20Marines%20in%20the%20Persian%20Gulf %2090-91%20The%203D%20MARINE%20AIRCRAFT%20WING %20%20PCN%2019000314900_2.pdf.

7. Paul W. Westermeyer, *US Marines in Battle: Al-Khafji* (Washington, D.C.: USMC History and Museums Division, 1991), http://www .marines.mil/Portals/59/Publications/U.S.%20Marines%20in%20 Battle%20Al-Khafji%20%20PCN%20106000400_5.pdf?ver=2012-10 -11-164151-183.

8. Colonel Charles J. Quilter II, *U.S. Marines in the Persian Gulf, 1990–1991: With the I Marine Expeditionary Force in Desert Shield and Desert Storm* (Washington, D.C.: USMC History and Museums Division, 1993), http://www.marines.mil/Portals/59/Publications/U.S.%20 MARINES%20IN%20THE%20PERSIAN%20GULF%201990-1991 %20EXPEDITIONARY%20FORCE%20PCN%2019000317200_1.pdf ?ver=2012-10-11-164211-400.

9. Lieutenant Colonel Ronald J. Brown, *U.S. Marines in the Persian Gulf, 1990–1991: With Marine Forces Afloat in Desert Shield and Desert Storm* (Washington, D.C.: USMC History and Museums Division, 1998), http://www.marines.mil/Portals/59/Publications/U.S.%20Marines

%20in%20the%20Persian%20Gulf,%201990-1991_With%20Marine
%20Forces%20Afloat%20in%20Desert%20Shield%20and%20
Desert%20Storm%20%20PCN%2019000314500_1.pdf.

10. Colonel Dennis P. Mroczkowski, *Restoring Hope: In Somalia with the United Task Force, 1992–1993* (Washington, D.C.: USMC History Division, 2005), http://www.marines.mil/Portals/59/Publications /Restoring%20Hope%20In%20Somalia%20with%20the%20Unified %20Task%20Force%201992-1993%20PCN%2019000413500_1.pdf.

11. James K. Sanborn, "Marine Aviation Deaths Hit 5-Year High," *Marine Times*, September 6, 2015, https://www.marinecorpstimes.com /story/military/2015/09/06/marine-aviation-deaths-hit-5-year-high /71665398/.

12. Richard P. Hallion, "D-Day 1944: Air Power over the Normandy Beaches and Beyond" (Air Force History and Museums Program, 1994), 2, http://www.dtic.mil/dtic/tr/fulltext/u2/a432943.pdf.

13. Ibid.

14. Fred H. Allison, "Perfecting Close Air Support in Korea," *Naval History Magazine* (U.S. Naval Institute), 20, no. 2 (April 2006), http://www.usni.org/magazines/navalhistory/2006-04/perfecting -close-air-support-korea.

15. Ibid.

16. David Axe, "How the US Marine Corps Bet Its Future on the F-35 Stealth Fighter (and Lost)," *The National Interest*, June 24, 2016.

17. Dave Majumdar, "U.S. Marines to Retire Harrier Fleet Earlier Than Planned, Extend Life of Hornets," *USNI News*, November 3, 2014.

18. Jeff Schogol, "The Marine Corps' Aviation Fleet Is in Peril," *Marine Corps Times*, April 26, 2016, https://www.marinecorpstimes.com /story/military/2016/04/26/fleet-peril-how-congressional-budget-cuts -are-crippling-the-marines-air-power/81974498/.

19. Donald Rumsfeld, Town Hall meeting, Camp Buehring, Kuwait, December 8, 2004; transcript available in "Troops Question Secretary of Defense Donald Rumsfeld about Armor," PBS *Newshour*, December 9, 2004, http://www.pbs.org/newshour/bb/military-july -dec04-armor_12-9/.

20. Mike Hixenbaugh and Jason Paladino, "Internal Navy Email: Safety of Helicopters in Question," *Virginian-Pilot*, February 6, 2015.

21. *Marine Aviation Plan 2016*, Office of the Deputy Commandant for

Aviation, https://marinecorpsconceptsandprograms.com/sites/default
/files/files/Marine%20Aviation%20Plan%202016%20FINAL.pdf.

22. Ibid.

23. Tyler Rogoway, "The Marine Corps' CH-53E Super Stallion
Fleet Is in Inexcusably Horrible Disrepair," *FoxtrotAlpha.com*, February
25, 2015.

24. Sanborn, "Marine Aviation Deaths Hit 5-Year High."

25. Chris D'Angelo, "Marine Corps Worries about Aging Helicopter Fleet after Deadly Hawaii Crash," *Huffington Post*, March 3, 2016.

26. *Marine Aviation Plan 2016*.

27. "Landing Craft, Air Cushion (LCAC)," *FAS Military Analysis
Network*, February 14, 2000.

28. "Assault Amphibious Vehicle (AAV7A1) Family of Vehicles
Upgrade," US Marine Corps Concepts and Programs, https://
marinecorpsconceptsandprograms.com/programs/ground-combat
-tactical-vehicles/assault-amphibious-vehicle-aav7a1-family-vehicles
-upgrade.

29. Bryan Clark and Jesse Sloman, "Amphibious Operations in
a Brave New World," *War on the Rocks*, November 15, 2016, http://
warontherocks.com/2016/11/amphibious-operations-in-a-brave-new
-world/.

30. Ibid.

31. Ibid.

32. Ibid.

33. Ibid.

CHAPTER XI. NAVAL REARMAMENT

1. "Iran May Seek Naval Bases in Yemen or Syria: Chief of Staff,"
Reuters, November 27, 2016, http://www.reuters.com/article/us-iran
-navy-yemen-syria-idUSKBN13M08M?il=0.

2. "An Analysis of the Navy's Fiscal Year 2016 Shipbuilding Plan,"
Congressional Budget Office, October 2015, https://www.cbo.gov/
sites/default/files/114th-congress-2015-2016/reports/50926-Shipbuild
ing_OneCol-2.pdf.

3. Admiral Paul F. Zukunft, "The State of the United States
Coast Guard, 2015," https://www.uscg.mil/seniorleadership/DOCS/
State%20of%20Coast%20Guard%20Address%202015%20SLP%20
Script.pdf.

4. Craig Whitlock and Bob Woodward, "Pentagon Buries Evidence of $125 Billion in Bureaucratic Waste," *Washington Post*, December 5, 2016, https://www.washingtonpost.com/investigations/pentagon-bur ies-evidence-of-125-billion-in-bureaucratic-waste/2016/12/05/e0668c76 -9af6-11e6-a0ed-ab0774c1eaa5_story.html?utm_term=.56330fa4903b.

5. Ibid.

6. Ibid.

7. Ibid.

CHAPTER XIII. THE MORALITY OF DEFENSE

1. George Washington, "The First State of the Union Address," January 8, 1790, http://ahp.gatech.edu/first_state_union_1790.html.

2. James Madison, "Special Message to Congress on the Foreign Policy Crisis," June 1, 1812, https://millercenter.org/the-presidency/ presidential-speeches/june-1-1812-special-message-congress-foreign-policy-crisis-war.

3. John Locke, *Second Treatise on Civil Government*, chapter 3, paragraph 17, http://www.earlymoderntexts.com/assets/pdfs/locke1689a.pdf.

4. Patrick Henry, speech delivered at St. John's Church, Richmond, Virginia, March 23, 1774, http://www.history.org/almanack/life/ politics/giveme.cfm.

5. Frederick Douglass, "Men of Color, To Arms," speech in Rochester, New York, March 2, 1863, http://www.blackpast.org/1863-freder ick-douglass-men-color-arms.

6. Peter Grier, "Weinberger Prepares for NATO Meeting. Talks Likely to Dwell on 'Star Wars' and Allies' Contributions to Defense," *Christian Science Monitor*, May 20, 1985, http://www.csmonitor.com /1985/0520/anato.html.

INDEX